Alaska's Place in the West

Alaska's Place in the West

FROM THE LAST FRONTIER TO THE LAST GREAT WILDERNESS

ROXANNE WILLIS

UNIVERSITY PRESS OF KANSAS

Published by the

University Press of Kansas

(Lawrence, Kansas 66045),

which was organized by the

Kansas Board of Regents and

is operated and funded by

Emporia State University,

Fort Hays State University,

Kansas State University,

Pittsburg State University,

the University of Kansas, and

Wichita State University

Chapter 1 first appeared as "A New Game in the North: Alaska Native Reindeer Herding, 1890–1940," *Western Historical Quarterly* 38 (Autumn 2006): 277–301. Copyright by the Western History Association. Reprinted by permission.

Library of Congress Cataloging-in-Publication Data

Willis, Roxanne.
  Alaska's place in the West : from the last frontier to the last great wilderness / Roxanne Willis.
     p. cm.
  Includes bibliographical references and index.
  ISBN 978-0-7006-1748-7 (cloth : alk. paper)
  1. Alaska—Environmental conditions. 2. Alaska—History. 3. Frontier and pioneer life—Alaska. 4. Wilderness areas—Alaska—History. 5. Nature—Effect of human beings on—Alaska—History. 6. Landscape changes—Alaska—History. 7. Alaska—Public opinion. 8. Public opinion—United States. 9. Regionalism—West (U.S.)—Case studies. 10. West (U.S.)—Environmental conditions—Case studies.   I. Title.
  GE155.A4W55 2010
  333.7209798—dc22   2010018063

British Library Cataloguing-in-Publication Data is available.
Printed in the United States of America

10 9 8 7 6 5 4 3 2 1

The paper used in this publication is recycled and contains 30 percent postconsumer waste. It is acid free and meets the minimum requirements of the American National Standard for Permanence of Paper for Printed Library Materials Z39.48–1992.

For everyone who has ever fallen in love with Alaska;
And for Ivan and Lydia—I cannot wait to take you there.

We want to create a different kind of society in our North, modern in every sense but in harmonious relationship to Nature. . . . Alaska, it has been said, may well be the last chance to do things right the first time.

—*Jay S. Hammond*

The question is not what you look at—but how you look & whether you see.

—*Henry David Thoreau*

Contents

Acknowledgments

First and foremost, I would like to thank John Mack Faragher, who supported this project through its crucial early phase. His wisdom, patience, and good humor were invaluable throughout the process. Without his help and advice, my desire to write about the history of Alaska would have remained only a dream.

Other scholars supported me during critical phases of my research and writing. I would like to thank Jean-Christophe Agnew, Susan Armitage, John Demos, Jay Gitlin, Alexander Nemerov, Colleen O'Neill, Stephen Pitti, Steven Stoll, Melody Webb, John Whitehead, and David Wrobel for their helpful insights into this project.

Stephen Haycox not only gave excellent advice on how to improve the manuscript, he also gave me an opportunity to present my work to an Alaskan audience. I am truly grateful for his support.

Kathryn Morse gave detailed and important feedback in the later stages of this project. She was a phenomenal help to me.

Friends and colleagues at Yale University read drafts, offered support, and gave me fabulous advice. I would like to thank Adam Arenson, Scott Gac, Paul Grant-Costa, Angela Pulley Hudson, Joseph Kip Kosek, Michael Kral, Mark Krasovic, Benjamin Madley, Karen Marrero, Christian McMillen, Robert Morrissey, Barry Muchnick, Amy Reading, Edith Rotkopf, Victorine Shepard, Taylor Spence, and Melissa Stuckey.

I am particularly grateful for Aaron Sachs's enthusiasm for my project, for his great advice, and for the opportunity he provided me to present my work to his colleagues in the American Studies Program at Cornell University. I received wonderful feedback from this group of scholars.

I had the privilege of receiving a fellowship from the Harvard University Center for the Environment, and I would like to thank Lawrence Buell, who served as my host. His kindness and wisdom were invaluable to me during my two years in Cambridge. I would also like to thank my colleagues in the fellowship program, in particular Peter Alagona, whose impressive knowledge of environmental history advanced this project tremendously.

I am grateful for the financial support—so crucial to doing research in Alaska—that came from the Howard R. Lamar Center for the Study of Frontiers and Borders, the Robert M. Leylan Fellowship, the Beinecke Rare Book and Manuscript Library, the John F. Enders Research Award, the John Perry Miller Fund, the Harvard University Center for the Environment, and the Harvard Alumni Association.

Librarians and archivists guided me to resources that I never would have discovered on my own. I would like to thank the helpful staff members at the following institutions: Rasmuson Library, Alaska and Polar Regions Collection, University of Alaska–Fairbanks (especially Rose Speranza); National Archives and Records Administration, Pacific-Alaska Region, Anchorage (especially Bruce Parham); Beinecke Rare Book and Manuscript Library, Yale University (especially George Miles); Consortium Library, University of Alaska–Anchorage; Alaska Resources Library and Information Services (ARLIS); Special Collections Division, University of Washington Libraries; University of Oregon, Special Collections and Archives; Yukon Archives; National Archives and Records Administration, College Park, Maryland; and National Library and Archives, Canada.

During the summer of 2003, I was graciously hosted by the Northern Studies Program at the University of Alaska, Fairbanks. I would like to thank Ross Coen, Judith Kleinfeld, and Julia Parczik for making me feel welcome at their university.

Some of the most interesting and rewarding experiences during my research came from trips into the Alaskan bush. For getting me there safely and sanely, I thank the staffs of Arctic Wild and the Northern Alaska Tour Company. I am also grateful to all the Alaskans who both formally and informally shared their stories with me during my many northern travels.

My editors at the University Press of Kansas, Kalyani Fernando and Ranjit Arab, were as helpful and encouraging as any editors could be. I am thankful for their support.

My parents, Margaret and Robert Willis, have stood by me in all my life's endeavors, and I appreciate their enthusiasm for this book project. I thank them for all the financial and emotional support they have given me. My parents-in-law, Susan and Craig Pynn, added a valuable source of emotional and financial assistance, above and beyond the obligation of in-laws, and to them I also owe an important debt of gratitude. My children, Ivan and Lydia, are an inspiration every day.

My husband, Geoffrey Pynn, has been there from start to finish, reading drafts, navigating my travels north, tending to our children, and listening to my countless theories about the meaning of Alaskan history. Without him, I could never have completed this project. I owe him more than words can say.

Introduction:
A Place for Alaska

I was disoriented. After a two-day, four-time-zone trek from New Haven to Fairbanks, I had finally arrived at the University of Alaska, jet-lagged, hungry, and more than a bit fatigued. It was late May, and I quickly settled into a small campus apartment for my three-month stint in the archives. Exploring the university grounds, I took in the sights and sounds of students about to leave for summer vacation. After asking one of these newly buoyant souls for the nearest source of food, I ended up in a modest bookstore café in which I would spend countless hours that summer sipping coffee and listening to the local chatter. The curvy script painted on the walls advised me to "listen to the wisdom of the taiga." I did not yet know what taiga was; I made a mental note to find out. Around me, patrons discussed summer plans—fishing, rafting, backpacking, gardening, and, most of all, traveling outside of Alaska. Just as I had arrived in my academic promised land, the academic types around me were planning to flee . . . to France, Hawaii, California—"anywhere but here," someone said. The customer next to me discussed his plans to travel along the East Coast. "I want to see Mount Vernon," he said. "You know, somewhere with some *history*. Unlike this place."

I wondered what this Alaskan would think if he knew I had come to this place precisely because I wanted to research its history. Had I not been so fatigued, I might have asked him. Instead, I mused over his comment, which bubbled to the surface of my thoughts again and again that summer as I worked in the archives. He had given me my charge: to shed light on the fact that Alaska had a history that was not only interesting, but important. Because, unbeknownst to him, my taiga-weary muse had echoed what I discovered to be an unstated but pervasive theme in the scholarly literature: Alaska history is regional history—irrelevant to the important questions being studied by scholars of American history and culture. It is quite common to write large synthetic texts in these fields and simply ignore Alaska or casually to bury its hundreds of millions of acres deep inside the footnotes. In many American history textbooks, Alaska disappears after the Klondike gold rush, never again to be mentioned in any significant way.

The reasons for the region's pervasive absence are quite simple. First, Alaska does not easily fit into our cultural assumptions about place. It takes the mellifluous phrase "from sea to shining sea" and adds the awkward qualifier "and a big chunk up by the Arctic Ocean." It adds tussocks and tundra—which few Americans could accurately define—to our comfortably familiar amber waves of grain. In addition, Alaska does not fit neatly into our accepted historical narratives. For example, when the Census Bureau declared the end of the frontier in 1890, the concept had scarcely been introduced in the north. Alaskan homesteaders were staking claims with snow machines and bush planes into the early 1980s. Alaska Natives ended up with corporations instead of reservations. The incongruities are numerous, and because of them, most Americans find Alaska *fascinating*—good material for travel essays, trivia questions, and wildlife documentaries—but not terribly important culturally or historically. As one Alaskan scholar has observed, the state's location on most national weather maps is quite telling.[1] If our local weather maps were to drop Alaska even deeper into the Pacific, how many of us would notice?[2]

It is because Alaska is so often overlooked that Alaska historians spend much of their analytic energy campaigning for the state's rightful inclusion into some larger historical narrative. They celebrate the cultural contributions made by (semi-)famous Alaskans—the aviator Carl Ben Eielson, the artist Sydney Lawrence, the politician Ernest Gruening. They point to Alaska's pivotal role in major historical events—World War II, the Cold War, global warming. Scholars take great pains to explain that present-day Alaska is more like the rest of the country than it is different, that "there is little in Alaska that resembles frontier settlement," as one historian noted. He went on to say that "most Alaskans . . . live in the state's urban centers, [and] life in Alaska's urban centers is nearly indistinguishable from life in the cities and towns that dot the landscape across the rest of the United States."[3] Historically,

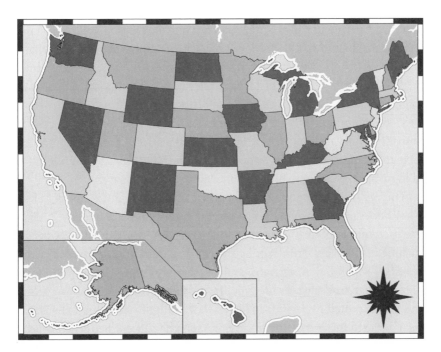

A typical reference map. License to publish this image was purchased from iStockphoto.

there were fewer cultural amenities in Alaska than in most other states, but even as long as a century ago, one historian has argued, "the Americans who went to [Alaska] forged a permanent, recognizably American subculture—Americanness—in an entirely novel environment."[4]

These arguments rail against the notion that Alaska is *exceptional*, that it is a place where people hunt for their own food, build their own houses, and live a rustic life "close to nature." This is the image perpetuated in popular literature, wildlife documentaries, and political cartoons, as well as in the ubiquitous urban myths about the region (including those I found myself debunking when discussing my research with non-Alaskans: Doesn't Alaska have six months of darkness followed by six months of light? Aren't there ten men for every woman in Alaska? Doesn't the federal government pay you to live up there?). It is hard to imagine another region of the country about which there are still so many outlandish myths in cultural circulation. The 2008 presidential election cycle—about which I will say more later—only added to the strange collection of cultural misunderstandings about Alaska and its inhabitants. These mistaken notions are ripe for scholarly correction.

Yet, I believe it is an oversimplification to say that instead of being exceptional, life in Alaska is more or less the same as in the rest of the United States. For one thing, there is no consistent experience of the American landscape, and residents of the Bronx, rural Nebraska, and Taos Pueblo live very different lives. Life in Alaska is different, too. Even if we set aside questions of race, class, and gender (which further complicate people's experiences of any given place), there is no way to say that a way of life is more or less American; there are no reliable criteria to determine that some place is more like "the rest of the United States" than it is different. By making this argument, historians are trying to correct the ever-widening gap between the Alaska of America's cultural imagination (polar bears, homesteads, and harsh winters) and the reality of most Alaskans' lives (fast food, strip malls, and, well, harsh winters). Their intent is sound, but I do not agree with their approach.

Heeding the lessons of environmental history, I maintain that there is something unique about Alaska—at least within the context of the United States. To put it succinctly, the place *cycles* differently.[5] Its days and nights, its weather and seasons, its natural migrations and cultural celebrations, are all in one way or another unique within the spectrum of American experience. Only in Alaska does daily life ebb and flow with the caribou migration, the midnight sun, the Iditarod, or the Inupiat whaling season. Only in Alaska are bear maulings, bush plane crashes, and hypothermia such common threats to life and limb. That is not to say Alaska is *exceptional*—it does share many characteristics with other American places and with other northern regions, particularly in Canada. But Alaska's differences from other American places are meaningful, and they have profoundly shaped the history of the region.

Another way scholars have tried to minimize Alaska's differences and to elevate its history is by claiming that the region should be considered within the rich historiography of the American West. As one historian has argued, "the idea of an exceptional Alaskan spirit continues to dominate representations of Alaska . . . but . . . there is more similarity to . . . western settlement . . . than there is real difference."[6] In his opinion, "Alaska history is . . . another chapter in the history of the American West."[7] Another scholar has claimed that, despite the fact that most prominent historians have largely ignored the region, "events in Alaska reflected the evolution of practically every other western territory or state."[8] Yet another historian mused that, "despite [Alaska's] far northern location, nearly everything about it evokes the West."9 I do not disagree that Alaska shares many characteristics with the western United States. In fact, I will argue later that much of Alaska settlement was self-consciously planned to imitate western development schemes. And modern-day Alaska does share many traits with parts of the continental American West, including a great distance from the centers of power, a concentrated urban population, and a large amount of federally controlled land. Still, simply attaching Alaska to the continental West fails to do justice to the region's rich and complex history.

The major problem with the attachment argument is that it takes dominant geographic frameworks—such as the "American West"—as givens. The only question then is whether Alaska is different ("exceptional") or instead fits somehow into something we already know (yet "another chapter" in a familiar story). But the truth is that what counts as the "American West"—or any other geographic space, for that matter—is itself up for debate, and the nature of that debate changes over time.10 After all, spaces are socially and culturally (as well as politically and materially) produced. As one environmental historian has argued, "historians have been notoriously inattentive to spatial issues. . . . We do usually regard space as a simple container for the political, social, or cultural. . . . Historians pay less attention than geographers to the social, as distinct from the strictly political production of these spaces. We take them as givens."11 But how we categorize geographic space is certainly *not* given, and that is nowhere more apparent than in Alaska. When we argue that Alaska should—or should not—be included in the history of the American West, we are debating the wrong question. Instead, we should be asking when we have believed that Alaska was part of something called "the American West," and why; how believing that Alaska is part of the American West changes the way we treat the Alaskan landscape and the peoples who inhabit it; what else we have imagined Alaska to be. (A quick glance into Alaska's past suggests there are many spaces—the West is but one example.) How does imaging Alaska as a different kind of place change the way we shape its natural environment?

As we examine Alaska's history, we see how the region has traveled among numerous spatial categories—from the north to the west, from the frontier to the wilderness, from the periphery to the spotlight and back again. And as Alaska gets defined and redefined in our cultural geography, the physical landscape changes as a result. In Alaska, we learn that places are not fixed in one objective geographic space. No, indeed—places *move*. This is true of every place, but it is precisely because of Alaska's outlier

Frontier book and gift shop building, Kodiak, 1945. Hans and Margaret Hafemeister Papers, Archives and Special Collections, University of Alaska–Anchorage.

status—the fact that in some ways the region *is* separate and distinct from the rest of the country—that Alaska's place in our cultural geography has been so frequently renegotiated. Alaska's understudied history gives us a unique window into the topic of space, place, and environmental change—an important subject for students of environmental history, and, indeed, for all historians. As one theorist put it, "there are no geographical concepts, terms, or metrics . . . that stand outside of language, history and politics. And therefore questions about exactly *where* something *is*, or what a space is, can only be perpetually negotiated, deferred, and contested."[12] In Alaska, we discover how our cultural maps shape the physical landscape; how the ways that we treat the environment materially are intricately tied to the ways we organize it conceptually. For that reason, if for none other, Alaska history should matter to everyone.

And there are other reasons to think critically about Alaska. But first we need to think a bit more about how this unique place cycles. In terms of sheer land area, Alaska is a huge part of America. At 375 million acres (586,000 square miles), Alaska's area equals 20 percent of the continental United States and is four times the size of California. All this land is extremely far north—between 51 and 72 degrees north latitude, to be exact. Because of Alaska, one-sixth of American land falls within a subarctic or arctic climate zone. These areas experience extreme fluctuations in the amount of daylight they have throughout the year. At Alaska's northernmost reach—350 miles above the Arctic Circle—there are sixty-seven days of continual darkness during the winter and eighty-four summer days when the sun never sets. Alaska spans as dramatically to the west as it does to the north. The reach from the southeastern panhandle to Attu—the westernmost Aleutian Island, almost due north of New Zealand—is about the distance between Atlanta and San Francisco (2,400 miles). The archipelago occupies both hemispheres, giving Alaska both the easternmost and westernmost points in the United States. Alaska also rises to impressive altitudes. Within the Alaska Range lies North America's highest peak, Denali, which reaches to an imposing 20,320 feet. Alaska's rocky shoreline has bragging rights, too—at 34,000 miles in length, it is 50 percent longer than the seacoasts of the forty-eight continental states combined. These statistics easily alchemize to sheer awesomeness—Alaska's geography is at once vast, extreme, diverse, and distinctive.

These same four adjectives can be readily applied to Alaska's natural environment. The Alaskan landscape is a rich collage of rain forests, swamps, arctic plains, fjords, glaciers, ice fields, volcanoes, mountain ranges, rugged coasts, frigid rivers, and countless streams and lakes. Navigating this breathtaking tapestry are significant populations of whales, walrus, sea otters, caribou, polar bears, moose, grizzly bears, lynx, wolves, wolverines, eagles, ptarmigan, halibut, grayling, and all five varieties of salmon, to name but a few species. A salient feature of Alaska's environment—typical of northern latitudes, but unique to American land—is permafrost, a layer of soil at varying depths beneath the earth's surface which has remained frozen for thousands of years. The northern third of Alaska (roughly, the section above the Arctic Circle) has continuous permafrost; most of the rest of the state has patches of frozen earth beneath the topsoil. In the subarctic regions, permafrost conditions create taiga—a high-latitude biome marked by a wide belt of coniferous trees. In Alaska, these are most often the scruffy (and reportedly wise) black spruce trees. In the high arctic, taiga gives way to tundra, a treeless, rocky plain padded with moss, lichen, and wildflowers.

The southeastern panhandle, the Kenai Peninsula, the Alaska Peninsula, and the Aleutian Islands are generally free of permafrost. These milder areas along the southerly coasts owe much of their character to the Japanese Current, a river of warm ocean water that flows north along the Japanese islands and westward through the North Pacific. This current creates climates that are significantly warmer than would be expected at such latitudes—for example, towns on the southeastern panhandle experience a mean annual temperature of about 45 degrees Fahrenheit. This is down-right balmy compared to Alaska's arctic region, which averages a mere 10 degrees over the calendar year. The vast interior of the state—the majority of Alaska's land area—is marked by extreme variations in temperature, with 80- or 90-degree days common during the short summer months, and several weeks of 40 or 50 degrees below zero during the long, dark winters. So, although patches of milder climates can be found, true to its stereotype, most of Alaska's weather is extreme and unforgiving.[13]

In spite of this harshness, human beings have flourished in this environment for thousands of years. Historically, Alaska has been home to a diverse group of Native inhabitants, including Eskimos, Indians, and Aleuts, whose combined population was approximately 80,000 at the time of first contact with Europeans. Traditionally, Eskimos occupied the northern and western coasts, living in semipermanent villages, traveling by dogsled, and hunting whales, caribou, and seals for subsistence.[14] Nine distinct groups of Athabascan Indians occupy the vast interior of Alaska. Historically, they were nomadic, hunting moose and caribou, gathering roots and berries, and fishing for salmon. The southeastern panhandle is home to groups of Tlingit and Haida Indians, who have historically taken advantage of a rich and hospitable climate, feasting on seals, deer, mountain goats, salmon, halibut, seaweed, clams, and the eggs of shorebirds. Their relatively sedentary lifestyle allowed for the evolution of an elaborate culture, which included the production of beautiful baskets, blankets, and totem poles; the staging of complex ceremonies called potlatches; and frequent warfare between rival groups. The Aleuts—whom linguists believe split from the Eskimos about 7,000 years ago—occupy the long archipelago that bears their name.[15] Traditionally, the Aleuts' subsistence came from the sea. Men used kayaks to hunt whales, sea otters, and sea lions, while women gathered eggs and crustaceans along the shore.

A rich diversity of Native cultures continues to thrive in Alaska. Although contact with Russians—and later with Americans—dramatically altered life for Alaska Natives, most of them still occupy their traditional homelands. In recent times, the Native population has hovered around 100,000 people—about 15 percent of Alaska's approximately 650,000 residents. Many Natives continue to practice elements of their traditional culture, producing distinctive clothing and artwork, participating in ritual activities, and hunting and fishing for subsistence.[16]

Alaska Native drying fish on the Lower Yukon, early twentieth century. Alaska State Library, Clarence Leroy Andrews Photograph Collection, Clarence Leroy Andrews, P45–0465.

Most of the Alaskan landscape is ecologically rich and geographically remote, but virtually none of it is untouched or unexplored. Alaska has been shaped and reshaped by human activity for thousands of years. In recent times, the pace of change has accelerated, as both development and conservation initiatives have increased in size and scope. And, as various groups have tried to sculpt the Alaskan landscape to meet their wants and needs, conflicts have arisen. This is the focus of my work—five major conflicts over environment and development in Alaska, including reindeer herding, the Matanuska Colony, the Alaska Highway, the Rampart Dam, and the Trans-Alaska Pipeline. Though far from a comprehensive history of Alaskan development, these five stories provide important insights into how and why a place called Alaska has changed over time. Development conflicts are an ideal window into the subject of space, place, and environmental change, since they reflect our attempts to manipulate the landscape in order to meet our expectations of it. As one scholar noted, "conflicts over nature always already entail struggles over the constitution of the world and its spaces."[17] How we define a place determines both how we want the landscape to look and what we expect the place to *do* for us.

The Matanuska Colony is a poignant illustration of how we can define a place before we know all the facts. This agricultural colony was a New Deal project, one of a series of rural rehabilitation initiatives designed to help families hardest hit by the Great Depression to start over with government assistance. In 1935, 202 families arrived in the south central region of Alaska called the Matanuska Valley and worked to settle the region with family farms. Not surprisingly, the Matanuska Colony began to crumble even before it got off the ground. The government underestimated the challenges involved with communication, transportation, and construction in a far northern environment. The isolation was debilitating for many settlers, who soon began to desert the project in large numbers. Agriculture, too, was almost impossible, and a short growing season, patchy permafrost, and poorly drained soil all conspired against the production of sizable crops. The government's dream of eventually populating Alaska with thousands of farming families quickly disintegrated.

The interesting historical question about the Matanuska Colony is not why it failed—the factors are too numerous to count—but rather why anyone would ever try to create an agricultural settlement in Alaska in the first place. It should have been clear from the outset, even without any studies to prove it, that farming in Alaska would be a challenging enterprise, but the federal government even had data to prove as much. Scientists had been performing agricultural experiments in Alaska since the gold rush days, with disappointing results.[18] Why send a group of already impoverished farming families to such a remote region with poor growing potential and no real agricultural market? The answer to this question lies deep within America's cultural geography and Alaska's place within it.

By the time the Matanuska colonists began their long journey north, Alaska had been part of the United States for almost seventy years. During this period, Alaska's place within America's cultural geography had already shifted greatly. When the United States purchased Alaska from Russia in 1867, the north was a foreign land, a place about which most Americans knew little. Although cultural mythology suggests that people of the time thought Alaska was "Seward's folly"—a reference to William H. Seward, the secretary of state who negotiated the deal—the majority of Americans actually responded favorably to the purchase.[19] Still, once the flurry of media attention around the $7.2 million transaction died down, most Americans gave little thought to the region. Remote and mysterious, Alaska did not attract settlers—or even very many visitors, for that matter. This vacuum of interest in the north created the space for a few visionaries to imagine interesting futures for the region.

One of the earliest explorers of Alaska, the famous conservationist John Muir, revered the northern landscape and believed that it should be preserved as a wilderness park in its entirety.[20] Muir, however, was in the minority, as most Americans saw the land as irrelevant to the *real* American landscape, and thus ripe for exploitation. A group of law enforcement officials suggested that Alaska be turned into a large penal colony, modeled after Australia's Botany Bay. Others proposed turning Alaska into a massive insane asylum, eliminating the need for such burdensome places in the contiguous United States.[21] Business entrepreneurs developed schemes to exploit Alaska's natural resources, often showing up in Sitka with nothing more than a dream to make it big in the salmon, timber, or ice business. Commercial fishing took off quickly, as did the resurrection of the Russian hunt for marine mammals, particularly on the Pribilof Islands. The American fur industry was quickly dominated by the firm of Hutchinson and Kohl, later renamed the Alaska Commercial Company. The company's managers opposed any settlement of Alaska, arguing that the region should remain a storehouse of natural resources to be exploited by private entrepreneurs like themselves.[22]

After a period of time, this ideology of Alaska as "extra" American land—simply a storehouse for resource extraction or a dumping ground for societal ills—gave way, and a few Alaska boosters began to see potential in the landscape. Initially they did so by looking to other northern places and finding permanent and profitable settlements there. One of the most significant examples of this new way of thinking was the importation of reindeer herds to northern Alaska. This idea—conceived by the Presbyterian missionary Sheldon Jackson—started as a modest plan to bring small groups of reindeer from Siberia to feed the Eskimos of western Alaska, whom Jackson mistakenly believed were facing starvation. The idea soon grew far beyond its original scale, as Jackson and his sympathizers began imagining a vast reindeer industry in which whites and Eskimos would work together to make Alaska's northern land profitable. Jackson modeled his vision on the reindeer industry of Scandinavian Lapland and hoped that someday reindeer herding would overtake the western cattle industry. He was mistaken, however, in assuming that the industry of one northern climate could be seamlessly transferred to another—too many natural factors were different in Alaska. This environmental misunderstanding ultimately led to the reindeer industry's downfall.

One problem with imagining Alaska as part of the circumpolar north is that such a geographic formulation kept the region distinct from the rest of the country. In fact, this model ran the risk of bringing Alaskan development schemes (such as reindeer herding) into direct competition with industries in the continental United States (such as western cattle ranching). It was not long before boosters looked away from the circumpolar north in an attempt to make Alaska more closely resemble the rest of the United States. This way of thinking emerged slowly, but its origins can be traced to several important events of the 1890s. In 1890, the Census Bureau reported that there was no longer a discernible frontier line, and the era of "free" American land had come to an end. Cultural anxiety ensued, as people wondered what consequences the end of the frontier would have on the American way of life. This anxiety only deepened in 1893, when the U.S. economy sank into a major depression.

That same year, Frederick Jackson Turner delivered his famous address "The Significance of the Frontier in American History" at the World's Fair in Chicago. Turner declared, "Up to our own day American history has been in a large degree the history of the colonization of the Great West. The existence of an area of free land, its continuous recession, and the advance of American settlement westward, explain American development."[23] Turner's frontier thesis took some time to gain widespread acceptance, but once it did, its influence was profound. Worries over the lost frontier escalated, and Americans began looking for new land to settle. While many politicians started promoting European-style colonialist expansion (and certainly, gestures were made in this direction), a few boosters reminded them that the United States already possessed an area of "free" land—Alaska— which was virtually uninhabited by white residents.[24]

But could Alaska really be the next frontier? Although a few boosters— such as John Muir and Sheldon Jackson—had readily embraced Alaska's untapped potential, most people, including the majority of Americans who had never seen Alaska, remained skeptical. Despite Americans' initial support of the purchase, derogatory nicknames for Alaska—"Icebergia," "Walrussia," and "Frigidia"—circulated widely in the media. One booster

Prospectors ascending the summit of Chilkoot Pass, 1898. Alaska State Library, Eric A. Hegg Photograph Collection, Eric A. Hegg, P124–03.

lamented Alaska's frequent portrayal as "a land of eternal winter, where perpetual gloom enshrouds a desolate landscape of snow and icebergs, peopled by a squalid and hopeless race of degraded Indians and Eskimo dogs."[25] This depressing image was difficult for Alaska to shake, but more promising ideas about the region soon came into play, especially after George Carmack discovered gold near the Klondike River in 1896. The strike brought thousands of people to the territory, quickly increasing Alaska's non-Native population from about 4,000 in 1890 to over 30,000 in 1900.[26] The enthusiastic stampede to the Klondike was soon followed by secondary rushes to Nome and Fairbanks. People were finally traveling north in large numbers. And Americans in the continental United States started thinking about Alaska as never before.

The information that got people thinking came from media reports, published narratives, and the miners' frequent letters home. The widely circulated image of determined prospectors marching up steep and icy Chilkoot Pass became the icon of the rush. Alaska provided the ultimate test of endurance, but it was a test that Americans seemed to be conquering head-on.

Or were they? Just as news of major success arrived from the goldfields, it was followed by reports of avalanches, lawlessness, and impending starvation. Americans waited anxiously to see who would win the familiar battle of man versus nature in the unfamiliar northern landscape. With time, it seemed that the miners had largely prevailed—if only, in most cases, by simply surviving—and their heroism was celebrated in poems, stories, and songs. The gold rush brought the Alaskan landscape to the forefront of the American cultural imagination, and famous writers such as Robert Service, Rex Beach, and Jack London portrayed it as the ultimate place for a man to test his mettle and ultimately to enrich his character.[27] Since the frontier had "closed" a decade before, places like this had been lacking. Perhaps the Alaskan environment had some assets worth exploiting after all.

With the stampede to the Klondike, the government also began imagining Alaska in a more positive light. Historically, gold rushes had opened the way for more permanent settlers; there was little reason to believe the situation in Alaska would be any different. So, around the turn of the twentieth century, the federal government brought the tools of American civilization to Alaska, including an expanded legal system, a homesteading law, and a provision for the incorporation of towns. The U.S. Department of Agriculture began sponsoring agricultural experiments in Alaska, and the U.S. Geological Survey explored for mineral deposits. To facilitate settlement, the federal government began plans for a railroad that would connect the coastal port of Seward with the mining interior at Fairbanks—the first American railroad built strictly to attract settlers.[28]

Consequently, in a moment of historical convergence, Alaska became "the last frontier." In one short phrase, the American North was conceptually attached to the rest of the United States, and expectations were sealed that Alaska's history and development should proceed in a manner similar to the way they proceeded on the western frontier. Prospectors and explorers would lead, followed by pioneer families who would settle into agricultural and industrial communities. The Natives would be civilized (or, in the gentler term of the day, "educated"), the wilderness tamed, and the American character would permeate the frozen landscape, transforming a foreign place into an authentic part of the United States. In return, Americans would get a chance to relive the heroic history of the frontier, testing their character against the elements and having an opportunity to be, in the words of Frederick Jackson Turner, "born again." Transforming Alaska into "the last frontier" served two important purposes. First, it lessened the culture's frontier anxiety by giving the United States a new "free land" to settle. Second, it rendered Alaska comprehensible to Americans. The frontier concept made Alaska part of America, and everyone could feel confident about how the future of the region would unfold.

And that future included agricultural settlement. So, now we can return to the Matanuska Colony and see the project in a new light. By the time those colonists were planting corn and cabbages at the foot of the Talkeetna Mountains, Alaska was no longer the frigid north, a place akin to Siberia and Lapland. Instead, it was a western frontier, like the Great Plains, Texas, and California had been before it. Because of Alaska's newly defined place in America's cultural geography, it seemed obvious to the proponents of Matanuska that Alaska would be an agriculturally productive place. Their conviction held firm even after years of failed agricultural experiments in the region. Thus, America's geographic imagination trumped any empirical knowledge of Alaska's environment. This would frequently be the case with Alaskan development schemes during the twentieth century. Projects that were obviously maladaptive in light of Alaska's environmental conditions were rendered completely logical by cultural geographic formulations. Alaska development proponents believed so powerfully in their ideas of what Alaskan geography *should* be that they continued to support massive projects that made no sense environmentally. America's changing cultural ideas of nature and place led developers down a path of continued ecological and economic destruction in Alaska.[29]

In order to fully understand this complicated history of Alaskan development, we need to ask what stories America has told itself about Alaska and how those stories have changed over time. The five development conflicts that I narrate in this project contain, in the words of one environmental historian, "not just stories about nature, but stories about stories about nature."[30]

Our stories about nature look very different depending on where we begin and end them. Too often, in Alaska history, the stories we tell are too short, overemphasizing some dramatic event—after all, the landscape lends itself to dramatic events—and we forget to uncover the longer story that can make sense of the drama. Take the construction of the Alaska Highway during World War II, for example. Perhaps no other episode of Alaska's history is so dramatically framed as a triumph of people over nature against countless obstacles. As one writer summarized the project, "[soldiers] fought their way through 1,600 miles of almost impenetrable wilderness, from Dawson Creek in Canada to Fairbanks, Alaska, and they left a highway behind them. . . . Yes, they had done their job. They had built The Road. And, just as roads last for centuries, so the story of their ingenuity, their endurance and their courage will live on and on, a stirring chapter in the American legend."[31]

The story is told in epic terms—brave men doing battle with the frigid north to defend their country from foreign invasion. The reality of the situation was far more complex. Although commonly believed to have been a last-minute response to the Japanese bombing of Pearl Harbor, the Alaska Highway was actually in the planning stages for at least a decade before the United States went to war. Boosters argued that a highway would facilitate settlement and encourage businesses in Seattle and Vancouver to invest in Alaska. Thus, when we take the long view, the Alaska Highway was not just an emergency military maneuver but also a long-term development scheme.

Before the war, however, it had been difficult for Americans and Canadians to agree on the logistics of construction. After the Japanese attack on Pearl Harbor, the two countries quickly agreed to build a 1,600-mile supply highway to Alaska for defense purposes. Construction was extremely difficult. The road began in the middle of nowhere—Dawson Creek, British Columbia, which was only accessible from the larger city of Edmonton by rail. Engineers working on the road had no experience with northern environments, and subarctic phenomena, such as permafrost, confounded them. The route chosen for the highway was meant to connect existing military airfields and failed to take topographical features into consideration. Construction crews would run into unexpected rivers or mountains and be forced to take massive detours to avoid them.

Before construction even began, military strategists argued that the highway would serve no useful purpose in the case of a Japanese invasion of Alaska. Boosters who had been lobbying for decades for a road along the Pacific Coast were angry that the route chosen did not take peacetime uses into consideration. Construction proceeded in the most destructive manner possible—trees were felled, heavy machinery and garbage were abandoned everywhere, and local communities were overwhelmed by thousands of U.S. military construction personnel. In the end, a highway was built, but it was a highway without an identifiable commercial or military purpose.

Symbolically, however, the road was important. In the context of the war, it communicated to Americans that they were safe from Japanese attack. More broadly, the highway connected the continental United States with Alaska. It worked to dissolve the uncomfortable geographic separation by attaching the two major pieces of American land with a quintessentially American road—a culturally significant move. It was now possible to go to and from Alaska entirely by land, which changed the scale of things.

And scale is another way in which Alaska's history has been profoundly shaped by America's cultural geography. Environment and development conflicts in Alaska are often framed as being conflicts between *regional* development interests and *national* environmental interests. This simple dichotomy is reflected in Alaska's historiography as well. Scholars write very different histories depending on whether they take a regional or a national perspective. For example, from a regional point of view, federal attempts to limit development in certain parts of Alaska can be considered intrusive, unfair, and unnecessary. As part of a national narrative, however, the protection of these wild landscapes can be portrayed as a political and moral victory for an overdeveloped country. Written in either of these two scales, Alaska history appears to be a simple conflict between regional development goals and national environmental desires. But this region/nation duality fails to capture the complexity of Alaska's story. For one thing, the national government has been the main proponent of development in Alaska, as my five stories will demonstrate. Conversely, it has often been local people (including Alaska Natives) who have opposed such projects and fought for conservation initiatives. There is no uncomplicated interest on either side.

In addition, there are many other scales in which to frame Alaska's story, including local, transnational, global, and some geographic scales that do not have an obvious name. Examining any episode in Alaska development requires us to consider the event from several vantage points. It is impossible to write a sound history of the region in any singular scale, since, as one environmental historian has argued, "if one scale inevitably interpenetrates others, if new scales can arise and superimpose themselves on others without erasing what was already there, then . . . it is better to think of scales best suited to problems and the intersection of numerous scales."[32] Thus, my history of Alaska does not embrace a simple regional-national dichotomy, although it recognizes that this formulation has shaped popular understanding of environment and development conflicts in the region. What appears to be a two-sided debate, however, usually proves to be far more complicated. In any environmental conflict in Alaska, you can find multiple, competing geographic scales.

Protesting the State of Alaska oil lease, 1969. Ward Wells, Ward Wells Collection, Anchorage Museum, B83.91.S4794.15.

The proposed Rampart Dam illustrates this phenomenon. First imagined in 1959, the project called for the damming of the Yukon River near Rampart Canyon, 130 miles northwest of Fairbanks. The Rampart Dam would have become the nation's largest hydroelectric project, eventually flooding the Yukon Flats region and creating a reservoir larger in surface area than Lake Erie.[33] Boosters began lobbying for the Rampart Dam with great fervor, led in their efforts by Ernest Gruening, former territorial governor and by this point U.S. senator from the forty-ninth state. Gruening used his position on the Senate Public Works Committee to promote the massive hydroelectric project, which was expected to cost $1.3 billion and generate 5 million kilowatts of electricity.[34]

It was apparently not an issue that Alaska did not need so much power; proponents argued that its availability would immediately attract metal, wood pulp, and cement industries to the region. Widespread Alaskan support for the dam, combined with Senator Gruening's influential position in Washington, would have all but assured the project's completion had it not been for one thing: the resistance of the national environmental movement. Environmentalists were quick to mobilize against Rampart, since the flooding of the Yukon Flats would destroy an area rich in salmon, moose, and fur-bearing animals. The flats were a primary nesting habitat for ducks and geese, a resource for both local Athabascan Indians and sportsmen in the Lower 48.

In 1960, with controversy mounting, Congress allocated $60 million for a feasibility study to be conducted by the Army Corps of Engineers. This study would investigate the potential benefits and risks of the dam, including its environmental impact on fish and wildlife. Meanwhile, proponents of the project joined together in a lobbying group, Yukon Power for America, predicting that after Rampart was built, "Alaska's dependence on seasonal construction activity and military spending [will be] replaced by a stable and growing economy."[35] Despite this group's promotional activities, opposition to the project continued to mount. Economic experts began to criticize the wisdom of building a dam in advance of any demand for electric power. Sportsmen complained that populations of game birds would decline and hunting would be compromised. Native residents also began raising objections. Thirteen Athabascan villages would be affected by the flooding, including seven that would be totally submerged by the reservoir.[36] The final blow, however, came in 1964, when the Fish and Wildlife Service—having conducted an environmental assessment for the Department of the Interior—reported that the Rampart Dam would pose "the greatest single threat to wildlife values of any project ever suggested in this country."[37] Although Gruening and others would continue to promote the project in the years to come, it would never again receive widespread support.

The political debates over the construction of the Rampart Dam—as with other Alaskan development conflicts—contain within them debates about the scale in which we tell stories about the past and the present. The dam's proponents recounted a regional history in which natural resources had always been abundant but economic development slow. The environmental movement told a national story of environmental decline, wherein landscapes as ecologically rich as the Yukon Flats had become rare. Alaska Natives thought in local terms about seasonal migrations and subsistence needs. Sportsmen in the Lower 48 created a transnational (or, perhaps more accurately, transregional) history of hunting migratory waterfowl, laying claim to a mobile natural resource.[38]

I do not wish to argue that one scale of thinking is better than another, but rather, to demonstrate how scale works to shape political debates in the short term and environmental storytelling in the longer term. By remaining aware of scale, we can recognize the ongoing contestation of spaces. We see how people and nature are spatially defined as well as how our historical narratives can come to redefine the spaces they inhabit. Alaska can be viewed as a group of local communities, a politically fixed region, a nation's last frontier, or part of a transnational circumpolar north. It just depends on how you scale the story. And the environmental history of Alaskan development will look very different depending on which scale you use.

On a national scale, the environmentalists' victory in the Rampart Dam debate began to change the way Alaska was imagined. For decades, the frontier motif had dominated the nation's image of the region. In 1968, massive oil deposits were discovered at Prudhoe Bay, and—ironically—it was the debate following this oil boom that called Alaska's frontier status into question. Soon after the initial strike, Alaska opened bidding on leases for North Slope lands—in a single day, the state became $900 million richer, with the promise of more to come. Three major oil companies—Atlantic Richfield (Arco), British Petroleum (BP), and Humble Oil and Refining Company (which would later become Exxon)—held most of the leases, and they vowed to get Alaskan oil to market as soon as possible.

This would not be easy. Retrieving oil from the desolate North Slope was going to require a massive engineering project that would dwarf even the construction of the Alaska Highway by comparison. The companies proposed building an 800-mile pipeline from Prudhoe Bay to the ice-free port of Valdez, after which oil would be loaded onto massive tankers. Pipeline construction would be managed by the Trans-Alaska Pipeline System (TAPS, later renamed Alyeska), which would be owned almost entirely by the "big three" oil companies.

In the months following the oil discovery, development activities proceeded in advance of any official decision about whether or not to build the pipeline. Oil companies sent bush pilots to patrol and "protect" the desolate oil fields; Alaska's governor, Walter Hickel (soon to become U.S. secretary of the interior), approved the construction of a winter "ice highway" to get supply trucks up to Prudhoe Bay; and TAPS representatives set up construction camps along the proposed pipeline corridor. Alaska boosters celebrated, as finally they had found a development scheme that promised to create jobs and to jump-start the Alaskan economy—and (as it was beginning to seem, at least) it would be constructed so fast that the opposition would scarcely have time to mobilize.[39]

Behind the scenes, environmentalists quietly acquiesced to the fact that oil drilling would indeed go forward. Their goal from the outset would be to minimize the environmental impact of the project as much as possible. They worried, however, that "the tide of petroleum and discovery and development has raced ahead of our understanding of its implications, to say nothing of our ability to put that knowledge to work."[40] Fortunately for the environmentalists, there would soon be an interruption in the seemingly unstoppable momentum toward pipeline construction.

This interruption had nothing to do with environmental concerns, however, but rather with settling Alaska Native land claims. The government had managed to sidestep the question of Native lands in Alaska for almost a century; soon after statehood, however, Alaska Natives began actively organizing against the state government's withdrawal of lands for economic development. Before a project as massive as the pipeline could be started, it was clear that the question of Native land claims had to be settled. In December 1971, after many months of intense negotiation, President Richard Nixon signed the Alaska Native Claims Settlement Act (ANCSA). ANCSA, which was largely viewed as a victory for Alaska Natives, awarded Native title to 40 million acres of land, provided over $900 million in exchange for the extinguishment of additional land claims, and created twelve regional corporations to administer the settlement.

With Native land issues out of the way, construction of the pipeline could proceed. The two years it took to pass ANCSA, however, had given the environmentalists time to mobilize. In the 1970s, national environmental consciousness was on the rise, and the powerful environmental lobby had recently shepherded both the Wilderness Act and the National Environmental Policy Act through Congress. Recognizing this as a decisive moment for Alaska's future, environmentalists convinced legislators to include a conservation provision in ANCSA. The 17(d)(2) stipulation authorized the secretary of the interior to withdraw up to 80 million acres of unreserved land for possible designation as national parks, forests, and wildlife refuges. So, while the construction of the pipeline went forward, the so-called "d-2 controversy" became the focus of national debates over Alaska's future. Environmentalists publicized their view of Alaska as America's "last great wilderness," and the phrase soon rivaled "the last frontier" in its association with the forty-ninth state. To the chagrin of

Alaska boosters, the environmentalists largely prevailed in their attempts to designate much of Alaska's land as wilderness. In 1980, after almost a decade of controversy, President Jimmy Carter signed the Alaska Lands Bill (formally called the Alaska National Interest Lands Conservation Act, or ANILCA) into law.[41]

The debate over ANILCA solidified Alaska's cultural standing as America's last great wilderness. While many Alaskans would continue to push for development and to think of themselves as settling America's last frontier, nature-minded residents of the Lower 48 now imagined Alaska quite differently. For a country anxious about the disappearance of wild places, Alaska had become the last American space where true nature could be found. Environmentalists celebrated Alaska as a scenic wonderland teeming with wildlife, untouched and pristine. The development history of the region was superseded by the notion that Alaska is—and should always remain—truly wild.

As one scholar has noted, "wilderness represents a flight from history."[42] Often, in designating an area "wild and free," people subconsciously erase any past alteration of the area by human beings. As Alaska became America's "last great wilderness," much of its history was indeed lost to the national narrative. Ironically, with the construction of the pipeline, the drive to settle and develop Alaska in the same manner as the western frontier was diffused, and the myth of an exceptional Alaskan environment—so disconcerting to many Alaskan historians—was born.[43]

America's cultural geography has been vital to the shaping of the Alaskan landscape. The course of Alaska's history has had as much to do with our ongoing desire to fit the region into some culturally coherent spatial category as with any environmental knowledge of the region. When we take this dynamic into consideration, the history of Alaskan development—which can appear haphazard and nonsensical at first glance—begins to make sense. And that man in the bookstore—the one who did not think Alaska had any history—well, his idea makes sense, too. After all, Alaska's standing as the last great American wilderness has largely moved the region into an ahistorical cultural space. But, ironically, it is precisely this wandering though unstable cultural geography that is at the heart of Alaska's history. And if past lessons hold true, Alaska will continue to travel in and out of various geographic categories and scales. Each move will leave a mark not only on the state of Alaska, but also on the larger American landscape that we all share.

A New Game in the North: Alaska Native Reindeer Herding

In the decades before American visionaries began importing frontier-style development schemes to Alaska, they imported reindeer. In the late nineteenth century, the Reverend Sheldon Jackson and his supporters saw Alaska as a fundamentally northern place—like Scandinavia—and they believed that economic development in the region could follow a trajectory similar to that of northern Europe. But Jackson's misreading of Alaska's Native culture and natural environment ultimately led to the downfall of his northern-style development scheme.

Before Jackson's reindeer importation project, Alaska had been one of the few places in the circumpolar north where reindeer husbandry was not practiced. Caribou are native to North America, but reindeer are not, and the differences between the two are largely historical rather than biological. Most scientists believe that the two groups of animals are members of the same species, *Rangifer tarandus*; they have similar genetic makeups and can usually interbreed. Many scholars speculate that the species originated in Eurasia and moved into North America when the Beringian land bridge existed between the two continents, around 15,000 years ago. The species evolved into two distinct groups after the land bridge closed, and that distinction was eventually codified in language, with the animals in Europe and Asia coming to be called "reindeer" and those inhabiting North America, "caribou."

The separate histories of reindeer and caribou collided at a very particular time and place: September 21, 1891, in western Alaska, when two men,

Reverend Sheldon Jackson and Captain Michael Healy, used the U.S. Revenue Cutter *Bear* to close the Beringian divide, sailing reindeer from Siberia and placing them squarely in Alaskan caribou country. Healy, the son of an Irish immigrant and his African slave, had run away from his home in the state of Georgia at a young age and begun "passing" for white. After jumping a British ship to Calcutta as a teenager, he began a successful seafaring career that would eventually take him to Alaska as an officer in the U.S. Revenue Cutter Service (the precursor to the Coast Guard) in 1874. By the early 1890s, the beginning of the reindeer project, Healy was well known among government officials for his far-reaching relationships with Alaska Natives, many of whom referred to him (ironically) as "the most famous white man in Alaska."[1]

These connections to Alaska Native communities were what made Healy an indispensable component of Sheldon Jackson's reindeer crusade. In all other ways, the unruly captain was an unlikely ally for someone like Jackson to embrace. Born in 1834 in upstate New York, Jackson was the son of a small shop owner and his young wife. Shortly after Jackson's birth, his parents made a public confession of their Christian faith and joined a local Presbyterian church. There was no question, after the family's conversion, that young Jackson would eventually enter the ministry, and once he graduated from the Princeton Theological Seminary, he began his career as a missionary among the Choctaw in Indian Country. Years of successful advancement in the church culminated in 1869, when he was appointed the new Rocky Mountain superintendent of missions.

It was during these years as superintendent that Jackson first became interested in Alaska. Once he had risen to the top of his profession in the West, the vast challenge of the territory, largely devoid of missionaries since the departure of many Russian Orthodox priests after 1867, appealed to him. Jackson proceeded to set up a few Presbyterian schools in the more populated areas of Alaska, and then decided that to continue his missionary work in the more remote areas of the territory, he would need the support of the government. He lobbied successfully for passage of the Organic Act of 1884, which established a civil government for Alaska and provided federal funding to develop a public school system there.[2] Jackson used the opportunity presented by the passage of the bill to nominate himself as the new general agent for education in Alaska, and, having no serious contenders for the position, he was soon confirmed by the necessary government officials.[3]

Reverend Sheldon Jackson, vice president of the Alaska Geographic Society, 1899. Alaska State Library, Alaska State Library Photograph Collection, Frank LaRoche, Sheldon Jackson-1.

Despite Jackson's initial success in the planning stages of his educational program for Alaska, he quickly discovered that even he could not overcome the vast challenges of Alaskan geography. Consequently, five years after his appointment as general agent of education, he was still just beginning to explore many of the coastal communities. As part of this ongoing endeavor, in the summer of 1890 Jackson joined Captain Healy aboard the

Bear, and the two men visited the Eskimo villages of western Alaska, while also taking a side trip to Siberia to visit and trade among the Chukchi people there.

During his time in the Arctic that summer, Jackson made two powerful observations. First, he concluded that, due to the avarice of the white man, the Eskimos of western Alaska were starving. In Jackson's words,

> from time immemorial [the Eskimos] have lived upon the whale, the walrus . . . and the caribou . . . of their vast inland plains. But fifty years ago American whalers . . . commenced for that section the slaughter and destruction of whales that went steadily forward. . . . With the advent of improved breech-loading firearms the [caribou] are . . . being killed off and frightened away to the remote and more inaccessible regions of the interior and another source of food supply is diminishing.[4]

Second, Jackson observed that, in comparison to the Eskimos, the Siberians were "fat." He found them to be "good-sized, robust, fleshy, well-fed, pagan, half-civilized, nomad people, living largely on their herds of reindeer."[5] Conversations between Jackson and Healy aboard the *Bear* that summer led both men to the same conclusion: The Eskimos were starving because they lacked a consistent food source, and at such extreme northern latitudes, only herds of reindeer could fill the gap.

While there is no doubt that Healy—and especially Jackson—believed deeply in the crisis they had identified, there are several reasons to believe that the problem of "Eskimo starvation" was not as acute as the two had thought. While it is true that the late nineteenth century saw a decline in some of the traditional food sources of western Alaska, it is probable that, especially in the case of the caribou, these declines were the result of natural cyclical variations in population and not a permanent decrease as a result of overhunting.[6] Also, Eskimos were used to temporary food shortages and would most likely not have perceived this particular one as a crisis.[7]

Eskimos had depended upon Alaska's air, sea, and land resources for thousands of years. They ate fish, caribou, seals, rabbits, berries, and occasionally bears, and usually food was plentiful enough for groups to live in semipermanent villages. When food supplies dropped, the Eskimos became nomadic, traveling long distances and increasing their trade with Siberian Natives and Indians from the Alaska interior. Since the 1850s, the Eskimos had also engaged in extensive trade with American whalers, who were increasingly desperate to find their prey and had begun to chase the whales as far north as the Arctic Ocean. Hunting in the north was difficult, however, and crews would spend up to eight months of the year locked in the ice offshore. The sailors would pass the long winters trading tools, flour, coffee, and liquor (which later became illegal) for the Eskimos' artwork, meat, and hides.[8]

By 1890 the Eskimos were still largely dependent on traditional foodstuffs, but they also had supplemental resources when times were lean. Nevertheless, the starvation problem was so severe in Jackson's eyes that he believed he could not begin to carry out his educational plans in the north until the Eskimos were sufficiently fattened up on reindeer. When his attempts to secure federal appropriations failed, Jackson redirected his efforts to canvassing for private donations. Over the course of the following year, Jackson placed stories about his reindeer plan in all the major eastern newspapers, and as a result he secured over $2,000 in donations to begin transporting reindeer from Siberia to Alaska.[9]

While Jackson was generating publicity and funding for the project, his vision for Alaskan reindeer herding began to expand. Although he had initially seen the project as simply a way to save destitute Eskimos from starvation, he now began to think of it more broadly as a means of bringing Alaska Natives into the modern world. During his years of working with Indian communities in the West, Jackson, like so many of his colleagues, had come to believe that the only way to help Native peoples was to get them to abandon their traditional cultures in favor of white, modern ways. In other respects, however, Jackson's experience in the north had convinced him that the situation of Alaska Natives was unique, as it certainly was—after all, Alaska Natives had not been militarily defeated, and with the notable exception of a few Native groups on the southeastern panhandle and in the Aleutians, few whites had yet to encroach on traditional Alaska Native lands.

Because of these circumstances, Jackson could not imagine implementing the policies of contemporary Indian reformers such as Henry Dawes, who sought to break up groups of Indians living on reservations through the allotment of privately owned land, or Richard Henry Pratt, founder of the famous Carlisle Indian School, who argued that young Natives should be separated from their communities and forced to learn the ways of white society. Instead, Jackson felt that Natives could—and should—be taught the ways of the modern world while remaining part of their communities and living on their traditional, communal homelands.[10] Jackson was not seeking to replicate western experiences in Alaska; he was seeking to do something different in what he saw as a distinctly northern place.

Jackson was able to generate a surprising amount of support for his plan. There were several reasons for his success. First, his seemingly philanthropic reindeer scheme appealed to a generation of Christian Indian advocates whose views of the West were largely typified by Helen Hunt Jackson's recently published polemic, *A Century of Dishonor*, which detailed some of the horrific consequences of the U.S. government's Indian policies on the frontier.[11] Second, Jackson's plan appealed to a broader group of easterners who were not Indian advocates per se, but whose developing progressive political views made them sympathetic to starving Alaskans whose food supply had reportedly been destroyed by white capitalist greed. Jackson's cause was furthered even more by the fact that the victims were Eskimos. The 1890s saw something of a minor "Eskimo fever" in the East as national events such as the 1893 World's Columbian Exposition in Chicago, Robert Peary's highly publicized trips to Greenland in his quest for the North Pole, and Franz Boas's 1897 Eskimo display at the American Museum of Natural History brought these "exotic" new people—and their northern lifeways— to the public's attention.

So, in the late summer of 1891, armed with the spoils of his solicitation campaign, Jackson joined Healy on another trip to Siberia, where the two men successfully traded guns, ammunition, cloth, and tobacco for sixteen head of reindeer. The deer finally arrived in Alaska on September 21, 1891— in Jackson's words, "trembling, hobbled and bruised"—at the harbor of Unalaska in the Aleutians, where they were left on the islands to see how well they would survive the winter.[12] The next summer, Jackson and Healy discovered that their small herd had actually increased by two, and they took this as evidence of their plan's success. The two men dedicated their summer to making five round trips to Siberia to purchase additional deer. This time, however, their destination was not the Aleutians. After much reconnaissance, they had selected Port Clarence on the Seward Peninsula as the location for the first reindeer herd. Jackson christened this new herding area the "Teller Reindeer Station," after his good friend and political ally in the Senate, Henry Teller. By the end of the summer, Healy and Jackson had brought a total of 171 reindeer to the station along with four Chukchi men, who had been hired to stay in Alaska to teach the Eskimos how to care for the deer.[13]

In the fall of 1892, Jackson returned to Washington in another attempt to secure government funding for the reindeer scheme. This time he was moderately successful, and in the spring of 1893 Congress allocated $6,000 for the project.[14] Meanwhile, Jackson appointed Miner Bruce, a journalist who had traveled extensively in Alaska, to be the superintendent of Teller Reindeer Station. During this first season, the deer did not change much about Inupiat life around Port Clarence, although Bruce reported that Natives traveled from hundreds of miles away to see the reindeer, wondering why the white men had brought them to Alaska. Ironically, because the government wanted to grow the herd as quickly as possible, the Inupiat were not yet allowed to kill any of the animals for food, a situation the Natives understandably found maddening, especially during the long, lean winter months.[15]

The biggest problem arising during the first year of the Teller Reindeer Station involved Miner Bruce's relationship with the four Siberian Chukchi herders. Bruce and his fellow government workers seemed to dislike the Chukchi men from the start, calling them foolishly superstitious and accusing them of exhibiting poor reindeer-handling techniques.[16] The Siberians had several ways of handling the reindeer that particularly horrified Bruce and the other government workers at Teller. First, when the men were thirsty, they would lasso a reindeer doe to the ground and drink directly from her bag of milk, "quaffing it with as much enjoyment as if it had been pure nectar."[17] The Chukchi also enjoyed feasting on the lice that would burrow themselves deep into the reindeers' fur.

Perhaps most disturbing to the Teller workers, however, was the Siberians' practice of herding reindeer using urine. The reindeer loved to drink human urine, and the Chukchi could effectively guide the herds in certain directions using urine streams as their beacons.[18] This seemingly "savage" herding practice likely sealed the Chukchi's fate as teachers of the Eskimos. By the spring of the first year, Bruce recommended that the Chukchi's contracts not be renewed, citing their inability to instruct the Inupiat effectively.[19] Bruce, Jackson, and the other champions of the project had claimed that reindeer herding would be an opportunity to civilize the Natives, and clearly the handling techniques taught by the Chukchi did not fit the white men's image of civilized, pastoral herding. By the end of the first winter at Teller, the government workers all agreed that the Siberians had to go.

For the reindeer program to survive, however, new teachers had to be identified quickly, and finding expert reindeer herders willing and able to move to Alaska was no easy task. After carefully considering what few options he had, Jackson set his sights on hiring experienced herders from Lapland. Lapland had a vast reindeer-herding industry, and, according to Jackson, "a moderate computation, based upon the statistics of Lapland, where similar climatic and other conditions exist, shows northern and central Alaska capable of supporting over nine million head of reindeer."[20] This was the beginning of Jackson's imagining the reindeer project on a new, larger scale. He sincerely believed that if reindeer herding worked so well in Scandinavia, it would surely be equally successful in Alaska.

After placing ads for Lapp herders in Scandinavian newspapers, Jackson received over 250 responses to his request, almost entirely from Scandinavians without any claim to Lapp (or Saami) heritage.[21] Most of these letters applauded Jackson's efforts to recruit Saami herders, but also stated that there were few, if any, full-blooded Saami in the United States. It soon became clear to Jackson that he would most likely have to travel to Lapland to recruit the herders he needed.

After raising over $100,000 in donations for the expensive trip to Europe, Jackson was able to send William Kjellmann, a Norwegian from Wisconsin, whom he had hired to work on the project, to Finnmark, where Kjellmann found it more difficult than he had expected to recruit willing participants. Kjellmann found that "Lapps, like the reindeer, cannot be crowded or forced in any way, and least of all in business matters."[22] Eventually, however, he managed to recruit sixteen Saami to sign three-year contracts to teach reindeer herding to Alaska Natives.[23] In signing these contracts the Saami recruits had to swear that they were upstanding members of the Christian church. While the Saami from Finnmark had been converted to Christianity by Lutheran missionaries in the sixteenth century, some of the Scandinavians who had written to Jackson warned that their conversion had been "incomplete" and that many Saami still practiced parts of their traditional religion. By inserting the Christianity clause into the contracts, Jackson aimed to guarantee that they would not only teach their apprentices the art of reindeer herding, but also act as behavioral role models for the Alaska Natives in a way that the Chukchi had not.

Luckily for Jackson, the Saami proved to be the kind of "civilized" Natives that Indian advocates of the day admired. Kjellmann and the group of Saami herders arrived in New York by ship on May 12, 1894, and spent the next few months traveling by rail to Seattle. The group created a media sensation during the course of the cross-country train trip, and the Saami were esteemed as talented, educated, and kind-hearted people who had selflessly

Saami woman milking reindeer in Teller, c. 1900. Fred Henton Collection, Anchorage Museum, B65.18.528.

come from far away to save the Alaska Natives from starvation and teach them how proper "civilized Natives" should act.[24] One reporter described the Saami as being "at the top . . . of the Esquimau group . . . in intelligence and morals."[25] Reporters noted that they could read and write, often in more than one language. Physically, the Saami were described as "better looking than the natives of Labrador or Alaska; they have light complexions, faded-looking hair, and are all blue-eyed."[26] The fact that the Saami were Christians was stressed, and, according to one report, "in Lapland the churches are three hundred miles apart, and [the Saami] frequently hitch up their reindeer on Friday, drive to church for the Sunday service, and return home on Tuesday."[27] Overall, the Saami were given an overwhelming stamp of approval from the media, which helped to generate more positive sentiment among the public for the Alaskan reindeer project.

On July 29, 1894, the Saami herders arrived at Teller Reindeer Station. Unlike the Chukchi, with whom the Inupiat had had a long-standing trade relationship, the Saami were complete strangers, and communication between the two groups was difficult. According to the reports of the white government workers, the Alaska Natives were initially hostile to the Saami, as they refused to take on subordinate student roles and instead tried to assert their dominance over their homeland. Despite these initial conflicts, however, it was not long before the Alaska Natives were inviting some of the

Saami along on their hunting and fishing expeditions. Soon, the Inupiat community tentatively embraced the newcomers, affectionately naming them the "Card People" because the Saami's traditional "Four Winds" hats reminded them of hats they had seen on playing cards.[28]

Nevertheless, the Inupiat continued to remain resistant to the nomadic way of life that these people represented. Reindeer herding required Eskimo men to leave their villages and families for up to four months at a time, as they had to travel continuously with the animals as they foraged for food. The apprentices found the work monotonous at best—far less exciting than hunting and fishing, and with far fewer tangible benefits. Although the contracts had stated that the Saami workers could use the animals in any way they desired, the Alaska Natives were still prohibited from slaughtering any deer, and they often ran off to see their families or visit a nearby village for the latest news and some companionship.[29]

Despite the discouraging reports he was receiving from the government workers at Teller, Jackson was eager to expand the reindeer program. In fact, studying the market for reindeer products in Scandinavia had convinced Jackson that more than the civilization of the Eskimos could be at stake with this project. Where he had once envisioned small subsistence herds living in and around Native villages, Jackson now began to imagine a "vast commercial industry" of reindeer herds in Alaska. Using comparisons with the reindeer economy of Lapland, he estimated that "Alaska, with its capacity for nine million two hundred thousand head of reindeer, [could] supply the markets of America with five hundred thousand carcasses of venison annually, together with tons of delicious hams and tongues, and the finest of leather."[30] With this newfound economic extrapolation, Jackson's vision for reindeer herding in Alaska expanded once again, and he began to believe that he could do even more than just feed the Eskimos or teach them to be civilized Christians—in fact, he could teach them to be successful capitalists—and develop Alaska's sluggish economy along the way.

Jackson soon convinced himself and some of his closest supporters that, given the right training and support, Alaska Natives could eventually control a vast economic empire in reindeer products. To grow the program, Captain Healy and his associates continued to barter with the Siberian Natives, importing a total of 1,280 reindeer to Alaska over the next few years.[31] In addition, the government workers decided to divide the Teller reindeer and distribute them among some of the other missionary outposts of western Alaska. Thus, in August 1894, reindeer were relocated to five stations along the coast of the Seward Peninsula and to one on the Yukon Delta. In addition, in order to try to convince the Eskimos of the tangible benefits of reindeer herding, in January 1895 the government loaned one Inupiat man, Charlie Antisarlook, 100 reindeer, promising him ownership of these animals and all calves born to them after an apprenticeship period of five years. During the next few years, more such deals would be made with individual Eskimo apprentices, and herds would be divided even further.

Of all the Native-controlled reindeer herds, however, Charlie Antisarlook's would become the most successful. In 1900, Antisarlook fell victim to the measles epidemic, and his wife, Mary Makrikoff Antisarlook, inherited her husband's herd of 272 reindeer. Because she lived in the Sinrock settlement near Cape Nome, she was often called "Sinrock Mary." Mary was the daughter of an Eskimo mother and a Russian father, and her ability to speak Russian, Inupiaq, and English made her a powerful figure in the region. She had served as an interpreter on government-sponsored explorations of Alaska and Siberia, and she often accompanied Sheldon Jackson on his travels. Mary had learned the techniques of reindeer herding alongside her husband, and after his death from the measles she fought hard to maintain legal control of their animals. Several times she moved the herd to avoid the negative influences of white gold seekers, and after remarrying, she adopted ten children, whom she taught to care for her deer, securing her legacy. At its peak, Sinrock Mary's herd totaled more than 1,500 animals, and she was even given a new nickname: "the Reindeer Queen of Alaska."[32]

Before Mary could become the Reindeer Queen, however, Jackson needed to increase the support for his great Alaska venture. Despite Jackson's media savvy and his strong network of connections in Washington, it is doubtful that he could have persuaded enough people of the need to expand the reindeer program much beyond its current state had it not been for one major—and, for Jackson, very well timed—event: the discovery of gold in the Klondike. Jackson happened to be traveling on a Yukon steamer with Kjellmann when he first got news of the gold rush, and the two men decided to make a trip to Dawson to check out the situation firsthand. According to Jackson's estimates, there were already between 4,000 and 5,000 miners in Dawson and Circle City, and he speculated that the group would be starving before the end of the winter, as it would be all but impossible to bring in supplies after the Yukon River froze. Other government officials, including the secretary of the interior and the secretary of war, shared Jackson's concerns, and soon news of an impending disaster had reached the media.[33]

Sinrock Mary with members of the Reindeer Committee, c. 1910. Lomen Family Papers, 1850–1969, UAF-1972–71–2278, Archives, University of Alaska–Fairbanks.

Fortunately—in his own eyes at least—Jackson had the perfect solution to the problem of the starving miners, and not surprisingly, it involved using reindeer to transport food and other supplies to the Klondike region.[34] Seeing no other obvious solution to the potential starvation crisis, Congress appropriated $200,000 for what soon became known as the "Yukon Relief Expedition." An atmosphere of impending doom started developing in Washington, and Jackson was ordered to leave immediately for Scandinavia to buy reindeer and hire herders.

Coincidentally, Kjellmann was already in Lapland, looking to replace four of the original Saami families who had chosen to return home after their three-year contracts expired. Once Jackson arrived, the two men worked quickly to purchase 539 draft reindeer, sleds, and enough lichen to feed the animals on the long trip back to the United States. Jackson and Kjellmann also worked with the three Saami families who had just returned from Alaska to recruit 113 men, women, and children to sign two-year contracts to live and work in the United States.[35] These new recruits would assist in the relief expedition and then stay in Alaska for the remainder of their two years of service, teaching Eskimos to herd. Jackson told the Saami about his vision for a vast reindeer industry in Alaska and promised them that they could profit from this new industry along with the Eskimos. Jackson also promised the Saami that they would be given the utmost respect in the United States and "be treated as white people."

After settling the contracts and securing the reindeer and supplies, Jackson and Kjellmann set out on the long journey home. Upon arriving in the United States, Jackson made an immediate trip to Washington, D.C., where government officials informed him that the Yukon Relief Expedition was no longer necessary, as the anticipated starvation crisis among the Klondike miners had never occurred.[36] Despite this development, Jackson recommended that the Saami and the reindeer continue on their journey to Alaska. The group made the long cross-country train trip to Seattle, where they stopped to await the arrival of the ship that would take them to Alaska. During this layover, a serious problem developed. After two false alarms with starvation over the past decade—first with the Eskimos, then with Klondike miners—there was finally an immediate and obvious hunger situation to worry about: the animals had run out of lichen. The reindeer were completely dependent upon arctic plant life, and attempting to feed them grasses from the local parks in Seattle only made their health deteriorate faster.[37] One by one, the reindeer began to starve. By the time the animals reached Alaska, only one-fifth of the original herd remained. Despite this embarrassing development, Jackson declared the expedition a success and pressed on with plans for his project.

Over the next ten years, reindeer were distributed throughout northwestern Alaska through government loans to mission stations, loans to independent Saami who had served out their contracts, and loans to individual Alaska Natives who were deemed "fit" to own herds.[38] The landscape became a moving patchwork of animals, ownership, and control. Although the Saami could do pretty much as they pleased, the government and the missions kept close watch over the Eskimo herders. Despite this formal difference in policy, some Eskimos and Saami worked closely together, and there were many marriages between the two groups, blurring the issue of ownership of the different herds. As the Eskimo herders improved their skills, the Saami treated them with increasing respect. For example, Tautook, a successful deer man from the village of Golofnin, was exalted by the Saami: "He is like a Laplander," they said.[39] Despite these examples of intercultural alliances, many Alaska Natives still felt increasing hostility toward the Saami, as they were given preference in reindeer ownership and much more freedom to sell and slaughter their animals.

The sharp differences between Saami and Eskimo interests were brought further to light in 1898, when three Swedish men struck gold at Anvil Creek near Nome. The ensuing gold rush brought tens of thousands of white men to the reindeer pastures of the Seward Peninsula.[40] The Saami used the opportunity presented by this influx of whites to establish a mail-delivery system (dubbed the "Reindeer Express"), to sell their reindeer for food and freight, and even occasionally to join forces with the white men panning for gold. Meanwhile, the majority of the Eskimos focused their energy on protecting their homes and hunting grounds. In addition, as if the threat of white encroachment were not bad enough, influenza and measles soon spread though the villages, and over half of the Native population in northwestern Alaska died by the end of 1900.

By 1905, there were an estimated 10,000 reindeer in Alaska. Many of the Eskimos who had been successfully "converted" to herding had died during the measles and influenza outbreaks, and the government, the mission schools, and the Saami still owned the majority of the herds. William Lopp, a mission teacher who had been involved with the reindeer scheme since its earliest stages, began to question whether the project had lost sight of its original goal: to improve life for the Eskimo communities of western Alaska. With Lopp's encouragement, the U.S. Department of the Interior began an independent investigation of reindeer affairs in Alaska, and Frank Churchill, an Indian agent and experienced investigator, traveled to several reindeer stations during the summer of 1905 to write a report on the subject. Churchill's findings singled out Jackson as the problem, arguing that his double role as general agent for education in Alaska and field agent for the Presbyterian Board of Home Missions presented a conflict of interest.

At the close of his report, Churchill recommended that the government reconfigure its policies so that the reindeer would benefit the Alaska Natives more directly. To this end, he recommended that the reindeer become a resource "for the natives only" and that visions of a reindeer industry be abolished. "The complete failure of the deer business as a lasting benefit to the natives will begin," he said, "with deer getting into the hands of white men wishing to build up a business for profits."[41] Jackson had hoped that the Eskimos would benefit from the development of a reindeer industry in Alaska, even imagining them as industry owners in charge of a vast economic empire, but Churchill found this belief to be naive. Suddenly finding his ideas under attack from every direction, Jackson officially resigned his position with the Bureau of Education, although he remained active in Alaskan affairs until his death in 1909.

William Lopp, the teacher who had initially brought Jackson's reindeer policy under scrutiny, replaced Jackson as the new general agent of education for Alaska. He began a major overhaul of herding in 1907 with the formation of the U.S. Reindeer Service, which set out immediately to secularize the reindeer program. The task of reindeer distribution was taken out of the hands of mission schoolteachers and given to school superintendents employed by the Bureau of Education. In order to get more reindeer into the hands of Alaska Natives, government herds were broken up and smaller reindeer stations were created in distant villages, so that more Eskimo men could learn the trade without having to travel so far from their homes.[42]

After the major cultural and geographical disruptions presented by the gold rush, a new sense of vulnerability among Alaska Natives made them more amenable to learning the reindeer-herding trade, and the government was doing everything in its power to make it easier for them to do so. For example, instead of having to go through some government- or mission-sponsored apprenticeship program to acquire a herd, Native Alaskans could now simply purchase reindeer from other herders. Despite the new ease with which Natives could acquire reindeer, there were many ways in which the Bureau of Education continued to control the terms of Native ownership. For example, Natives were not allowed to sell female deer to non-Natives, so that reindeer would necessarily continue to concentrate into Native hands. To this end, the government's new policy was extremely successful, and by 1915 two-thirds of the approximately 70,000 reindeer in Alaska were owned by Eskimo herders.[43]

These successes notwithstanding, individual Eskimo herds remained small, disparate, and disorganized. In an effort to remedy the situation, the Bureau of Education, led by the vision of one of its school superintendents, Walter Shields, developed the concept of "Eskimo Reindeer Fairs." Beginning in 1915, the fairs were held in centrally located villages in northern Alaska, and all the reindeer herders and their families were invited to attend. Activities ranged from lassoing, sled pulling, and butchering contests to reindeer parades, singing, and storytelling.[44] The activities were carefully designed by the bureau to convince the Eskimo herders that reindeer herding was an integral part of their culture and their future.

Eskimo herders at a Reindeer Fair in Shishmaref, c. 1923. Lomen Brothers, Karen Krogseng Collection, Anchorage Museum, B81.36.15.

And, in many ways, the plan worked. The Natives who came together for these fairs embraced their roles as herders by writing songs, sharing reindeer recipes, and devising better strategies for reindeer management. They also started to form their own village herding associations and pledged to work together to bring reindeer products to local markets. Because of the carefully crafted fair strategy put in place by Walter Shields—as well as the spontaneous creation of an Eskimo reindeer culture that the fairs facilitated—Alaska Natives began embracing reindeer herding as their own. They began to believe that reindeer could uniquely enhance the livelihood of Eskimo peoples; as the herder Cudluck Oquilluk put it, "the deer help us very well. The deer is just like money. We all say to the government, thank you, because he bring us deer in Alaska for the Eskimos."[45]

In 1914, however, amid the work and excitement of planning the first reindeer fair, a quiet but important transaction had taken place, one that would eventually challenge the developing Eskimo reindeer culture. Alfred Nilima, a Saami herder from the Kotzebue area, sold his herd of 1,200 reindeer to Carl Lomen, a white man from Nome. Despite the protests of many Reindeer Service employees, Lomen's transactions were found to be legally sound. Although Bureau of Education regulations prohibited Alaska Natives from selling their female reindeer to white men, no such limitations had ever been placed upon the Saami owners. By exploiting this small but powerful loophole in the bureau's herding policy, Carl Lomen, a white man, was suddenly in the reindeer business.

Carl Lomen had come to Nome in 1900 with his family to take advantage of the gold excitement. Gudbrand Lomen, Carl's father, was a Norwegian American attorney who had brought his family from St. Paul, Minnesota, to Alaska with the hope of making a business for himself sorting out conflicting mining claims. There was more than enough work for him to do, and his five sons, including Carl, quickly found other mining-related activities to invest in, from photography to prospecting to the drugstore business. By the time Carl purchased his first herd of reindeer, the Lomens had formed a loose conglomeration of Alaskan business interests that they called "Lomen & Company."

The family had decided to invest in the reindeer business with the financial backing of a Norwegian miner who had become wealthy during the early Nome gold strikes. From the beginning, it was clear that the Lomens planned on making the industry big, and they immediately invested in the construction of cold storage plants and investigated transportation possibilities to bring reindeer products to national markets. In order to placate the worries of Eskimo herders, who had just begun, with the Bureau of Education's support, to think about selling some of their meat and hides to white Alaskans, the Lomens gave assurances that there would be no competition between the two groups. The family promised that they would focus on developing national markets and leave the local customers to the Natives.[46] Of course, it would have been no secret to the Lomens that by this point, with the gold rush all but over, most of the potential local customers had already left Alaska.

Nevertheless, the Bureau of Education was cautiously optimistic during the early years of the Lomen reindeer business that white and Native reindeer herders could operate side by side.[47] Carl Lomen initially endeared himself to both bureau officials and the Eskimo herders by offering to buy excess steers from the Natives at a generous $10 per head. He also hired Eskimo herders to work with his employees in the field.[48] While small gestures such as these may have initially kept the peace in the pastures of northwestern Alaska, behind the scenes, Lomen was already working to ensure his family's future dominance in all aspects of the reindeer industry. He spent much of his time building networks of support in major eastern cities, styling himself as the "Reindeer King of Alaska."[49] Lomen's success was overwhelming. Within two years, he had organized the Lomen Reindeer and

Trading Corporation, with holdings of 40,000 reindeer and capital stock worth over $1.5 million.

Unfortunately, the Native herders in western Alaska (with a few notable exceptions, such as Sinrock Mary) were not enjoying a similar degree of success with the reindeer enterprise. A terrible outbreak of influenza during the winter of 1918–1919 had taken the lives of many of the herders, and much of the cultural momentum put in place by the reindeer fairs was lost. In addition, the decrease in the number of Eskimo herders meant that most of the Native-owned reindeer were now wandering freely around western Alaska. The number of animals was growing at an astonishing rate. By the early 1920s, it was no longer possible to tell which reindeer belonged to whose herd. William Lopp, who remained in charge of the Alaska Division of the Bureau of Education, suggested that Natives consolidate their reindeer into cooperatively managed herds, or "companies."[50] In most cases, these herds were organized as join stock companies or ownership cooperatives, issuing one share of stock per deer to each member–owner.[51]

This new corporate structure seemed to overturn the philosophy of small, subsistence herds that Lopp and his Reindeer Service colleagues had established fifteen years before. In many ways, however, the new structure was the inevitable outgrowth of the original Reindeer Service plan, which had resulted in too many individually owned herds drifting together on the same open landscape. The developing Lomen enterprise must have been an important factor as well. After all, this new corporate structure—whether intentionally or not—directed the Eskimo herders toward a competitive, capitalist mind-set, the exact thing that had caused Lopp to criticize Sheldon Jackson's policy fifteen years before. Now that the Lomens were working to create a large-scale reindeer industry, the Bureau had quickly decided that the Natives should be doing the same.

Not surprisingly, the Lomens were much faster and more effective than the Bureau of Education in attempting to create markets for reindeer products in the United States. They used radio and print ads to convince the American public that Alaskan reindeer meat could provide a readily available and cheaper alternative to beef. And to make this new meal option seem attractive, Carl Lomen did everything in his power to get the meat "taste-tested" by prominent critics, particularly in eastern cities. One positive reviewer proclaimed that "all who have tasted the meat like and become fond of it and pronounce it delicious. The fat is nutty and can be eaten in small cubes with as much relish as we down caramels or marsh-mallows."[52] Unfortunately for the Lomens, however, not everyone took to the northern delicacy with such enthusiasm. One set of New York critics bemoaned, "If any meat is worse than reindeer meat we are at a loss to think what it is, unless it would be mule meat. The tenderest steak of a reindeer is tough, coarse, and stringy. . . . It is dark and horrible in appearance. Reindeer meat is so bad that there ought to be a law against it."[53] Despite critical setbacks such as these, the Lomens were successful in getting a number of urban restaurants interested in reindeer as a high-end specialty meat.

The Lomen family also explored more creative outlets for their company's products. They spoke with the U.S. Army about the desirability of reindeer hides for making lightweight, waterproof suits that could be worn by soldiers and pilots. They advertised their product to pet-food manufacturers, successfully convincing the White Rover Company to try marketing a dog food made entirely of reindeer meat.[54] And, perhaps inevitably, the Lomens also worked to capitalize on the mythological and cultural significance of reindeer. They marketed live, harness-broken animals for use in Christmas parades and holiday displays, eventually securing contracts from department stores across the country, including Macy's. To contribute to the authenticity of their product, the Lomens would offer their customers the possibility of having one or more Eskimo herders accompany the animals on their trip south. After caring for the deer, these "authentic Alaskan Eskimos" would then act the part of Santa's helpers for the Christmas spectacle.

The Lomens' efforts were at least moderately successful, as almost 6.5 million pounds of reindeer and reindeer products were sold in the United States by 1929.[55] The vast majority of the sales benefited the Lomen Corporation, although the Bureau of Education did make some sales on behalf of the Eskimo herders. Still, these sales represented only 5 percent of the estimated 640,000 deer that then existed in western Alaska.[56] Demand simply could not keep pace with supply, and the supply of reindeer was soaring dangerously out of control.

As their numbers grew, the reindeer were forced into ever more distant arctic landscapes. As one observer astutely noted, "Alaska's food, the reindeer, is eating up Alaska. . . . Lack of market and capital make it impossible to ship out the deer and lack of pasturage will make it impossible to keep them there much longer."[57] Although the Lomens were having some

Eskimo man at a Christmas performance, 1920s. University of Washington Libraries. Special Collections, UW25939x.

success selling their reindeer products, their operating costs were so high that they were simply not making a profit. Consequently, the company was unable to build more slaughterhouses or cold storage facilities to process more deer. Meanwhile, the Eskimo herders, most of whom had never seen a profit from their reindeer, stepped up their attacks on the Lomen Corporation and asked the federal government to step in on their behalf.[58]

In 1929, the secretary of the interior decided that the reindeer situation was an Alaskan problem, and he officially transferred responsibility for the program from the Bureau of Education to the office of Alaska's governor. In the midst of this governmental transfer, a federal Reindeer Committee was appointed to investigate the current conflicts and problems with reindeer herding in Alaska. The Lomens used this chaotic window of opportunity to lobby for favorable range regulations, marketing privileges, and the dismissal of Native complaints against them.[59] The Lomens were fairly successful in their lobbying efforts, but the economic benefits to their company were ultimately minimal, as their export market crashed with the onset of the Great Depression.

While the Lomens were attempting to assess the extent of their company's financial losses, the Reindeer Committee was attempting to assess what was really happening on the reindeer ranges of Alaska. The committee had much to investigate, as accusations of wrongdoing flew from every direction. The Eskimos accused the Lomens of abusing their monopoly on slaughterhouses and transportation facilities, of stealing Native reindeer by deliberately manipulating branding marks, and of only paying Eskimos for reindeer with credit at their trading stores.[60] The Lomens accused the government of undervaluing their role as an employer of Alaska Natives and of deliberately ruining their company's profit margins by flooding the market with underpriced Native reindeer meat. Both groups accused one another of monopolizing grazing lands, of not taking care of their animals, and of causing the problem of reindeer overpopulation.[61]

In February and March 1931, the Reindeer Committee presented the results of their investigation at a series of Reindeer Hearings in Washington, D.C. The group concluded that there were too many reindeer wandering unattended around the Alaskan landscape and that there were simply not enough profitable ways for their owners to dispose of them. The committee recommended that a roundup of all Alaskan reindeer take place as soon as possible so that the ownership of all animals could be determined and carefully marked. It was also suggested that the government work harder to develop secure markets for reindeer products in the continental United States. Although, on face value, the committee's recommendations appeared fairly benign, if uninspired, much of the rhetoric of its final report clearly favored the Lomen Company. The group uniformly dismissed many of the complaints of the Natives, and at the close of the hearings, one member of the committee said, "I do not believe that the record has established anything in the way of serious criticism of either [the Lomen] company or others connected with the production of reindeer. To me [the investigation] has revealed just the ordinary controversies that arise in connection with such an industry."[62] The Native herders and their supporters were naturally upset by the results of the investigation.

With no meaningful way to implement the committee's investigations, nothing came of the original report, and complaints against the Lomens continued to mount. The Department of the Interior quickly ordered another investigation, the recommendations of which took on a similar tone to those of the 1931 Reindeer Committee Hearings.[63] The report maintained the legality of the Lomens' business dealings and concluded that, although it should make some efforts on behalf of marketing reindeer products, "the government should not purchase existing reindeer marketing facilities or establish competitive agencies."[64] Meanwhile, advocates for the Native herders became increasingly aggressive and vocal in their cause, which had expanded to include nothing less than bringing down the Lomen Corporation. The Native herders openly attacked the latest reindeer investigation in the media, and one Native herder was quoted as saying that the government's recommendations served "as an official White Wash for all things Lomen. . . . The three special investigators can truly be styled, the three yes men of the Lomen interests."[65] The Eskimo herders became increasingly politically active during this period, and they managed to attract a number of prominent Indian advocates to their cause.

The most important of these sympathetic Indian advocates was John Collier, the new commissioner of Indian affairs. Collier came to this position having spent the past decade working for the Indian Defense Association, which opposed the Dawes General Allotment Act of 1887. Inspired by his experiences in the Indian Southwest, Collier worked to reformulate federal Indian policy around the concept of cultural pluralism, and the centerpiece of his new policy was the Indian Reorganization Act, or "Indian New Deal," of 1934. This legislation encouraged Native peoples to create tribal governments and engage in cooperative economic activities on reservations. Although the Indian New Deal did not apply to Alaska Natives—even simple concepts such as "tribes" and "reservations" were simply not applicable there—Collier was eager to include Alaska in his vision for federal Indian policy. Thus, he helped to promote the passage of the 1936 Alaska Reorganization Act, which encouraged Alaska Natives to form village governments and offered them loans from a federal credit fund to promote the development of Native economic activities.[66]

This act was not nearly as comprehensive as the Indian Reorganization Act, and it did not apply directly to reindeer matters. However, during the course of crafting the legislation, the Office of Indian Affairs conducted its own investigation into the Alaskan reindeer controversy. After studying the subject, Collier concluded that reindeer herding was part of the Eskimos' heritage and should be promoted for the exclusive betterment of the Alaska Natives.[67] What Jackson had promoted as a means of Eskimo *assimilation* almost forty years earlier now became, in Collier's view, an important part of Eskimo *culture* that should be preserved for their benefit.

Collier's investigation into Alaska Native affairs was one important factor changing the tone of the reindeer debates in Washington. Another was the financial status of the Lomen Corporation. After the economic downturn of 1929, the Lomens were forced to ask for a government loan to keep their business afloat. This loan was approved in 1933 on the basis of the company's importance as an "employer of Eskimos." As a result, however, the government decided to audit the company. The auditor found that "the condition of the [Lomen Corporation] and subsidiary companies . . . should be of great concern to the officers and stockholders of this enterprise. The companies have experienced heavy losses, resulting in a deficit of over five hundred thousand dollars for the period covered by this report."[68] By the conclusion of the audit, it had become clear to almost everyone, including the Lomens, that the company would probably not survive much longer. The family became amenable to a buyout.

Although it was difficult to convince many members of Congress to purchase private property in Alaska at a time when economic conditions could not have been worse, a strong desire to end the whole reindeer mess won over many skeptics. On September 1, 1937, Congress passed the Reindeer Act, which restricted the ownership of domestic reindeer in Alaska to Natives only and transferred control of the program to the Alaska Division of the Office of Indian Affairs. The legislation also set in motion the administrative machinery for the eventual government purchase of all non-Native-owned deer and industry-related supplies.[69] Although it took several years to complete the appraisal of the Lomens' assets, the government eventually purchased the entirety of their enterprise for just under $500,000. And with the signing of the check, Carl Lomen, a white man, was suddenly out of the reindeer business.

Though the Reindeer Act was understood to be a complete victory for Alaska Natives, there was one group for whom it was a complete disaster: the Saami herders. The Saami had largely kept out of the reindeer controversy, managing their private herds and working with both the Lomens and the Eskimos when they felt it was appropriate. Although they never imagined that the political controversy over white ownership had anything to do with them, for the purposes of the Reindeer Act, the Saami were defined as "non-Native," and thus the legislation compelled them to sell their herds back to the government. A throwaway promise made by Sheldon Jackson to their immigrant parents forty years before had suddenly come true: In America, the Saami were indeed "treated as white people." But in a strange twist of power dynamics, some of the Saami herders who remained in Alaska ended up working for the Eskimos, the people they had once been hired to teach.

The years immediately following the government buyout of non-Native deer were mysterious ones, referred to in Yupik oral history as "the great die-out" or "the crash."[70] In 1930, about 640,000 reindeer were estimated to exist in Alaska. By 1940, the number had fallen to 250,000, and by 1950, only 25,000 reindeer remained.[71] No one knows exactly how this population crash occurred, though there were several probable causes. The first theory was starvation. The reindeer had overgrazed much of northern and western Alaska, and the ecosystem had simply reached its carrying capacity. The second theory was predation. The rise in the reindeer population had led to an increase in the wolf population, which then naturally lowered the numbers of reindeer back to manageable levels. The third theory, and the one favored by most of the Eskimo herders at the time, was that the reindeer had "gone caribou."[72] The years leading up to the reindeer's disappearance coincided with the in-migration of hundreds of thousands of caribou to the Seward Peninsula. The Eskimos believed that the reindeer no longer wanted to be herded, so they ran off with the migration, joining their ancient relatives and "passing," as it were, for caribou.[73]

Regardless of the cause of "the crash," few Eskimo herders saw the departure of the reindeer as much of a problem. Despite the fact that the Office of Indian Affairs had worked so hard to preserve this important aspect of Eskimo "culture," it had become clear to many Natives that the reindeer brought them more work than reward, and most of the herders had never really taken to the nomadic lifestyle that herding required. Now that the Natives had secured the reindeer as their own, they were free to let them go. Many Natives were happy to watch the reindeer run off with the caribou, so they could concentrate on hunting and fishing again.[74] The reindeer would not disappear forever, though, and years later, Natives would again embrace herding as part of their culture and livelihood. That, however, is the story of another time.

One of the first major development projects in Alaska was a distinctly northern one. Although it was modeled after profitable reindeer herding in other parts of the circumpolar north, the project could not successfully be replicated in Alaska. The government introduced reindeer herding as a tool of assimilation—a way to move Eskimos away from traditional lifeways and toward an engagement with market culture—but the Native experience with the project was far from linear. Rather than wholeheartedly embracing the enterprise—or universally rejecting it in favor of more traditional activities—Natives instead considered reindeer herding as one of many economic options available to them at different times throughout the twentieth century. Rather than moving Alaska's economy along a tested northern development path, the reindeer's presence would instead ebb and flow with the needs of Eskimo communities and changes in the Alaskan environment—a reflection of the Alaska Native herders whose culture quietly but definitively shaped the project.

Alaskan Pastoral:
The Matanuska Colony

Tourists in Alaska are often surprised to find—among its more famous mountains, glaciers, and wildlife—that the state is also home to a small but tenacious agricultural community. Next to their "last frontier" license plates, Alaska residents often place "Buy Alaska Grown" bumper stickers, evincing an agricultural pride that might seem more appropriate in the Midwest or the Great Plains. Yet, for Alaskans, agriculture is as much a part of their history as gold mining and oil drilling. Alaska's agricultural heyday came during the 1930s, when Americans suffering from the Great Depression became interested in a renewed pastoral mythology. Thus, Alaska was refashioned as America's last frontier, a place of inevitable agricultural settlement and economic growth. The government sent a group of settlers north, with the expectation that these pioneers would start an agricultural empire in Alaska. This experiment quickly failed, however, as the depression-era farmers could not sustain meaningful crop production in Alaska's harsh subarctic environment.

Boosters began speculating about the possibility of arctic agriculture as soon as the land was purchased from Russia in 1867, although serious consideration of farming in Alaska did not begin until after the Klondike gold rush of 1897.[1] Prior to 1897, the white population was under 5,000—too small a number for anyone to worry much about the potential for northern food production. At the end of the century, Alaska's wide-open spaces were also not a huge draw for farmers. Families looking to homestead could still find free land in Montana and the Dakotas, and there was no need to travel so far to such a challenging country when easier options existed closer to home.[2] The few white people who did venture north were often looking for a pioneer lifestyle that included hunting and fishing, and they did not demand an abundance of vegetables and grains to supplement their diets.[3] Alaska had very few "white foods" on the shelves of its remote trading stores, but there were very few white people who wanted them. Most people were satisfied with the choices available to them.

The situation changed dramatically at the end of the century. In August 1896, George Carmack and his brother-in-law, a Tagish Indian named Charlie, discovered gold in the sands of Bonanza Creek near the Klondike River. The news of their strike spread quickly, and by the summer of 1897, the rush was on. Some 35,000 gold seekers stampeded through Alaska to reach the Canadian banks of the Yukon River. Most men came unprepared to survive the northern winter, and politicians and the media predicted mass starvation. Some Alaska boosters, such as the missionary Sheldon Jackson, called for the importation of reindeer from Lapland to feed the men. Others, less sympathetic to wayward prospectors heading off into an icy borderland—a "no man's country" of sorts—looked to the Canadian government to solve the problem.[4] Still other Alaskan advocates, Alaska Governor John Brady among them, called on the government to invest in northern agriculture so that Alaska could become a self-supporting land. This was a major shift in thinking about Alaskan development. Instead of looking to civilize the Natives or exploiting Alaska's northern resources, boosters now began imagining more frontier-like settlement in the region. And it seemed impossible to imagine Alaska as a potential American homeland without a steady and familiar food supply—for many Alaska proponents, this was the first and foremost condition for settlement. The supposed gold-rush crisis provided an opportunity to promote the agricultural opportunities that would attract permanent residents.

At first the call for Alaskan agriculture was dismissed in favor of more immediate solutions. When three Scandinavians struck gold on the shores of Nome in 1898, however, the crisis deepened, and suddenly more people were listening to the agricultural advocates.[5] By 1900, the number of white men in Alaska had increased to 63,000, and there did not seem to be enough food to go around. In addition, with the high price of goods in Alaska, most prospectors could not afford to purchase a meal even if they could find one.[6] While, in most cases, Canadian and U.S. government rations prevented starvation in the short term, government officials soon decided that a more lasting solution to Alaska's "food problem" needed to be found.

Though this conviction was strong enough for the government to start investing in northern agriculture, the process did not exactly take off quickly. Despite the efforts of a small number of agricultural enthusiasts, such as Governor Brady, most people in the continental United States still believed that Alaska was too cold, too icy, and too barren to grow crops. Nevertheless, in 1898 the U.S. Department of Agriculture made a modest investment in the possibility of Alaskan farming by sending three officials (including Sheldon Jackson) to consider the agricultural potential of several regions in the district. After stating that farming was difficult in the north, the men nevertheless reported that it was possible to grow things, and in fact, some vegetable gardening and cattle raising were already taking place in select regions, often by aging prospectors and trappers fallen on hard times.[7] While their conclusions were clearly mixed, the three men were more optimistic than most people had expected.[8]

As a result of the preliminary recommendations made in this report, the government took another step forward in its investigation and opened a number of agricultural experiment stations.[9] This process, however, was tentative, and few researchers were actually deployed to Alaska to work on the agricultural question. Some of the government workers were intrigued by the possibility of Alaskan farming, but few were willing to commit significant resources to the project, especially after the crisis of starving gold miners had ended. Still, officials continued to allocate just enough money for the agricultural investigation to trickle on. In part, the government believed that, if Alaska were ever to be permanently settled by white people, it would need to follow the "normal course of development," which included establishing farms in the region.[10] Although settling Alaska was not at the top of everyone's priority lists, opening the land to farming still seemed like an important project to undertake, so the experiments continued. The first agricultural station was built in 1898 in Sitka (then the capital), and over the next decade five more opened— in Kenai, Kodiak, Rampart, Copper Center, and Fairbanks.[11]

Among the people who worked at the experiment stations, the most important was Charles Christian Georgeson, a native of Denmark who had immigrated to the United States in 1873 to further his education in agricultural science. By the time he was appointed by the secretary of agriculture to head the Alaska agricultural project, he had become a well-known and well-traveled professor of agriculture in Texas, Kansas, and Japan, and he was considered one of the world's foremost experts in the Danish dairy industry. Georgeson's move north caused him to refocus his academic work

Cabbage growing at the Matanuska Agricultural Experiment Station, 1935. Alaska State Library, Mary Nan Gamble Photograph Collection, P270–714.

on Alaskan farming, however, and it was not long before he was a true believer in the possibilities for arctic agriculture. Before he even arrived in the north, Georgeson did some cursory research, and he was soon preaching the philosophy that "latitude determines the land" and comparing Alaska's growing potential with that of Scandinavian countries.[12]

Because of his status as an "expert" in the field, Georgeson's opinions were taken more seriously than those of the equally enthusiastic but less knowledgeable boosters such as Jackson and Brady. In fact, it was not long before Georgeson replaced Alaska's Governor Brady as the unofficial spokesperson for Alaskan agriculture. Even before the experiment stations had had a chance to demonstrate the feasibility of Alaskan agriculture, Georgeson began arguing for the importance of pursuing farming in the district: "The white population of the Territory is dependent upon the farmers of the States for maintenance, but what this means can scarcely be realized by those who are not familiar with the conditions. . . . It stands to reason that if the means to support life can be produced within the boundaries of the Territory all the other resources will become more valuable."[13]

Despite the fact that Georgeson began the agricultural experiments shrouded in optimism, early results were less than promising. Researchers reported that the soil was "sour and sadly in need of drainage." Norwegian varieties of clover, radishes, peas, carrots, and beans were all "total failures." "Young plants languished, turned yellow, and died."[14] Grain crops—so important to the possibility of ever raising livestock in Alaska—were flattened by wind and rainstorms before they could be harvested.[15] In spite of these setbacks, it was a testament to the power of belief, perhaps, when observers noted, "the barley and oats made their best growth on old ground in Governor Brady's garden."[16]

Governor Brady was not the only one who claimed to have a good harvest, and Georgeson's disappointment with the early results at Sitka was tempered by the testimonials he collected from Alaskans who said they had successfully grown vegetables in the territory. These agricultural proponents countered the results from the experiment stations by claiming that government workers were not planting crops in the most fertile areas or using the correct growing techniques for northern conditions. A settler in Wrangell argued that "only ignorance of their opportunities prevents them from growing much. . . . All of the hardier vegetables grow in the greatest luxuriance."[17] Another proponent claimed that while farming in Alaska was not "as easy as falling off a log," food production *was* possible, once farmers learned the particulars of the northern environment.[18]

Hopeful speculation such as this kept the agricultural project going through the early years of questionable results at the experiment stations. And although the government farmers could never claim general success, they did begin to see more promising results as time went on. During the particularly warm summer of 1906, a government worker at the village of Coldfoot, 60 miles north of the Arctic Circle, claimed to have grown 8-pound cabbages and 16-pound turnips.[19] In 1907, a picturesque experiment station was established at Fairbanks, and photographs featuring the newly planted crops and grazing livestock were quickly publicized as being "typical" of Alaskan farms.[20] Researchers at Barrow, Alaska's northernmost village, claimed to have planted gardens near the shores of the Arctic Ocean where continuous sunlight produced mature vegetables in twenty-seven days.[21] It was not long before boosters and the media were using these "incredible, but true" stories to wax fantastic about the possibilities of "farming in a bowl of ice."[22]

While for most Americans, arctic agriculture was nothing more than a fascinating oddity, for Alaska boosters the 16-pound turnips were serious business. In part, the possibility of agricultural settlement in the region fueled a slow but growing movement in Washington focused on developing the northern land. In 1912, Alaska officially became a "territory" (as opposed to a military "district") when the government passed the Second Organic Act. As a territory, Alaska became entitled to an elected legislature, and the region lost something of its colonial status. Because the new territory lacked any real economic base, however, the federal government still needed to play a prominent role in Alaska's development. To this end, the Second Organic Act granted the president the authority to establish a railway that would "develop the country and resources thereof for the use of the people of the United States."[23] The idea of an Alaska railroad had been tossed around since the gold-rush period, when boosters were trying to create an all-American path to the Canadian Klondike region. Debates over the proper route, however, had kept private investors from ever establishing a completed rail.

In 1914, however, under the president's direction, Congress allocated $35 million to fund the construction of a railway from the coastal port of Seward to the interior mining town of Fairbanks—the first railroad built strictly to attract settlers. For Alaska advocates, this was an exciting development. Construction would bring thousands of jobs to the territory, and the railroad would provide potential residents with reliable transportation to the interior of Alaska, where they could build homes and businesses. The Department of the Interior established a construction camp on Cook Inlet, which soon became Anchorage, a city of 6,000 people where previously there had been none. Despite the large numbers of people working on the project, the railroad took more than eight years to build, as the challenges of construction were monumental.[24] President Warren G. Harding finally completed the project by driving in the golden spike on July 15, 1923.

The Alaska Railroad concentrated boosters' attention on the areas along its route; if development were to take off, they reasoned, surely it would be here.[25] In particular, Alaska advocates focused on the Matanuska Valley, a "newly-discovered" region of about 500 square miles, situated about 40 miles north of the new city of Anchorage.[26] The valley was picturesque, encircled by the snowy Talkeetna Mountains to the west and the rocky Chugach Mountains to the north and east. The mountains protected the valley from harsh winds, and the climate was "mild" by Alaskan standards—reaching above 60 degrees Fahrenheit in the summer and rarely dipping under 20 degrees below zero in the winter. Rainfall averaged about 16 inches per year.[27] The lakes and forests of the valley were rich with fish and game, and several hundred Athabascan Indians regularly visited the area to hunt for food. The quality of the soil varied considerably, although certain patches were visibly dark and fertile. It was not long before writers were dubbing Matanuska "the California of Alaska."[28] The Department of Agriculture soon joined in the chorus of hopeful speculation, and government workers opened Alaska's last agricultural experiment station in the valley in 1917.

As soon as construction began on The Alaska Railroad, settlers started moving to Matanuska, albeit at a slower rate than the most optimistic boosters had predicted. In 1923—the year President Harding pounded in the golden spike—there were a total of ninety farmers in possession of 22,000 acres of "agricultural land," only 1,400 acres of which were actually cultivated.[29] The railroad began an aggressive campaign to attract more settlers to the area, touting the claim that "Alaska, America's last frontier, offers 160-acre free homesteads, exempt from taxes, adjacent to The Alaska Railroad, and near established markets, to persons of like vision, sinew and spirit that urged our forefathers to pioneer and develop our West States."[30] Enthusiasm for settling the last frontier seemed to go hand in hand with the belief in the possibility of arctic agriculture. In 1921, a farmers association in Fairbanks took a symbolic leap of faith in the forecasted development and built a grain mill to process the wheat that speculators predicted would soon be produced in the region.[31] Still, few Americans heeded the call north, and those who did often failed at their attempts to farm and left the territory disillusioned. According to one observer, during the 1920s, "450 farmers settled in the Matanuska Valley near the Alaska railroad. All of them . . . left the country after their second year there, or . . . abandoned their farms, most of them having lost every dollar they took in with them, all of them bitterly damning the misrepresentations that induced them to go."[32]

By 1929, The Alaska Railroad was running at an annual loss, and the region along the rail was still importing $2 million worth of food every year.[33] Still, Alaska boosters did not give up their dream that one day Americans would realize the vast agricultural potential of the north. The railroad continued to churn out promotional literature, and the government continued to fund the agricultural experiment stations, hoping upon hope that something would eventually draw settlers to the sparsely populated northern territory.

What Alaska boosters could not have predicted was that the something that eventually turned people's attention to Alaska was not a northern boom, but a southern bust. When the stock market crashed in 1929, over one-quarter of Americans lost their jobs, leading to poverty, hunger, and desperation in both rural and urban areas of the country. Oddly enough,

Alaska was not significantly affected, since its economy had never shared in the prosperity of the 1920s—or any prosperity at all, for that matter.[34] Initially, many Alaska promoters continued their work without changing tactics, seemingly unfazed by the national economic crisis. For example, in 1929, Otto Ohlson, the new general manager of The Alaska Railroad, opened an office in Chicago with the sole purpose of promoting tourism and immigration to Alaska. Ohlson was an energetic military officer who had managed railroads in France during World War I, and he worked with the same kind of military diligence to promote settlement in the north. "The Colonel"—as he became known in Alaskan circles—designed numerous pamphlets and posters that were distributed in the agricultural heartland during the early 1930s.[35] He also negotiated with continental railroads and steamship lines to transport willing immigrants, their material possessions, and their animal companions to Alaska, all at very affordable rates.

Yet, despite Ohlson's diligence, not everything remained the same after 1929. For one thing, the ongoing national crisis caused the government to drop its support for the Alaska agricultural experiment stations in 1931. Funding for the railroad was also cut. Despite these setbacks—which could only be expected, given the state of the economy—people began talking more optimistically about Alaska than they had since the gold-rush days. The reasons for this were several. First, many scholars and politicians blamed the depressed economy on the paucity of unsettled territory left to be developed. In 1890, the U.S. Census Bureau had declared that the era of "free land" had ended, and the American frontier was officially "closed." Three years after this symbolic announcement, the historian Frederick Jackson Turner argued for the centrality of the frontier to American prosperity and culture in his seminal essay, "The Significance of the Frontier in American History."[36] In the early 1930s, many writers continued to espouse Turner's ideas in their explanations for the economic disaster that had struck America: "Many an observer has pointed out that past U.S. depressions were relieved by mass migrations to the frontier . . . [and] that the present depression is uniquely acute because that safety-valve is gone," wrote one reporter.[37] Many Americans worried that the depression would endure because the impoverished had nowhere to go to begin anew.

The "closed frontier" theory of depression, as this idea came to be known, was actually not a new concept; some turn-of-the-century economists had reasoned that the closing of the continental frontier had resulted in the economic downturn of the 1890s. The view was more widespread in the 1930s, however, because of the presidency of Franklin Delano Roosevelt. Roosevelt—a former student of Frederick Jackson Turner's at Harvard College—was a true believer in the frontier thesis. Something of an agrarian romantic, Roosevelt had always idealized the notion of farmers and western pioneers making their living from the land. In 1932, the year he successfully defeated Herbert Hoover in the race for the White House, the newly elected president theorized about the importance of the frontier to the American way of life. He argued that

> depressions could, and did, come and go; but they could not alter the fundamental fact that most of the people lived partly by selling their labor and partly by extracting their livelihood from the soil. . . . At the very worst there was always the possibility of climbing into a covered wagon and moving west where the untilled prairies afforded a haven for men to whom the East did not provide a place. . . . Traditionally, when depression came a new section of land was opened in the West; and even our temporary misfortune served our manifest destiny.[38]

Although this "closed frontier" theory of depression seemed to leave little room for hope, Roosevelt's plan to improve the U.S. economy—his "new deal for the American people"—also addressed the so-called "frontier problem." He advocated a government-sponsored turn away from the industrial life that had failed so many Americans and a move "back to the land."[39] According to this philosophy, men could regain their economic independence by making their living directly from the earth, as the eighteenth- and nineteenth-century pioneers had supposedly done. As one back-to-the-land proponent argued,

> individual independence shall be achieved by millions of men and women, walking in the sunshine without fear of want. . . . In response to the loving labor of their hands, the earth shall answer their prayer: "Give us this day our daily bread." . . . Theirs shall be the life of the open . . . fragrant with the breath of flowers, more fragrant with the spirit of fellowship, which makes the good of one the concern of all, and raises the individual by raising the masses.[40]

As this agrarian suggests, life on the frontier should be different than in years past. One of Roosevelt's advisers explained that "the keynote of the new frontier [will be] cooperation, just as that of the old frontier was individual competition."[41] In 1933, Congress invested in Roosevelt's "socialist frontier" by allocating $25 million for the president's use in promoting the relocation of urban poor to rural regions. During the 1930s, approximately 100 communities were created from this back-to-the-land ideology.

So, it was in this atmosphere of national mourning for the closed frontier and growing support for collective rural resettlement that people began to look at Alaska in an increasingly optimistic light. As the country slowly stopped bemoaning the onset of the depression and began looking for ways out of their despair, one writer acknowledged that "the United States does have an unexploited frontier. Ever since the Depression cast its blight upon this country, economists . . . in common with the general public, have overlooked the fact that in Alaska we have vast territory, unsettled and undeveloped, which is most certainly capable of supporting many more people than those now regarded as unneeded in the congested industrial areas."[42]

Ever since the United States had purchased Alaska from the Russians in 1867, boosters had been looking for something to do with all this land. Now, decades later, it seemed that those in the Lower 48, having spread from coast to coast, might finally need a new land to settle. Expectation had met opportunity, and the time was right to do something about Alaska. In the summer of 1934, President Roosevelt met with Ernest Gruening, the new head of his Division of Territories and Island Possessions of the Department of the Interior, and told him, "Alaska needs more people and we ought to do something to promote agriculture. Next spring I would like you to move a thousand or fifteen hundred people from the drought-stricken areas of the Middle West and give them a chance to start life anew in Alaska."[43]

Soon after Roosevelt suggested that Gruening start investigating the possibility of an agricultural settlement in Alaska, a plan was set into motion.[44] Gruening met with Harry Hopkins, the head of Roosevelt's Federal Emergency Relief Administration (FERA), and Hopkins agreed to fund the project. Hopkins, a close of confidant of Roosevelt's, believed strongly in the redemptive power of hard work, and the idea of an agricultural colony appealed to him. After a brief survey of possible settlement locations, Hopkins decided to coordinate FERA's resources with the (largely unsuccessful) efforts of "The Colonel," Otto Ohlson, manager of The Alaska Railroad, to bring farmers to the Matanuska Valley.

Ohlson advised sending only a few hundred families at first, so they would not produce more than the local market could absorb.[45] President Roosevelt agreed to start small, but he also wanted to get the project going quickly. He issued an executive order on February 4, 1935, banning further homesteading in the valley and setting aside all remaining land for the settlers. Many details were sacrificed in favor of expediency. The entire plan was developed in a matter of months, unleashed on the American people by a group of government officials with hopeful but hazy information about a northern promised land called the Matanuska Valley.[46]

When news of the proposed Alaska colony spread, thousands of poverty-stricken Americans wrote to the government begging to be part of the program. They expressed a deep frustration with the opportunities available to them in their local communities, and they described their hopes and expectations for a better life in Alaska. Letters arrived from people in every desperate corner of the country, and they flooded the desks of officials at all levels of government.[47] Annie Holdaway, a teenager from the Great Plains, wrote to President Roosevelt,

> We see in the paper where 2,500 families are going to be sent to the Matanuska Valley, Alaska. I decided to write and tell you how very, very much we wish we could be one of those families. My father, Roscoe Holdaway, is fifty years old. . . . Daddy has always had such a hard time. For the last eight years the crops have been almost a complete failure on account of the drouth [sic] and boll weevils. It gets a little worse each year. For the last two years we haven't been financially able to make a crop. . . . We think if we could get to go [to Matanuska] that we could get on our feet again. We have always wanted to go to Alaska. It seems like a land of promise, a Canaan, to us. . . . We want to go so bad. Maybe we could get a [farm?] of our own.[48]

The situation was every Alaska booster's dream. Suddenly volunteers to settle Alaska were too numerous to count—provided the government covered all the expenses, of course. Families with ten or more children volunteered to abandon their farms; homeless factory workers begged for transportation up north; women asked whether there were men in Alaska who "needed wives." The entire population of Jones County, Texas, exhausted by years of heat and drought, demanded to be taken to a northern climate en masse.[49] Gruening believed that the colonists should be chosen from the approximately 15,000 applicants who had pled their cases in excruciating detail. Hopkins, who by now was officially leading the project, disagreed, preferring to use a more "scientific" method of selection. He argued that settlers should be chosen from the Great Lakes cutover region—the northern parts of Minnesota, Wisconsin, and Michigan—reasoning that the midwestern climate most closely resembled that of the Matanuska Valley. In addition, a high percentage of midwestern residents were of northern European ancestry, which Hopkins believed made them well suited to a pioneer lifestyle. So, despite Gruening's arguments to the contrary, government officials sent rejection letters to the hopeful Annie Holdaway and thousands like her, and instead turned their attention to another group of desperate families: the federal aid recipients in the Great Lakes region.

Times were hard everywhere, but they were particularly hard in the Midwest, and the list of federal aid recipients was long. In every county of the region, people were destitute and defeated. The depression had left the many midwestern miners and lumberjacks out of work. Agriculture in the Great Lakes region had always been difficult—tree stumps, rocky terrain, and infertile soil were perpetual problems—but now severe drought made farming almost impossible. Government services in this area were either unavailable or unreliable. Residents suffered from both isolation and poverty, and many families were prime candidates for relocation. Nobody doubted that there would be a long list of volunteers to move to Alaska. The question was how government officials would choose among them.

As part of Roosevelt's economic recovery efforts, each state had a large staff of social workers dealing with local poverty and unemployment. Harry Hopkins—a former social worker himself—decided that these men and women should be in charge of choosing the colonists. In the spring of 1935, the social workers met in Washington, D.C., to work with Hopkins's staff to establish selection criteria. The group decided that besides being eligible for federal aid, colonists should be between twenty-five and thirty-five years old, married, and have between one and six children. All members of the family had to be in good mental and physical health and be familiar with life in a cold climate. Urban residents were not to be considered, since they might experience "culture shock" in Alaska. The women needed only to be hardworking, although teaching and nursing abilities would also be considered. The men should have experience with subsistence farming, and it was preferable for them to also have a vocational skill such as carpentry, blacksmithing, or machine work. A high-school education for the adults was desirable. Regular church attendance was a must.

Charged with this monumental task, the workers returned to their home states to begin the interview process. Despite the rigid selection criteria, the 201 families who were ultimately chosen—66 from Minnesota, 67 from Michigan, and 68 from Wisconsin—often strayed widely from Hopkins's ideal.[50] For example, 18 of the men had no farming experience at all, and 27 others had little to speak of. Sixty-one colonists were over the age of thirty-five, and 12 were less than twenty-five years old.[51] Some colonists had a history of criminal convictions or alcohol abuse, and a few had health problems—including 8 with active tuberculosis, 4 with asthma, 1 with a wooden leg, and another who had to be committed to a mental asylum before the group even reached Alaska.[52]

It is unclear whether potential colonists misrepresented themselves during the application process, or social workers strayed—intentionally or not—from Hopkins's guidelines when making their selections. It can also never be known for sure how accurately the workers described the colonization project to the applicants. These questions would be the source of contentious debate in the years that followed. In fact, it was not long before Matanuska Colony administrators were openly accusing social workers of choosing inappropriate families because they "were naturally interested in eliminating misfits and inexperienced farmers" from their states' relief rolls.[53] At the time, however, no one suggested that the social workers were acting inappropriately, and so the decisions they made were respected.

After the families were chosen, the government quickly started to promote the project. Newspapers across the country announced that "around one thousand people from relief rolls of three Great Lakes states will begin a 3,500 mile trek by land and water next month to Alaska. There they will build their homes in the wooded valley of Matanuska and begin clearance of land for a truck gardening and dairying community."[54] Once this news spread, officials in Washington were inundated with more letters. Many were from angry citizens who thought that their families deserved to be part of the colony. Some writers praised the government's plan and inquired how they could secure a spot in the next group of colonists chosen. Many more, however, Alaskans included, questioned the wisdom of the resettlement, citing the many examples of failed farming efforts in the north.

The more aggressive of these letters actually accused the government of insensitivity and foolishness. One woman scolded President Roosevelt:

> To me, it is the most inconceivable thing in the world, that anyone mentally outstanding enough to be chosen one of our government representatives in Washington, could be so lacking in judgment as to vote to send a group of poverty stricken Americans to Alaska to establish new homes. . . . Alaska! Where at most, summer prevails only four months of

the year, and anything in the way of gardening has to be produced in that time; where the seasons require at least three outfits of clothing to meet the demands of weather comfortably and healthfully. . . . After all, the [depression] can and will not go on forever. . . . So why not have kept the few families with us until that time, rather than make them feel like the Russians must have felt on departing for Siberia?[55]

Despite this scathing criticism, the positive fanfare surrounding the project increased exponentially as the colonists' departure drew closer. The families traveled in three contingents, each according to its state of origin, and a large number of reporters joined each group as it journeyed west by rail. For the first group of families from Minnesota, the exciting cross-country trip reached a high point in San Francisco, where a brass band greeted them with an enthusiastic rendition of "Happy Days Are Here Again."[56] A crowd of local residents cheered as a fleet of taxis transferred the colonists to their posh hotels, where "in the room of each family was a basket of fruit, candy, Hills Brothers coffee, identification tags, movie tickets, schedule of events, a yard of streetcar tickets, fresh nightgowns for the mothers, diapers for the babies, and toys for the youngsters."[57] The next few days were filled with joy and excitement as the mayor treated the families to theater shows, elaborate meals, and street parades.

A week or so before the first group of families departed, a shipment of tents, cots, stoves, food, and farm equipment was loaded aboard the *North Star* to set sail ahead of the colonists. Also aboard this ship were a group of government supervisors, a doctor, some nurses, a photographer, and several hundred "transient workers," who were charged with breaking camp prior to the colonists' arrival.[58] On May 1, amid a cacophony of hillbilly music and patriotic cheering, the Minnesotans departed San Francisco on the *St. Mihiel*, continuing on toward their new home in Alaska.

The five-day voyage was the first real hardship for many colonists, as unusually choppy waters made many people ill. For those who managed to avoid seasickness, however, the scenery was breathtaking. The boat traveled north through the icy glaciers of Alaska's Inside Passage,[59] where cresting whales, soaring eagles, and the beckoning beauty of misty fjords greeted them, a scene that must have amazed these passengers so accustomed to midwestern landscapes. The group landed in Seward and was welcomed by another local celebration. The colonists were told that they had made it to the promised land of Alaska, "far from the vicissitudes of the make-believe, tinsel civilization Outside."[60] From Seward, the group boarded a train and continued on to Anchorage, where the mayor had declared May 10 a local holiday so that the entire city could attend the welcoming party for the colonists.

Finally, after all the fanfare, the colonists continued north by rail to the tiny town of Palmer, the official headquarters of the new colony. This time, however, the families did not arrive to find celebratory dinners, theater tickets, or even Hills Brothers coffee. In fact, the only thing waiting for them at the end of their journey was an unfinished tent city that could barely shield them from the muddy spring rain.[61] Still, the enthusiasm of the group could not be dampened. They had finally set foot in their land of opportunity. They had made it to the Matanuska Valley.

As the colonists familiarized themselves with their new home, the natural environment in the valley—about which they had all speculated for so long—slowly made itself known. Despite the muddy conditions, the colonists' first impressions were overwhelmingly positive.[62] The Alaskan landscape was phenomenal, and the Matanuska Valley offered Alaskan scenery at its best. The Chugach Mountains, which bound the valley to the south and east, and the Talkeetnas, which bound the valley to the north, jutted dramatically toward an open sky. Purple, yellow, and white wildflowers enlivened the groundcover. Moose, caribou, and bears could be spotted in the west end of the valley as it opened out to the level, poorly drained Susitna River Valley. Soil formations were mostly loessial or wind-blown. Two glacially fed rivers—the Matanuska and the Knik—ran through the region, and there was an abundance of lakes and streams brimming with trout and salmon.

Despite the portentous rain during the weeks following the colonists' arrival, the rainy season would not normally begin until July, after which mosquitoes would appear in frightening numbers. The valley's location at 62 degrees north latitude meant that the summer seasons would be short (averaging 108 frost-free days), but the summer days were long (averaging seventeen hours of sunlight).[63] Although the abundant sunshine gave some colonists all the hope they needed that first summer, even the most optimistic among them would soon learn that the winter had another whole set of natural extremes.

These impending months of cold and darkness made everyone a bit uneasy about the amount of work that had to be done in such a short time. The makeshift tent city erected by the transient workers would never make it through the first snowfall, and with snow possible as early as September,

Colonists arriving in Palmer, May 10, 1935. Alaska State Library, Mary Nan Gamble Photograph Collection, P270–124.

construction of the houses needed to begin right away. Don Irwin, a cheerful government worker who had previously managed the Matanuska Agricultural Experiment Station, had been appointed by Harry Hopkins to run the colony, and he decided that families should draw lots to determine who would live in which part of the valley.

As dozens of reporters watched, the men gathered around an improvised stage made of wooden planks and oil drums, each picking a number that corresponded with a 40-acre lot. Much was at stake. The soil in the valley varied considerably from place to place—rich in some areas, rocky in others. The luckiest men drew lots on which there was an abandoned homestead and perhaps even a few acres of cleared land. Some lots were close to the town and railroad station; others were on forested land more than 10 miles away. After each man realized his fate, the bargaining began in earnest, as families traded lots with one another to try to improve upon their locations.[64] Inevitably, perhaps, fighting broke out among the colonists, and many families were unhappy with the land they ultimately received.

So, the complaining began. Some colonists claimed that social workers back home had told them that they could locate their homesteads anywhere they pleased, and they were furious with having to build on their assigned lot.[65] The men were supposed to help the transient workers with the actual construction of the houses, but many refused, often because they believed it was the government's responsibility or because they were angry at the order in which the houses were being built. The transient workers took advantage of the long hours of sunlight and worked on construction projects both day and night, waking babies and irritating the colonists and their dogs.

Even as construction got under way, new problems arose. The first major supply ship was wrecked off the Alaska coast, and even when supplies finally showed up, they were mostly useless: coffee beans arrived without grinders; horses without wagons; grindstones without axes. Perishable food spoiled because there were no cold storage units. Stoves and hardware rusted out in the open. The colonists requested more overalls and underwear, but 5 tons of paper towels were delivered instead. The early rainfall brought mosquitoes, and men swatted and swore at the swarming insects while women tended to the children's bites. All the while, reporters hounded the colonists with questions and photographed everyone's every move, hoping to gain some insight into life on the last frontier.[66]

Many of the colonists added to the carnival of complaints while trying, with varying levels of ingenuity, to solve the problems that had overtaken their daily lives. Nine of the families simply packed up and left, selling their possessions to secure passage home. Although there was always a core group of families who claimed to be happy, even more became angry after a young boy received inadequate medical care and died from the measles. Most families were displeased with the prices charged for supplies at the commissary, and they began to accrue debts far beyond the original $3,000 allotted them. Minor concerns became major complaints, and colonists nearly rioted over missing the audio program "Amos 'n Andy" because of the shortage of plugs for radios.

A group of unhappy women—no doubt brought to Alaska by overly exuberant husbands—attempted to steal the transient workers' identification badges, disguise themselves as men, and return to the United States. As more and more troublesome stories such as these made their way to Washington, the senators from Michigan, Minnesota, and Wisconsin became increasingly critical of the colonization scheme. After receiving a telegram from a group of unhappy families, Arthur Vandenberg, the junior senator from Michigan,

Some of the colonists returning home after gathering wood for cabin construction, 1935. Alaska State Library, Mary Nan Gamble Photograph Collection, P270–264.

interrupted debate on the Senate floor to accuse the government of sending unsuspecting citizens off on a "crazy Alaskan adventure." The senator complained that the colony was terribly mismanaged—construction of houses was slow, fresh food was scarce, and medical care was poor.[67]

Congressional debates over the administration of Matanuska raised the profile of an already well-publicized venture. On June 24, Hopkins reported to Congress on the progress being made on construction projects, arguing that food and medical care were more than adequate, given the remoteness of the colony. Many government officials defended Hopkins's point of view, the most vocal of which was Senator Homer T. Bone of Washington, who begged everyone to remember the poor conditions from which the colonists had come. Senator Bone described the success of the new community in patriotic terms, arguing that the colony offered the best of the frontier experience without any of the hardships.[68] Those in favor of rehabilitation programs argued that the colony embodied the values of democratic individualism, as it sought to make self-sustaining farmers out of 200 families formerly dependent on government handouts.[69]

As politicians back east speculated about the ideological implications of the Matanuska settlement, colonists up north worried about the material projects that needed to be completed before their first Alaska winter. In his effort to expand the management of the colony, Harry Hopkins had sent Samuel Fuller, a New York industrialist, to oversee the construction work. Fuller halted construction of everything but the colonists' homes, and he cut the prices on supplies being sold to families.[70] When Fuller was called away on business, Hopkins replaced him with Leroy Hunt, a colonel in the Marines, who continued Fuller's attempt to win back the confidence of the colonists. Hunt, like Don Irwin, wanted to please everyone. "The Happy Colonel," as he was known, easily agreed to most of the colonists' requests, whether or not they were practically feasible. Still, by the end of that first summer, one out of every six families had abandoned the colony, and many more were threatening to leave.

By early September, only 28 houses had been completed, and the families became increasingly concerned as the weather turned colder. Under Hunt's enthusiastic supervision, however, an enlarged construction crew managed to build another 112 unfurnished homes by the end of October, and—much to the colonists' relief—all the remaining houses were finished by late November. Hunt demanded that construction of common buildings continue through the winter, despite the difficulty and cost.[71] At this first sign of progress, Harry Hopkins handed over management of the colony from the Federal Emergency Relief Organization to the Alaska Rural Rehabilitation Corporation. Although funding for the project would still come from the federal government, Hopkins was eager to move immediate responsibility for the controversial project into local hands.

Once the rainy summer passed and the colonists were at least minimally housed, much of their collective anger dissipated, and the families settled into a semblance of community life. While the colony school remained unfinished, children began to attend classes in the nearby towns of Matanuska and Wasilla. Both Protestant and Catholic churches were opened, and traveling teachers and clergymen took up residence in the community. Jack Allman, a former newsman living near the colony, started an upbeat newspaper, the *Matanuska Valley Pioneer*, which he published out of one of the abandoned tents. Many families occupied themselves with catching and canning fish, and—although technically illegal without a license—some men tested their frontier fitness by hunting for moose, bear, and Dall sheep. A few colonists used the late summer and early autumn to begin clearing their land. For the most part, however, little agricultural work was done, as

Colonists displaying beets and lettuce grown in their garden, 1935. Alaska State Library, Mary Nan Gamble Photograph Collection, P270–742.

many of the families claimed that the government had promised to clear the first 12 acres on each homestead, and they were simply waiting for this promise to be fulfilled.[72] Although that first winter was not particularly severe by Alaska standards, the long hours of cold and darkness were more than many colonists could take, and by spring only 158 of the original 201 families were still living in the valley. These remaining colonists found ways to fill their days, and discontent within the community temporarily waned.

The summer of 1936 brought some of the dirtiest work—both literally and figuratively—that had yet to be done. The government agreed to pay the colonists to cut down the trees on their land so that the bulldozers could come in and clear the rest. The work was slow and difficult. The land was covered with stumps, brush, and moss, and pockets of permafrost lurked beneath the topsoil. The colonists became bitterly divided over whether the government should provide them with a stump-pulling machine.[73] As angry debates slowed down the tedious work, government officials privately confessed that it would be a miracle if each colonist got 5 acres cleared that year—not enough land to support a family, let alone bring crops to market.[74] Most colonists started by vegetable gardening, since they did not have sufficient acreage to grow grain or raise livestock. A few families tried their luck with small numbers of chickens and dairy cows.

As these first farms got under way, the government began taking surveys of the colonists' land—and their mounting debt. With so few crops being planted—let alone going to market—families had little money on hand, and they bought almost everything on credit. The ostensible budget for the commissary was $45 per family per month, but most colonists exceeded that limit, and at least one family was forced to withdraw from the colony when the father began stockpiling commissary goods and selling them for cash.[75] In an attempt to get the colony out of this financial quagmire, the government started issuing allowances in "bingles" instead of cash. Bingles were only accepted at colony stores, and they could never be used to buy alcohol, luxury items, or passage back to the United States.[76] For many colonists, this level of governmental paternalism was more than they could tolerate. Still, complain as they did, they had little choice but to comply—at least in the short term.

So, what did the colony demonstrate about the potential for Alaskan agriculture? The answer to this question is not straightforward. At a minimum, the colony confirmed that it was possible to grow things in Alaska. Not everything thrived at northern latitudes—"hot crops," such as corn, tomatoes, cucumbers, and squash, all languished in the cold. Potatoes, cabbage, strawberries, and small grain crops, though, could be successfully cultivated. Clearing the willows, spruce, and birch brush from the land was always difficult, particularly when it came to removing tree stumps. Once the ground was cleared, however, pigs, chickens, and dairy cows could root and graze, although the majority of their feed still had to be imported from the continental United States. Despite these obstacles, Alaskan agriculture grew slowly during the war years. By the summer of 1943, there were 250 farms in the valley, over half of which had been established by the Alaska Rural Rehabilitation Corporation.[77] Clearly, Matanuska farmers were proving that Alaskan agriculture was possible.

The fact that farming was possible, however, did not necessarily mean that it was environmentally desirable or economically profitable. At first, questions about the feasibility of farming were overshadowed by the sheer excitement that anyone was growing anything at all. Instead of talking about the size of the harvest, the managers of the colony focused on the size of individual plants, bragging of 6-foot pea plants and 4½-foot oats.[78] Alaska's long hours of summer sunshine produced large vegetables in a short time, and these potent symbols of fertility initially helped build morale among the farmers. What the colony's extraordinarily large vegetables belied, however, was the fact that permafrost and an early freeze could make sizable yields difficult to achieve. And it is the size of yearly harvests—not the size of individual plants—that ultimately determines the success of agricultural life.

After a few bad harvests, some farmers completely abandoned the idea of raising crops and focused on producing eggs and dairy products. During the early 1940s, a group of colonists started delivering Grade A milk to Anchorage under the "Matanuska Maid" label.[79] World War II brought an influx of military personnel to the growing city, and the farmers had a larger market than ever before. Still, even with the help of the Alaska Rural Rehabilitation Corporation, production could not keep pace with demand. Imported feed was expensive, and caring for the animals through the long winters was difficult. Many farmers slowly drifted into mining, fishing, or military work. Even those who continued dairy or mixed vegetable farming had to rely on government subsidies or second jobs to cover their expenses. Still, the pursuit of Alaskan agriculture continued—as it does today.

Every summer since 1936, Matanuska Valley farmers have hosted the Alaska State Fair in Palmer.[80] The fair, which celebrates the history of the Matanuska Colony, showcases the best produce grown in the region, including cabbages, grains, carrots, onions, celery, peas, and other vegetables. In 1941, Colonel Otto Ohlson offered $25 for the heaviest cabbage, beginning the famous "largest cabbage contest," which continues to the present day. In 2000, a local woman set the record with a 105-pound cabbage. The fair currently attracts more than 300,000 visitors annually—many of them tourists from the "make-believe, tinsel civilization Outside."[81] Fair officials find that visitors are often "surprised to learn that vegetables and grains will grow in Alaska."[82]

During the late 1930s and early 1940s, national discussions about the Matanuska Colony largely served as springboards for debates over the frontier, collectivism, and the New Deal. In Alaska, however, the focus remained on developing an attractive agricultural community in the north, and local debates were still focused on what—if anything—could be profitably grown there. For many farmers, the answer was "nothing," and by 1948, only 63 of the original 201 families remained.[83] Some of the families left for the continental United States; others found work in Alaska, usually mining, fishing, or working for the military. After the start of the war, the public lost interest in the colonization project, and its "national mission" to rehabilitate the poor gave way to other goals. Government officials ended up settling most of the colonists' debts, at a cost of $1.2 million.[84] The families who remained in the colony made an uneasy truce with the Alaska Rural Rehabilitation Corporation, although rules and contracts were constantly being renegotiated.

The most surprising fact, given all the dissatisfaction and upheaval, is that some farmers managed to cultivate crops. Although the climate and soil quality made it nearly impossible to grow large-scale commodities such as wheat or corn, some farmers had modest luck with dairy products, eggs, or mixed vegetable gardening. They were able to capitalize on the novelty of oversized vegetables (although some critics complained that these larger vegetables lacked vitamins and flavor).[85] Most farmers were forced to accept second jobs to make ends meet, but there were a few families who never gave up—albeit a very few. The Matanuska Colony never really ended—it merely faded into a minor agricultural community that continues to be supported by loans from the Alaska Rural Rehabilitation Corporation.

Supermarkets in Anchorage still proudly showcase produce from the Matanuska Valley. In 2008, however, Alaska only had 0.2 percent of its land under cultivation, and the state was ranked fifty out of fifty in terms of its agricultural output—which is not a particularly impressive figure, even before the state's size is taken into consideration.[86] Slightly fewer than 500 families were trying to making a living through agriculture in 2008, and most rural residents privately admit that farming is tough, even under the best of circumstances.[87]

Ironically, Alaska's largest agricultural commodities are aquaculture and vegetables grown in greenhouses or nurseries.[88] Still, the Matanuska Colony inserted farming into Alaska's sense of itself, and there are many residents for whom the agrarian ideal remains important. For the time being, small numbers of farmers will continue to grow crops and graze livestock underneath the snowcapped mountain ranges of Alaska. After all, even if farming does not contribute much to the economy, the symbolic power of agriculture cannot be underestimated—it brought the ideology of the frontier to the northernmost state; indeed, farming is part of what makes the Alaskan landscape recognizably American. In a foreign environment of glaciers, permafrost, tussocks, and tundra, pastures and hay bales are comfortably familiar. And the giant vegetables certainly make a fascinating display at the fair.

The Road to Nowhere:
The Alaska Highway as a
Northern Development Project

On November 20, 1942, U.S. and Canadian officials gathered at Soldier's Summit, a remote spot near Kluane Lake in the Yukon Territory. With great fanfare—broadcast to the North American public by radio—representatives from the two countries announced the completion of the Alaska Highway, a transnational engineering feat spanning 1,422 miles from Dawson Creek, British Columbia, to Delta Junction, Alaska.[1] Although the project was not technically finished—since it was barely passable and needed to be rebuilt during the coming summer—the pathway that had been opened was shrouded in symbolic importance, particularly for the United States.

After the outbreak of World War II, the United States feared that the Japanese might target Alaska for invasion. The Alaska Highway was built in response to this perceived threat—in the event of an attack, its proponents argued, the road would serve as an important supply route to the remote territory. The highway was also a demonstration of political will. In nine short months, the almost 20,000 soldiers and civilian workers who built the road had shown their Japanese foes—and indeed the world—the lengths to which Americans would go to defend their homeland. Although the Alaska Highway was never used for military traffic, its construction became an important wartime success story. The sheer magnitude of the project impressed Americans, regardless of the highway's ultimate failure to serve its advertised purpose. In contemporary media coverage, the construction workers were portrayed as war heroes, men (and women) who had braved a harsh northern environment to keep their country safe from the Japanese.

The popular historical interpretation of the highway has changed little from its 1940s' formulation. Scholarly treatments of the project have rarely looked beyond the immediate wartime context to put the highway into a longer view.² A recently acclaimed documentary of the Alaska Highway falls victim to this shortsightedness. As one astute Canadian reviewer observed, "most of the [documentary's] narrative could well have been written in 1942, for it is distinctly triumphalist in tone, with much use of words such as 'conquer,' 'hardships,' 'challenge,' and the like. There is no mention at all of the considerable harm done to the environment, nor of the negative effects on the indigenous communities that lay in the highway's path."³

While focusing on the project's value (or lack thereof) to U.S. wartime strategy elicits a certain set of historical questions, taking a longer perspective on the Alaska Highway automatically brings the social, cultural, and environmental aspects of the project into focus. In this longer view, global war becomes only a passing backdrop to a different kind of drama—the ongoing attempts by the United States to settle and develop the Alaskan landscape. As always, ideas about how Alaska fits into the national narrative shaped the project in profound ways. When the highway project was first imagined, it was based on the idea of Alaska as the last frontier, a place whose settlement and economic development would be facilitated by easier access from the contiguous United States—an idea that had persisted for decades. After the outbreak of war, Alaska became a place on the forefront of national defense, and the highway became a means of accessing this potential military stronghold. Ultimately, however, the road that was built served neither an economic nor a military purpose.

Prior to the construction of the highway and the advent of air travel, most visitors (or settlers with all their worldly goods) voyaged to Alaska by steamship. The journey was long, difficult, and expensive, and it is not surprising that travelers yearned for an easier alternative. Many Alaska boosters felt that a land route was the key to attracting more permanent settlers.⁴ As early as 1865, the Western Union Telegraph Company identified the Rocky Mountain Trench—the valley between the Pacific Coast Range and the Rocky Mountains that stretches from the Gulf of California through western Canada to Alaska—as a probable route for a telegraph line and road from the United States across the Bering Strait to Asia and Europe. Northerners were excited by the prospect of a permanent trail to Alaska. The company began construction of the telegraph but abandoned its plans when the American merchant Cyrus Field successfully laid a transatlantic telegraph cable between North America and Europe, eliminating the need for a Pacific line.[5]

After the abandonment of the telegraph trail, many people continued to call for the construction of an overland route. However, the next serious proposal was not crafted until 1899. Its creator, Edward Henry Harriman, was a wealthy railroad magnate who owned the Southern Pacific, Union Pacific, and Illinois Central lines. He made a name for himself in the north by financing an Alaskan voyage for artists, scientists, and writers, which he casually dubbed "the Harriman Expedition." While cruising and conversing with prominent intellectuals such as John Muir, George Bird Grinnell, and Edward Curtis, Harriman conceived of the idea for a permanent connection between the United States and Alaska by way of rail through British Columbia and the Yukon.[6] His goal was to promote commercial development along the route as well as to provide a convenient mode of transportation.

Similar ideas had been circulating among entrepreneurs since the United States purchased Alaska in 1867, but no one's vision was quite as ambitious as Harriman's. His plan included a railroad bridge over the Bering Strait to Asia, where the American track would hook up with a proposed Russian railroad. Although a few prominent officials rallied in support of Harriman's plan, it was ultimately abandoned after 1905 when the Russians lost the Russo-Japanese War, which rendered them unable to build their part of the rail.[7] After Harriman's proposal died, there continued to be talk of a Canadian line from Edmonton to the Yukon Basin. However, with U.S. and Canadian leaders disagreeing over who should pay for the project, nothing ever came to fruition.[8]

As the automobile rose to prominence, mumblings about a northern rail gave way to rumblings about a northern road. During the 1920s, the government engineer Donald MacDonald proposed constructing a "Pacific-Yukon Highway" that would be part of an international road system linking Alaska to Argentina. Soon other northern boosters were promoting the idea.[9] Although there were disagreements over the proper route, most people assumed the road would follow the coast from Seattle north through British Columbia and the Yukon. In 1929, citizen-based International Highway Associations were created in Fairbanks and Dawson City to research and promote this northern highway. According to these associations, the benefits of construction would include access to timber and mineral resources, increased tourism, assistance to air travel, and the promotion of goodwill between the United States and Canada.[10]

Proponents of the highway in the United States could easily summarize their reasoning in a rhetorical flourish: "We are seeking to expand the frontier. We are seeking to enlarge the opportunities for happiness and success for the people of Canada and the United States."[11] In other words, open a path and settlers (and their money) would begin to flow north, just as they had once flowed west. Some Canadians agreed with this notion. Simon Fraser Tolmie, the Conservative premier of British Columbia, became the most prominent supporter of the Pacific-Yukon Highway. He believed that a coastal road through British Columbia would bring huge economic benefits to the province. Not sensing that he could garner much support from the Canadian government—then led by the Liberal prime minister William Lyon Mackenzie King—Tolmie turned to President Herbert Hoover to investigate the potential advantages of the proposed road.[12]

Hoover, who was hopeful that the Pacific-Yukon Highway would stimulate industry in northwestern cities such as Seattle, assembled a commission to study the proposal. In 1933, the group reported back to the president, concluding that "the project was feasible from an engineering and constructional standpoint [and] that substantial benefits would accrue from the project, but . . . more information was necessary before it could be definitely determined that the project was economically sound."[13] The commission noted that the highway's northern location would increase all the expenses associated with its construction and limit most of its benefits to the more temperate months of the year. Still, the commission concluded in favor of the idea, with the assumption that the United States would jointly finance the project with Canada based on the relative length of road in each country. With less than one-sixth of the proposed highway on U.S. soil, the United States would only be responsible for $2 million, while Canada would have to invest an estimated $12 million.[14] American proponents—with fingers crossed—tried to defend the financial arrangement by claiming that "the benefits to be derived from each road by the two nations will be in proximate ratio to the funds expended by each."[15] Not surprisingly, President Hoover supported this reasoning, and Prime Minister King did not. Alaska boosters were outraged: Canada was blocking the settlement of America's last frontier, not only geographically, but now politically as well.

As a result, the project failed to move forward, and discussions of an international highway were tabled while the United States and Canada faced the mounting crises of the Great Depression. In 1937, the highway plan resurfaced when President Franklin Roosevelt became interested in building a northern road for military purposes after the outbreak of the Second Sino-Japanese War. U.S. sympathy was settling with the Chinese, and consequently, a Japanese threat began rising to the West. With Japan only 750 miles from the United States' "back door," Roosevelt publicly wondered if a highway to Alaska could help the United States defend the vulnerable territory in case of an invasion.

While defense had always been one of the many justifications for the proposed highway, at this moment, it shifted to center stage. Anthony Dimond, Alaska's nonvoting delegate to Congress, agreed that Alaska's defenses should be improved, and he began promoting a highway as a defensive military project.[16] (Dimond had also lobbied for the Pacific-Yukon Highway in the early 1930s. Typical of many highway boosters, Dimond was genuinely concerned with Alaska's defense, but he was also content to employ whatever reasoning would get his northern road built.[17])

Prime minister King remained skeptical about investing Canadian money in what now seemed like a preemptive military maneuver by the United States against Japan. However, the new premier of British Columbia, Thomas Pattullo, was as excited about the project as his predecessor had been. Pattullo's enthusiasm was based on the projected economic benefits it would bring his province rather than any desire to promote international cooperation or to support U.S. military strategy. Regardless of Pattullo's motives, Roosevelt was able to use his visible enthusiasm to convince Congress to fund the Alaskan International Highway Commission to research a possible highway to Alaska. Thanks to relentless lobbying by Premier Pattullo, a similar commission was set up in Canada, and the two groups were instructed to work cooperatively.[18]

While the commissions carried on with their work, some Canadians began complaining that "the Canadian committee [has] no real power." According to one scholar, "the reaction of Canadian politicians—with the notable exception of British Columbia Premier Tolmie—was cool and noncommittal, for they were wary to . . . schemes that might foster American dominance of the northwest."[19] Still, even with flagging Canadian enthusiasm, the Alaskan International Highway Commission conducted its investigation and concluded that "the construction of the highway is a worthy project."[20] After much aerial reconnaissance, the commission reported favorably on two potential routes for the highway. Route A—also called the coastal route—would link Seattle with Alaska by way of Vancouver, Hazelton, and Whitehorse. Route B—also called the Rocky Mountain Trench route—would nearly follow the old telegraph trail, running north from Prince George to Dawson City and on to Alaska.[21]

Tensions between the U.S. and Canadian commissions partially grew out of a disagreement over the preferred route. The Americans strongly favored Route A, even while quietly admitting that a coastal road would be more difficult to construct. Route A ensured that Seattle would remain "the gateway to Alaska," as it had always been with water travel. Also, Route A would make it easy for small feeder roads to connect the highway to Skagway, Juneau, and other Alaskan port cities, facilitating the movement of people and goods into southeastern Alaska. Both of these features could have significant economic benefits for the United States.[22] After all, the Americans' primary goal was to settle Alaska and to promote economic development there; in this respect, Canada was merely an obstacle to be overcome.

The Canadian commission did not sympathize with the American point of view. The Canadians argued that a Route A would be more vulnerable to foreign invasion, while an inland route would be safer, cheaper, and easier to build. In addition, Route B would provide an all-Canadian route to Dawson City, then the capital of the Yukon Territory. Canadian officials had been working to revitalize Dawson's sluggish economy since the end of the gold rush. At a joint meeting of the two commissions in 1939, the Americans strongly advocated for their preference, although the Canadians successfully pressured them to state that "the matter of the route to be selected through Canadian territory was primarily one for decision by Canada."[23] Even after this admission, however, the United States did not back down, and the disagreement continued to simmer. Meanwhile, in Europe and Asia, more serious conflicts were escalating into war.

When Hitler invaded Poland in 1939, Canadian surveyors were hard at work studying the Northwest Staging Route. Conceived in the early 1930s, the route was a series of airfields in western Canada and Alaska spanning the shortest route (called the "Great Circle Route") from North America to Asia. The United States and Canada had initially been interested in using the airfields as a commercial connection with the so-called "Orient." After 1939, however, the Dominion of Canada was at war along with the rest of the British Empire, and the project took on new meaning. While the Americans and Canadians continued to squabble over a possible highway, they easily agreed upon a strategy for the airfields. The Northwest Staging Route moved quickly from surveillance to construction, and Canada soon built fields at Grande Prairie, Fort St. John, Fort Nelson, Watson Lake, and

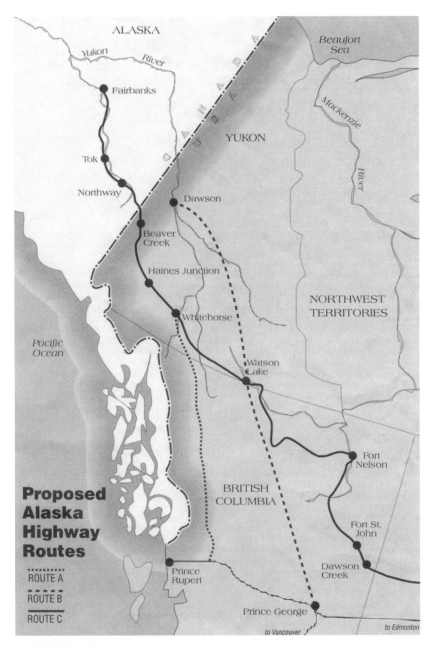

The three major proposed routes for the Alaska Highway, c. 1940. From Fern Chandonnet, ed., *Alaska at War, 1941–1945: The Forgotten War Remembered* (Anchorage: University of Alaska Press, 2007). Provided courtesy of the University of Alaska Press.

Whitehorse. A large U.S. air base—Ladd Field—was already in place at Fairbanks.[24] When completed, the Northwest Staging Route comprised fifteen airfields from Great Falls, Montana, to Nome. The fields were available for daytime use in September 1941.

While working together on the staging route, the United States and Canada formed the Permanent Joint Board to consider more cooperative measures for the defense of North America. At its first meeting, the board decided that Alaska was the most vulnerable area on the continent and that more should be done to defend it. The group stopped short, however, of recommending the construction of a northern highway.[25] In part, the Canadians were nervous. If a major war broke out in the Pacific, it was possible that the United States would be involved while the British Empire remained neutral. Would giving the U.S. military the right of way through Canada be akin to supporting the U.S. war effort?[26] Moreover, while some U.S. board members believed that a highway could help with Alaska's defense, the Canadians were less sure about its usefulness for their own country. Some speculated that a highway could even be harmful. If Alaska fell, they wondered, could the road actually facilitate a Japanese invasion of Canada?[27]

Now that the possibility of a U.S. military conflict was growing, the U.S. Army began voicing its own reservations. A road originally intended to facilitate the settlement of America's last frontier had magically transformed into a military project. Despite the crescendo of support from President Roosevelt, Alaska Delegate Anthony Dimond, and other politicians, military strategists were not completely convinced of the highway's utility. In 1940, the U.S. Navy concluded that a northern highway would be "useless" in the event of a war.[28] The War Department engaged in an extensive study of the project and decided that "the value of the proposed highway as a defense measure [would be] negligible."[29]

The military's view was partially based on General George Marshall's opinion that a Japanese invasion of North America was "highly improbable."[30] In addition, War Department officials realized that the construction of a northern highway would be tedious and that the project could divert money, equipment, and soldiers away from more valuable operations. Military leaders also claimed that water travel would be sufficient to meet the defense needs of Alaska, even in the event of an attack. Not surprisingly, the military's position further dampened Canada's enthusiasm for the project. As a Canadian official wryly observed, "if and when the Canadian Government should decide to co-operate in the Alaska highway project, they would probably wish to represent their co-operation as a contribution to the defence of this hemisphere."[31]

In Alaska, highway boosters condemned the War Department's assessment and accused the military of continuing to ignore northern defense needs, as it had since the Alaska purchase in 1867. Although the War Department's position made it more difficult to lobby for the highway in Congress or Parliament, local associations in Canada and Alaska continued to organize in favor of construction. In fact, new groups of outspoken residents on the Canadian Prairies and the American Great Plains had begun to promote a new route for the highway that began in Edmonton, Alberta, and followed most of the cities on the Northwest Staging Route northwest to Fairbanks. Advocates claimed that a prairie road would provide "cheap construction, better climate conditions, productive . . . farming and mining, and also scenic beauty" when compared to the previously proposed Routes A and B.[32]

Because Edmonton would become the economic center of the project, the premier of Alberta, William Aberhart, was soon enthusiastically promoting the "Prairie Route," or "Route C," to Canadian and U.S. leaders. While Aberhart was busy lobbying for his preferred route, another prominent advocate for the highway emerged: The polar explorer Vilhjalmur Stefansson—internationally famous for his anthropological fieldwork among the Canadian Inuit—published a report in support of the highway. Stefansson had his own vision for the road, however, and he rejected the three extant proposals in favor of an inland route that traveled north from Edmonton through the Mackenzie River Valley.[33] Stefansson's proposition became known as "Route D." So, by 1941, there were four proposed highways to Alaska.

Despite the obvious lack of support from U.S. military officials, Delegate Dimond introduced a bill in the House of Representatives on February 5, 1941, authorizing the construction of a highway to Alaska, following whichever route President Roosevelt saw fit. After the introduction of the bill, the president once again requested the Army War Plans Division to research the possible advantages of a highway; again, the military's report concluded there would be few—if any—strategic benefits to construction. This was early June. Several weeks later, on June 22, the situation changed. Hitler invaded the Soviet Union, easily uprooting the Russian Empire and unsettling military officials in the United States. True, Japan had signed a neutrality agreement with the Soviet Union in April 1941; still, there was always a possibility that the Japanese would invade Siberia if Soviet armies collapsed.[34] The Japanese threat to Alaska seemed to be growing.

The Nazi invasion of the Soviet Union concerned both President Roosevelt and British Prime Minister Winston Churchill. Although neither leader was fond of Stalin, they agreed that Hitler was the bigger threat. The United States and Britain decided to join together in support of the Soviet Union against Germany. As a primary part of their aid, the two countries designed a "lend-lease" program that would ferry aircraft to the Soviet Union via the Northwest Staging Route. Each country pledged to transport 1,800 aircraft between October 1941 and June 1942.[35] For better or worse, the north was now an important part of wartime strategy.

The new international situation had consequences for the highway as well. Two days after the invasion, General Marshall advised that the U.S. Army's recent report be rewritten. Marshall concluded that a highway was now "desirable as a long range defense measure, providing this construction is controlled so as not to delay or interfere with other more pressing military requirements."[36] Although this was far from an enthusiastic endorsement, it was more than enough for Roosevelt, Dimond, and the local boosters, who had all been waiting for any stamp of approval from the military. Canadian officials remained dubious, but U.S. political support coalesced quickly after the military's tepid endorsement appeared.

The urgency of the international situation escalated both politically and rhetorically as the highway advocates lobbied for construction. Anthony Dimond claimed that "Alaska is the most central place in the world for aircraft, and that is true . . . of Europe, Asia, or North America. . . . He who holds Alaska will hold the world."[37] One highway enthusiast famously warned skeptics: "We [can] either build a highway up to Alaska or the Japanese will build it down for us."[38] The various groups of advocates for each of the proposed routes began jockeying for attention from politicians and the media. Meanwhile, the most stalwart of Alaska boosters could relax in their conviction that "the route is incidental. . . . The road is going to be built."[39] There would still be a comfortable window of time to sort out the details.

Then, on December 7, 1941, the Japanese bombed Pearl Harbor, and that window of time shattered. Rhetorical urgency became genuine panic. The United States was at war, and the enemy had attacked American soil. In order to appear strong at home and abroad, officials needed to decide quickly whether or not to act on one of the highway proposals. On January 12, 1942,

Delegate Dimond gave a speech to the House of Representatives arguing for the immediate passage of his highway bill. On January 16, President Roosevelt convened a cabinet committee to consider the timely construction of an overland route to Alaska, and two short weeks later, the committee concluded that a highway should be built at once. It would connect the airfields of the Northwest Staging Route, loosely following "Route C."[40]

"This route," wrote Ernest Gruening, "was disappointing to Alaskans who hoped for one nearer the coast which would ultimately permit connecting roads with the coastal cities of Juneau and Ketchikan."[41] The committee members ultimately chose the prairie over the coastal route because they felt the road could be used to supply the airfields, and conversely, planes using the airfields could drop food and equipment to construction workers. Never mind that the majority of Alaskans and Canadians wanted a route that would be useful for decades to come; the decision was made only to facilitate rapid construction to meet the military's needs.[42]

Although members of the cabinet committee decided in favor of the highway, they—like many defense strategists—remained somewhat skeptical of the immediate military advantages of the road. The highway would take a minimum of two years to build, so it would be of no help if the Japanese were to invade Alaska in the meantime. The committee also agreed with the War Department that the most vulnerable areas of the territory— such as the Aleutian Islands, the Kenai Peninsula, and the southeastern panhandle—would not benefit from the highway and would still depend upon naval defense. Construction would require a huge commitment of money, equipment, and soldiers, rendering these resources unavailable for combat situations.

Still, the group decided that a road to Alaska would probably be built eventually and that the United States should "take advantage of the present war to secure the necessary agreements from Canada to start work now and finish perhaps many years to come."[43] If it was military reasoning that ultimately got Alaskans their highway, so be it. In addition, the road could have tremendous symbolic power, assuring Americans that they were safe at home and perhaps dissuading the Japanese from further attack. Such a demonstration of American will could be extremely powerful at this particular moment.

For those who already supported the highway—such as army officials and President Roosevelt—the committee's reasoning was more than sufficient. On February 6, 1942, the U.S. army chief of staff approved the construction of a road from Dawson Creek, British Columbia, to Big Delta, Alaska. Five days later the president authorized the measure. As far as the Americans were concerned, the Alaska Highway was going to be built. The only obstacle now was Ottawa. How would the Americans convince Canada to invest in a project that one of its leaders infamously dubbed a "dubious egg"?[44]

After preliminary conversations with Canadian officials, the answer turned out to be rather straightforward: The United States must agree to pay for the entire cost of construction. In exchange, Canada agreed to give the United States the right-of-way, to permit use of local timber and gravel, and to waive all import and employment taxes associated with building the road. The United States would return full control of the highway corridor to Canada six months after the end of the war.[45] Prime Minister King officially authorized the agreement on March 18, 1942, and construction of the highway began immediately.[46]

The Alaska Highway was built twice. As part of the army's strategy to open a path to Alaska as quickly as possible, Brigadier General Clarence L. Sturdevant devised a construction plan with two phases. First, the Army Corps of Engineers would punch a trail through the wilderness posthaste; contractors with the Public Roads Administration would follow a year later and upgrade the army's "pioneer road" into a permanent highway (military officials also asked some civilian contractors to help with the initial clearing). Despite the popular myth of the Army Corps of Engineers expertly carving a long road to Alaska in eight short months, in reality the military only opened the crudest of pathways. This path would not become a road until at least a year later, when the civilian contractors had completed their work.

The military's plan sounded simple enough, but it would prove daunting in practice. A road normally emerges from a well-traveled path; decades or even centuries of trial and error might dictate its course. By contrast, the Alaska Highway was artificial, created where no road had naturally evolved. Consequently, unlike some of the other proposed routes, this road did not follow even the most obvious contours of the rugged landscape. The land through which the highway would be built was heavily wooded and often swampy (as one military official quipped, "whoever named this the 'Prairie Route' never saw the country").[47] The soldiers needed to link the airfields along the Northwest Staging Route, but their lines of connection would waver as they worked to avoid the most formidable mountain peaks (including those of the Canadian Rockies) as well as rivers and large areas of foliage-filled swampland (called muskeg). After the original pioneer road

Mud and muskeg complicate the construction of the Alaska Highway, c. 1942–1943. Alaska State Library, Alaska Highway Photograph Collection, P193–015.

was completed, the Public Roads Administration planned to reroute long sections in order to make it safe for highway traffic (defined as vehicles traveling up to 70 miles per hour).

In March 1942, the construction process began. Ten thousand soldiers and all their supplies headed north. Part of the controversy surrounding the chosen route arose from the fact that the southern terminus of the road—Dawson Creek—was only accessible by rail from Edmonton (one fair-weather road did exist, but it was not regularly maintained).[48] This made it exceedingly difficult to bring in the heavy equipment. Further complicating the situation, construction of the highway would commence simultaneously at three points—Dawson Creek, Whitehorse (which was connected by the Yukon Route to Skagway), and Big Delta (which was connected to Fairbanks by the Richardson Highway). A lengthy combination of air, land, and water travel was needed to bring supplies to these three northern locations.[49] From all three points of contact, transportation was difficult. Food, clothing, workers, and machinery were often stuck in transit—sometimes for the duration.

One supply problem for both the operation of the Northwest Staging Route and the construction of the Alaska Highway was the difficulty of getting enough fuel on-site for construction vehicles. As part of his proposal for the Alaska Highway, the explorer Vilhjalmur Stefansson had advocated for the construction of a pipeline from the Norman Oil Wells—long ago discovered but mostly unexploited—to Whitehorse, so that fuel would be more readily available for the defense of northern Canada and Alaska.[50] In the spring of 1941, Secretary of the Interior Harold Ickes studied the proposal and decided it was impractical. After Pearl Harbor, however, the idea re-emerged in an atmosphere of urgency.

The army supported the idea, echoing Stefansson's arguments that construction of the highway necessitated the pipeline. Critics, however, seethed: "The idea of a pipeline . . . is completely cockeyed," said one. "The Fort Norman field is of unknown potentiality; it would be built entirely within Canada at our expense; it is doubtful if it could be maintained, for any fifth columnist could easily bribe an Indian for $25.00 to wreck it in a dozen places."[51] Still, as the navy admitted it could not guarantee the security of Alaskan shipping lanes, the army's position prevailed. In April 1942, the U.S. government decided to go forward with the project, offering to cover all the costs and to sell the pipeline after the war for whatever price Canada deemed fair. Ottawa—seeing very little to lose—quietly agreed. The Army Corps of Engineers was ordered to build all 500 miles of the "Canol" (short for "Canadian Oil") pipeline over the coming summer months.

This triumvirate of northern projects—the Northwest Staging Route, the Alaska Highway, and Canol—occupied a large share of U.S. military resources in the spring of 1942. Just as countless numbers of men and machines were being moved into the northern interior, however, everyone's worst fear came true. In the early hours of June 3, the Japanese bombed the U.S. Naval installation at Dutch Harbor on Unalaska Island in the Aleutians. Several days later, Japanese forces occupied the more remote islands of Kiska and Attu, taking their few residents—Aleuts, missionaries, and weathermen—hostage.[52] The Japanese were now on American soil. The psychological blow to Americans was devastating. An intense battle over the two islands began, although efforts on both sides were hampered by the fog, wind, and rocky terrain characteristic of the Aleutians. Reclaiming the islands for the United States would not be easy. As the reality of the situation set in, some officials wondered what possible use the highway would be to this battle.

For the Army Corps of Engineers, however, the Japanese invasion was a perfect incentive to get the northern construction projects completed on schedule. The Army Corps was the workhorse of the military, especially during wartime. The Corps was often used to build camps, bridges, and airfields, and during World War II it supported military personnel in both Europe and Asia and built the facilities for home-front operations, such as the Manhattan Project.[53] Corps engineers knew how to build infrastructure quickly in the midst of war; what they did not know, however, was how to build it in a challenging subarctic environment. Northerners—whether Native or non-Native—were not consulted in the planning of the highway. The army did not take advantage of local knowledge; it would have to learn the rules of the northern construction on its own.

When the soldiers and civilian workers—30,000 in total—arrived in the tiny towns of Dawson Creek, Fort St. John, Watson Lake, and Big Delta, the north was as unprepared for them as they were for it. Stores, hotels, and restaurants were few; more sophisticated cultural resources were lacking altogether. Dawson City was the largest town, with just over 1,000 residents. Many "towns" were only seasonal villages, inhabited by Natives who continued to live a seminomadic existence. Residents—both Native and non-Native—were used to a predictable lifestyle dictated by the rhythm of the seasons, not by governments in the midst of an international war. Still, they were forced to adapt as Americans drove bulldozers through their yards, fields, and hunting grounds. Some residents took advantage of a rare opportunity to work for substantial cash wages; others tried to continue their normal activities as best they could. Often, however, the soldiers brought pestilence that was difficult to ignore—such as disease, alcohol, and a steady market for prostitution.[54]

In April 1942, local residents watched as massive tent cities sprang up in Dawson Creek, Big Delta, and many tiny villages in between. Because of the difficulty of communicating in the north, the project was divided into two commands—one headquartered in Whitehorse and the other in Fort St. John. Seven regiments worked on the highway, three of which were African American. During World War II, the military was still segregated by race, and white and black troops did not work together (although the officers commanding black troops were all white). The military claimed that African Americans were not effective in combat, so their service was often limited to auxiliary work. On the highway, too, the black regiments were initially assigned to perform menial tasks in support of the white troops who built the road. Many people believed that African Americans lacked the intellect and experience to work the heavy construction equipment, and still others worried that they would be unable to work efficiently in a cold climate. In time, however, it became clear that in order to finish the highway on schedule, every available soldier—black or white—would have to work on construction.[55] The army's beliefs were put to the test as black and white regiments performed identical tasks.[56]

This work proceeded in more or less the same manner in all sections. Officers determined the route as they went along through a combination of aerial photography and ground surveillance. Often the path was determined solely by "sight engineering," in which the lead man would stand atop his machine and point in the direction that seemed to offer the fewest obstacles. The lead bulldozers (which the soldiers called "cats") smashed through a pathway, and those who followed removed fallen trees and widened the trail. Because the soil was frozen close to the surface, "the trees, even the largest, were easily knocked over. . . . The roots [spread] out in shallow fans, which popped out when the big bulldozers crashed against the trunks."[57]

Felling trees might have been unusually easy, but the challenges were many. After the trees were cut and cleared, the road had to be filled and graded to meet even the crudest of transportation standards. In the southern parts of the road, there was muskeg, into which machinery would sink, sometimes never to be recovered. In most cases, the road had to be completely rerouted around the swampy land. The northern troops had their own construction nightmare in the form of permafrost. This permanently frozen soil just below the surface would melt when vehicles drove above it, turning a seemingly stable roadbed into mush. After many failed repairs, engineers discovered they could insulate the frozen ground with logs (called "corduroy") and build the road on top of it. Corduroying the highway was tedious, however, and construction in northern areas eventually slowed to about 1 mile per day.[58]

Living and working conditions were difficult. Because the subarctic summer offered almost continuous sunlight, officers would sometimes pressure soldiers to work impossibly long days in extreme environmental conditions. As one soldier succinctly reported, "it just about freezes at night, and its [sic] hotter than hell in the daytime."[59] The smoke from forest fires—a regular part of northern life—compromised visibility and irritated sensitive eyes and throats.[60] The living facilities were substandard at best;

soldiers complained that they often "camped in a swamp and slept in water."[61] With the swamps came bugs, and even military head nets could not keep out the swarms of mosquitoes and biting flies. The wet conditions facilitated the spread of disease, and sickness moved quickly through the camps. Fresh meat and vegetables were scarce; meals often consisted of canned World War I rations. As summer turned to autumn, days turned from impossibly warm to frigidly cold. Frostbite became common. Perhaps worst of all was the monotony: each day as difficult as the one before, and precious few distractions. When asked what it was like to work on the highway, one soldier famously declared, "It's miles and miles of nothing but miles and miles."[62] Everyone involved agreed that construction "would, indeed, be a 'Long Trail.'"[63]

While the highway workers struggled to complete the arduous task set before them, the media celebrated the highway as a monumental American achievement in an otherwise difficult year. As the U.S. military suffered multiple defeats abroad (in every battle but Midway), headlines boasted of "Our Glory Road to Tokyo" and claimed "Alaska Highway [is] an Engineering Epic: Mosquitoes, Mud, and Muskeg [are] Minor Obstacles."[64] The highway was built with an awareness of spectacle—though many other scenes from the war were censored, reporters could freely capture countless images of soldiers working diligently on the road, and civilians at home could feel comforted by their efforts.[65] The supposed urgency of the project, combined with the unforgiving quality of the natural environment, led both soldiers and reporters to imagine that the Army Corps was literally doing battle with a hostile enemy, blurring the distinction between battlefield and home front and allowing soldiers to claim genuine victory over the wilderness.

While soldiers did battle with their northern environmental foe, and reporters and civilians celebrated, some highway advocates quietly mourned the way in which the highway was being constructed. Alaska boosters had long lobbied for an overland route that would be commercially useful in peacetime, and the Alaska Highway was far from fitting the bill. Donald MacDonald, the longtime highway advocate and former member of President Roosevelt's Alaska International Highway Commission, was terribly disappointed with the route. He complained, "You [cannot] call the misbegotten thing we have from Dawson Creek to Fairbanks a highway. . . . It is crooked as hell. Actually it is a belated abortion. . . . The Alcan Highway is not and never will become the main supply road to Alaska."[66]

Soldiers build signs along the highway route, c. 1942–1943. Alaska State Library, Alaska Highway Photograph Collection, P193–161.

MacDonald was not alone in his criticisms. Delegate Anthony Dimond, who had also lobbied hard for the highway's construction, now found himself in the difficult position of opposing the existing road, arguing that "it would be a mistake to even suggest that the construction of this highway will solve the immediate and pressing problem of adequate land transportation to Alaska, and through Alaska. The highway so built leads directly from Alaska into the great central plains of Canada and the United States, but does not afford anything but the most circuitous and roundabout connection with the Pacific Coast."[67] The highway provided an opportunity to make Alaska part of the greater Pacific Northwest, and it that sense, this route had obviously failed. Indeed, the Alaska Highway seemed to lack an obvious objective—it began and ended in remote locations, proceeded haphazardly across the landscape, and failed to connect Alaska with major cities in either the United States or Canada. Aside from giving lend-lease pilots a direct path by which to navigate—an important service in the short term—it was unclear what advantage the highway might be in times of either war or peace. In fact, construction of the highway had hardly begun when Anthony Dimond began lobbying for a second road along the Pacific Coast.

Perhaps the biggest tragedy, however, was not *where* the highway was built, but *how*. Because of the backdrop of the war, speed was the only concern—breaking through a passable road in the shortest possible amount of time. The natural environment was destroyed in and around the highway as countless trees were felled to open the path, to create corduroy for the road, and to use as firewood. Cold but careless soldiers often started forest fires, and the men often shot deer, caribou, and bears for food, fur, and fun.[68] Excess supplies were often burned or buried alongside the camps. Workers reported that "no one was allowed to remove *anything*—blankets, dishes, foods such as jams—but they were all piled and either buried or bulldozed over."[69] Broken, rusted, or surplus machinery was simply left alongside the roadbed, and many locals joked that the Americans were building an "oil can" highway to Alaska (a play on the colloquial term "Alcan").[70] The road was truly a collision course of waste and destruction.

Collisions along the road were cultural as well as environmental. Many white officers and civilians simply could not accept the presence of African American troops in the north. The belief that blacks would wither and die in cold climates had long worked to justify keeping African Americans from migrating to Alaska. The pressing need for soldiers to build the highway, however, forced the military to bring black men to a region into which few had gone before. Still, officials hoped to keep their presence temporary. As one general argued,

> the thing which I have opposed has been [the black soldiers'] establishment as port troops for the unloading of transports at our docks. The very high wages offered to unskilled labor here would attract a large number of them and cause them to remain and settle after the war, with the natural result that they would interbreed with the Indians and Eskimos and produce an astonishingly objectionable race of mongrels which would be a problem here from now on.[71]

While officials initially tried to limit the kinds of work that African Americans performed, the need for speedy construction meant that black troops ultimately came to perform the same tasks as white troops—and, to the surprise of many, they proved to be among the most efficient regiments in all the work they completed.[72]

Still, racial conflict and discrimination were omnipresent during construction. African Americans served in segregated units and were issued clothing, food, and equipment that were far inferior to those of white troops. Black soldiers reported to white officers, who kept them in wilderness areas and out of the towns because it was believed they would upset the locals.[73] In a northern replay of racist southern politics, black men who were caught interacting with white women were often accused of sexual predation, and after a few such incidents, black troops were banned from entering the city of Fairbanks. Most of the white officers were ignorant of southern cultures and dialects, and a few dozen black soldiers spoke a French patois that made even basic communication difficult.[74]

Not surprisingly, however, this racial conflict was erased from contemporary media accounts of the Alaska Highway. One of the most important icons of road construction was a staged photograph of a black soldier shaking hands with a white soldier at the meeting point for the northern and southern units, 20 miles east of the Canadian border. To Americans at home, it appeared as though blacks and whites were working harmoniously together—in segregated units, maybe, but without major complaints or conflicts.

Alaska and Yukon Natives experienced their own cultural collisions. Some Natives chose to serve in the Army Corps for cash wages, and in many ways, their experience was better than that of African Americans. They were not forced to serve in segregated units, for example, and they

Some of the African American soldiers who helped to build the highway, c. 1944. James Monroe ("Pat") James Photograph Collection, UAF-2004-92-1, Archives, University of Alaska–Fairbanks.

were familiar with all the challenges of working in a northern environment. Still, Natives, too, suffered from language barriers and cultural prejudices, and they were often accused of being lazier and less productive than white soldiers. Cash wages allowed Natives to obtain access to new communication and transportation technologies, but the coming of the highway also threatened many traditional activities, particularly hunting. Trigger-happy soldiers and habitat destruction threatened many populations of game. Although northern Natives would adapt to the changes brought by the highway—just as they had always adapted to changing circumstances—most elders recognized construction as a critical moment of cultural upheaval. As one Yukon Native explained, "before the highway came and split us all in different ways, we used to feed ourselves good from the country."75

Cultural and environmental collisions aside, the Army Corps of Engineers succeeded in its mission to open a pathway to Alaska. Just nine months and six days after the start of construction, the pioneer highway was completed. Despite its extremely crude condition, defense convoys were traveling north by December, and in 1943 the Public Roads Administration finished upgrading the highway (the group had started its work even before the pioneer road was done). The Canol pipeline was also completed in 1943, and oil was in the pipe by December. Although expenses were difficult to estimate, the government officially stated that the entire project had cost the United States about $135 million—slightly more than $51,000 per mile. In reality, the highway may have cost up to $300 million.[76] Either way, the expenses were a far cry from the $2 million that officials had initially imagined investing in a northern road. By 1943 it had become apparent that, other than providing some support to the airfields and the lend-lease program, the highway would be of little use during wartime.[77] With the military justification for the project now in tatters, talk turned to possible uses for the road when peace was declared.

On April 1, 1946, Canada was given control of a meandering road to nowhere. Although Ottawa was not particularly interested in acquiring this engineering monstrosity, the United States was more than happy to honor the terms of the original agreement and to give the Canadian portions of the road (about 1,200 of 1,400 miles) back to Canada. Ottawa seriously considered abandoning the highway, but pressure from the United States, and the fear of international embarrassment, convinced the Canadians to maintain—and even to upgrade—the road.[78] This would be a huge and expensive task—all for a highway that most of Canada never really wanted. Local communities were ambivalent at best about the highway, and residents who had survived the construction did not want additional workers trampling through their homes and hunting grounds. But it seemed that they had no choice, as the Alaska Highway was now a permanent part of Canadian and Alaskan life.

Returning the vast majority of the road to Canada allowed U.S. leaders to evade much of their responsibility for the wasteful project. The Alaska Highway was no longer an American problem, and Alaska boosters—who had wanted a road, but certainly not *this* road—had no choice but to promote the Alaska Highway as the gateway to the last frontier. The route was open to public traffic in 1948, and while boosters promoted this new means of getting to Alaska, skeptics quietly wondered whether, "taking the great length of the Highway into consideration . . . people with money wishing to reach Alaska or the Yukon for a holiday might not in the future prefer to travel by plane."[79] While most travelers did—and continue to—prefer to travel to Alaska by air, the road attracted a surprising number of tourists in its first year—almost 19,000, to be exact. By 1950, the number rose to almost 50,000, and it increased steadily thereafter, reaching about 350,000 travelers annually in recent times.[80] That may not be an astonishing number of tourists, but it becomes impressive when you consider the remoteness of the road and the paucity of creature comforts along its corridor.

Although the Alaska Highway eventually made a modest contribution to tourism, it has never become a boon for northern development. Many other wartime projects contributed more to Alaska's economy and infrastructure.[81] Like many other schemes to settle Alaska, however, the road was conceived of by boosters who believed that it could be the magic bullet to solve the perceived problem of underdevelopment in the north. Highway proponents believed that better transportation could turn Alaska into the next seemingly successful chapter in the settlement of the American West. As with other such plans, however, a project intended to improve life in the North ended up doing irreparable harm to local peoples and the natural environment. In the case of the highway, the urgency of wartime construction exacerbated this damage—and it is precisely the mythology of wartime victory that has kept the true extent of this damage from ever being assessed.[82]

The Alaska Highway is part of America—if not geographically, at least conceptually. Though residing primarily in Canada, the road remains steeped in the heroic framework of World War II and the U.S. commitment to defend Alaska from foreign invasion. Few people remember the history of the highway as a northern development scheme, and most scholars writing on the subject continue to focus on how the Alaska Highway might have shaped the war, rather than on how the war might have shaped the Alaska Highway. If the war had not happened as it did, would a different road have been built? Would the social, cultural, and environmental dynamics of construction have been different during peacetime? Might a truly useful transnational development project have emerged in a different historical moment? Or was the idea of an international northern road doomed from the start? A long view of the Alaska Highway suggests a new set of historical questions that are yet to be explored. Alaska's road to nowhere is one of many northern development topics ripe for further investigation.

Alaska Submerged: The Rampart Dam Controversy

The Yukon is a major—but unassuming—river. It is the longest waterway in Alaska, carving a 1,400-mile arc from the Canadian border through the center of the state out to the Bering Sea. Add the 600 miles the river flows from its headwaters in Canada to the Alaskan border, and the Yukon becomes the fifth-longest river in North America. The Yukon drains more than 300,000 miles of Alaska, British Columbia, and the Yukon, and its tributary basins include major rivers such as the Tanana, the Koyukuk, and the Porcupine. Despite its size, however, and its familiar sobriquet—"the Mighty Yukon," the river is unimpressive at first encounter. Its banks are low and swampy, its water brown and cloudy, and its swirling current seemingly angry at the world. The river creates a prime habitat for mosquitoes and other biting insects, making visits to the Yukon unbearable even during the summer season. Still, the river is in many ways the heart of Alaska—a life-giving artery that has shaped both the natural and human history of the region through the many things that have happened here—and even some things that have not.

And things that never happen move history along in profound ways. Nonevents may not shape the way a landscape looks, but they inevitably shape the ways in which a landscape is imagined. The Rampart Dam, which was never built, is nonetheless an important event in the history of the Yukon and Alaska. From the point of its proposal onward, the flats along the central Yukon River (about 100 miles northwest of Fairbanks) became the place where the Rampart Dam was *not*. The dam project was conceived by Alaska boosters who imagined developing and urbanizing Alaska on a scale suitable to the region's size. If Alaska could not be an agricultural frontier, they surmised, surely it could be an industrial frontier. But their project would never materialize, as, once again, development proponents failed to understand the realities of the Alaskan natural environment and the culture of Alaska Natives.

Long before the Yukon River became nationally known as the site of nondevelopment, however, the region was already an area of both ecological and cultural importance. A maze of shallow river channels and more than 40,000 ponds and lakes, the Yukon Flats were the primary nesting area for millions of waterfowl and shorebirds. Athabascan Indians (Gwich'ins and Koyukons) had used the area for hunting, fishing, and trapping for thousands of years. Three species of salmon—the chinook, chum, and coho—traveled more than 1,000 miles from the sea to the Yukon, and many species of fur-bearing mammals—including moose, lynx, muskrats, foxes, wolves, wolverines, and rabbits—lived along its banks. Because of the abundance of food and fur, the river had long been a center of trade, and dozens of permanent Native settlements dotted the shoreline. During the nineteenth century, white trappers and gold seekers passed through the flats on their way to and from the Canadian and Alaskan interiors.[1] Many things happened along this section of the Yukon River before one important project did not.

This project—the Rampart Dam—got its start in 1959, shortly after Alaska officially became a state, when the Senate Public Works Committee allocated a small sum to study "the feasibility of a hydroelectric facility at Rampart Canyon on the Yukon River."[2] The proposed dam would be 530 feet high, and it would flood 6.8 million acres in the Yukon Flats region, an area greater in size than Lake Erie. After the twenty years it would take the reservoir to fill, the site would produce an estimated 5 million kilowatts (34.2 billion kilowatt-hours—enough to power 10 million homes) of electricity per year, more than twice the capacity of the Grand Coulee on the Columbia River, the nation's largest dam.

Never mind that Alaska had nothing close to an adequate market for such power; proponents believed that inexpensive and readily available power would attract both settlers and industry to the northernmost state, since, to their minds, modern America was "a strange and wonderful monster with a completely insatiable appetite for electric power."[3] Alaska boosters had long believed that the state could be home to at least 5 million people; now, they were claiming that "the development of the state's

A mail boat crossing the Yukon, c. 1925. Frederick B. Drane Collection, UAF-1991-46-516, Archives, University of Alaska–Fairbanks.

hydroelectric resources [could] contribute to that transformation."[4] It was estimated that the massive dam would cost $1.3 billion.[5]

As with many development schemes in Alaska, the Rampart Dam was facilitated by the confluence of national and regional events. At the national level, the 1902 Reclamation Act had authorized the government to pursue "water improvements" in the West, to irrigate arid regions, and to facilitate economic development. These initiatives accelerated after the severe droughts of the 1930s, and famous Great Depression–era projects included the Hoover Dam, the Grand Coulee Dam, and the Central Valley Project in California. The demand for hydroelectric power soared during the 1940s, when the nation's need for power far outstripped its available sources. What were once primarily irrigation projects now became crucial sources of hydroelectric power for a nation in the midst of a global war. After the war, hydroelectricity remained in demand, and industries moved west to take advantage of the cheap power. Reclamation began to look like an economic panacea—a sure way to jumpstart agricultural and industrial production in sluggish western economies.[6]

And then there was the Cold War. The Soviets had recently made enormous strides in hydroelectric power, and there was immense political pressure for the United States to do the same.[7] In 1948, the Department of the Interior created the Bureau of Reclamation, and together with the Army Corps of Engineers, government workers began identifying potential dam

Alaskan congressional delegation members, including Senator Ernest Gruening (*left*) and Representative Ralph J. Rivers (*right*), examining the Rampart Dam site with Alaska District Engineer Colonel Christian Hanburger, 1960s. Ernest H. Gruening Papers, 1914–[1959–1969]1974, UAF-1976-21-55322, Archives, University of Alaska–Fairbanks.

sites in the Territory of Alaska. One site on the Yukon River, the Rampart Canyon, a gorge 100 miles southwest of the Yukon Flats, particularly appealed to the engineers. In addition to being a geologically appealing site for a dam, any hydroelectric facility built in this area would easily "dwarf any power plant now in production anywhere in the world." Proponents of the project were quick to note that "even the Russians, making rapid strides in the development of hydroelectric energy, do not yet have anything as big as Rampart, though dams as big are said to be on Soviet drawing boards."[8] At the level of foreign policy, officials felt major pressure to build a massive project somewhere in the United States—and Rampart provided them with the opportunity to do just that.

From a regional standpoint, the year in which the Senate Public Works Committee introduced the bill to study Rampart—1959—was a monumental year. President Dwight D. Eisenhower had formally admitted Alaska to the union as the forty-ninth state on January 3. Statehood was long in coming. After World War II, Alaska's territorial governor, Ernest Gruening, became increasing frustrated with the paucity of infrastructure in the territory. He believed that the only way Alaska could obtain adequate roads, hospitals, schools, and homesteading regulations was to put voting representatives in the U.S. House and Senate. Under Gruening's leadership, the Alaska State-hood Association was formed in 1946. It took more than a decade of stops and starts before the group saw its dream realized.[9]

With all the privileges of statehood, however, also came responsibilities. The new state wanted—and needed—to decrease federal control in the re-gion and to build a strong economy. It was time, once and for all, to settle and develop the last frontier. The perplexing question was how. Histori-cally, even with heavy federal investment, the Alaska economy had never enjoyed a period of steady growth. In this atmosphere of relative despera-tion, Alaska's leaders were open to almost any scheme that might lift the new state into economic independence and prosperity. And that is how a prominent group of Alaskans latched onto—as one of its opponents fa-mously dubbed it—"the plot to drown Alaska."[10]

But before there was "the plot to drown Alaska," however, there was a plot to blow it up. The explosive plan—code-named "Chariot"—was part of Operation Plowshare, an Atomic Energy Commission (AEC) initiative to investigate peaceful uses for nuclear weapons. The AEC established Plowshare in 1957 to demonstrate that nuclear technology could benefit so-ciety—primarily by rearranging the natural environment in seemingly pro-ductive ways (a process dubbed "geographical engineering" by its propo-nents). Plowshare scientists believed that nuclear explosions could effectively reroute rivers, carve tunnels through mountains, and release otherwise inaccessible minerals from the ground. As Edward Teller, the so-called "father of the hydrogen bomb" and head of the AEC laboratory, put it, "if your mountain is not in the right place, just drop us a card."[11] While moving mountains and rerouting rivers, the Plowshare project would also (conveniently) provide a legal mechanism to detonate nuclear weapons during an official moratorium on testing.

Members of the AEC planned numerous experiments to resurface the American landscape, but it was Edward Teller's pet project to create an arti-ficial deepwater harbor through multiple underground explosions that re-ceived the lion's share of public attention. Locating a site for the experiment was difficult, however, as public unease with nuclear devices was growing, especially around traditional testing sites in Nevada. The Army Corps of Engineers was tasked with finding the most appropriate location for the project, and the AEC asked its advisers to minimize potential hazards to people and wildlife and to maximize the project's potential economic benefits.[12] After the army made its recommendations, the AEC settled on Ogotoruk Creek, near Cape Thompson, Alaska, as the site for the harbor. The 1958 decision to situate the project in northern Alaska was based on the mistaken belief that the area was virtually uninhabited and the optimistic assumption that a harbor could be used to promote mineral exploration in an otherwise remote region. A 2.4-million-ton explosion was tentatively planned for the summer of 1959.[13]

Thirty-one miles south of the proposed explosion sat the village of Point Hope, one of the longest continually occupied sites in North America. The 300-person Inupiat Eskimo community lived largely by hunting and fishing, and their culture was intimately tied to the arctic landscape and its abundant natural resources. The Eskimos had interacted with white whalers and missionaries for hundreds of years, and they had successfully integrated modern tools and amenities into their subsistence lifestyle. Still, Ogotoruk Creek, a traditional hunting area, remained important to the community, and it was not long before Natives were organizing against Project Chariot. Edward Teller argued that the Eskimos would benefit from the employment opportunities created by the new harbor, but local residents were not interested in changing their lifestyle. As villager Kitty Kinneeveauk explained, "we really don't want to see the Cape Thompson blasted because it is our home. . . . I'm pretty much sure you don't like to see your home blasted by some other people who don't live in your place like we live in Point Hope."[14]

The Natives were not the only group opposed to the project. Although some Alaska boosters thought the project would "center world scientific and economic attention on Alaska just at the time when we are moving into statehood and inviting development," others were not convinced.[15] Critics pointed out that Cape Thompson was icebound nine or ten months of the year, and potential mining sites were located well on the other side of the Brooks Range. Private business investors were not terribly interested. Even Chariot's proponents had to admit that there was little need for a harbor in that location: "The only trouble with the plan," said one, "is that we haven't been able to find anyone who really wants a harbor there."[16] The AEC scrambled to increase public support by scrapping the idea of a harbor, decreasing the size of the blast, and reclassifying the project as a "scientific experiment." This raised the eyebrows of many, including Soviet officials, who noted that the so-called experiment would take place only 180 miles from the Siberian border.

Biologists at the University of Alaska (loosely affiliated as the Alaska Conservation Society) began to add their voices to the chorus of Chariot opponents. In 1959, a group of fifty Alaskans concerned about radioactivity—led by a member of the Matanuska Valley Farmers' Cooperative Association—came together as the "Commission for the Study of Atomic Testing in Alaska." Both groups were skeptical of the assurances given to them by the AEC that "there is no evidence that the damage will be widespread or will have any long-range effect on the environment."[17] They wanted independent scientific investigations of the blast's potential impact on wildlife and human health.[18]

Of particular concern were the Native communities throughout northern Alaska who relied on caribou as a primary food source. Caribou eat lichen, and lichen get most of their nutrients from dust particles in the air. Scientists discovered that the atomic blasts of 1945 had contaminated Alaskan lichen with radionuclides. Because they grow slowly, lichens can absorb huge amounts of radioactivity, and this radioactivity gets concentrated quickly as it moves up the short arctic food chain, severely damaging the cellular systems in both plants and animals and resulting in cancer, genetic mutation, and even death.[19] It did not take much research to discover that the fallout from Chariot would likely have serious consequences for the arctic environment and the people who lived there.

The controversy quickly captured the attention of the burgeoning national environmental movement. In particular, Olaus Murie, an arctic biologist who had spent many months researching in Alaska, declared that his conservation organization, the Wilderness Society, would actively oppose Project Chariot. The Sierra Club soon followed suit. Because of mounting public pressure, the AEC appointed a commission to study the environmental effects of the blast. The group soon concluded that there were "no biological objections to the shooting based on our investigations" and recommended that the detonation take place during the spring, when the ground would be protected from radiation by a blanket of snow.[20]

Biologists at the University of Alaska disagreed with the AEC's conclusions, arguing that low precipitation and high winds made the area especially vulnerable to radioactive damage; moreover, spring was the season during which Natives hunted in the immediate vicinity of Ogotoruk Creek. In November 1961, environmental and Native opposition to the project culminated in the highly publicized Inupiat Paitot, a gathering of Eskimo people in the village of Barrow. Within a year, the AEC announced that it was no longer pursuing Project Chariot, although its members maintained that the cancellation was for scientific reasons and not because of Native or environmental opposition to the proposed blast.

The failure of Project Chariot increased the concern of Gruening and other boosters about Alaska's seemingly underdeveloped economy. Decades of unsuccessful attempts to attract businesses and settlers to the region left many with a general sense of desperation; the achievement of statehood—viewed as a profound victory by many Alaskans—also carried with it the visible burden of greater economic independence. Alaskans had fought for more control over their governance, and now that they had achieved it, leaders wondered what was to be done next. As part of the Alaska Statehood Act, the government authorized the state to withdraw more than 103 million acres of unreserved federal land—slightly less than one-third of Alaska's total area—over the next twenty-five years. The decision regarding when and where to withdraw land would largely determine the state's economic development strategy. Salmon fishing, gold mining, and federal military spending were all on the decline. Although timber and petroleum still held some economic promise, Alaska would also need to find new and innovative industries to promote significant growth and development.[21]

When Alaska became a state, its leaders shuffled positions to take advantage of the region's new political power. Former territorial governor Ernest Gruening—along with the previous nonvoting delegate Edward "Bob" Bartlett—became the U.S. senators from the forty-ninth state. Former territorial attorney general Ralph Rivers represented Alaska in the House of Representatives, and native-born William A. Egan became the state of Alaska's first governor. All had been active in the statehood movement, but it was Ernest Gruening who had campaigned the hardest, and it was he who had emerged as the most passionate—and powerful—advocate for the union's newest state.

After serving on the Alaska International Highway Commission during the 1930s, Gruening became Alaska's territorial governor in 1939, a seat he occupied for almost fourteen years. During that time and the years that followed, Gruening worked to convince Alaskans that they needed to free themselves from the "yoke" of federal control, to preserve the seeming freedom and independence of frontier life, and to achieve economic prosperity by whatever means necessary. Even after statehood was achieved, these would continue to be his primary goals, particularly during the decade he would represent Alaska in Washington.[22]

While Gruening and other Alaska boosters celebrated the increase in local autonomy accompanying statehood, they quietly lamented the decrease in federal dollars that came with their newfound political freedom. Statehood proponents had managed to shepherd an omnibus bill through Congress along with the statehood act, and this gave Alaska five years of continuing federal support before the state would need to take over many of its own financial responsibilities. But still, time was short, and potential sources of income seemed few. Alaskans—both statehood supporters and the minority of opponents—were overwhelmingly against the idea of taxation, arguing that statehood had promised to bring less government intrusion into their lives, not more. Although commercial oil exploration had already begun in some arctic regions, few boosters truly believed that petroleum would be the long-term answer to Alaska's economic woes. For most Alaskans, hydroelectric power seemed the brightest possibility on the horizon, and it was not long before the newly minted senator from Alaska—conveniently a member of the Senate Public Works Committee—began his obsessive quest to build the Rampart Dam.

Gruening believed that Rampart had the potential to be "the greatest peacetime project in the history of the free world."[23] Gruening, a Harvard-educated-doctor-turned-journalist-turned-politician, threw himself into whatever he did with the enthusiasm of a zealot, and after almost two decades of advocating for Alaska, he saw Rampart as a panacea for the state's low population and seemingly underdeveloped economy. The Senate Public Works Committee allocated $49,000 in 1959 for the Army Corps of Engineers to begin studying the project; by October of that year, Alaska Governor William Egan announced that preliminary work on the Rampart proposal had begun.[24] In 1961, Congress allocated an additional $225,000 to continue the Rampart investigation.[25] With serious studies under way, the public relations campaign began in earnest—with Ernest Gruening at the helm.

Rampart's proponents initially were fighting an uphill battle in the realm of national publicity. Unlike many areas in the continental West, Alaska obviously had "no sizable market for electric power." Even optimistic calculations estimated that "mining and sylvaculture, as extractive industries primarily supplying outside markets, would never require more than a fifth of Rampart's product even at its minimum capacity."[26] It was easy for residents in the Lower 48 states to dismiss Rampart as a crazy scheme with poor economic rationale—especially in the wake of Project Chariot. For Alaskans, however, the Rampart Dam soon "acquired the same mystical aura of promise as, for example, steel mills to India," wrote a reporter for the *Washington Post*. "It is a symbol of economic independence to a land very recently emerged from colonial status. More materially, the dam is a vessel of hope for a state suffering [from] a peculiarly unstable economy."[27]

The hope came from the theory that Alaska should provide power availability in advance of current needs, so that businesses and industry would have an incentive to move north.[28] Most of Alaska's leadership found this theory convincing, and they repeated it at every opportunity: *Provide the power, and the market will come.* In particular, boosters believed that hydroelectricity would attract numerous light metal, wood pulp, and cement industries to the region and that any unused power could be exported to Canada or Japan for a significant profit. As Alaska State Representative Jay Hammond—one of the few politicians who doubted this reasoning—surmised, most Alaskan leaders would "stand up and face Mecca whenever someone said Rampart."[29]

Rampart's proponents joined forces in 1963 and created an organization called "Operation Rampart," quickly renamed Yukon Power for America (YPA). The organization was spearheaded by the publishers of Alaska's two major newspapers, the *Anchorage Daily Times* and the *Fairbanks Day News-Miner*, and its membership comprised businessmen, political leaders, chambers of commerce, and numerous private citizens. Future Alaska senator Ted Stevens, a trustee for the group, claimed that YPA was "not a private lobby group" but rather "a group of public-spirited citizens who have donated their time."[30] Stevens's comment notwithstanding, the group immediately began lobbying (ultimately unsuccessfully) for the inclusion of the $1.3 billion Rampart Dam project in the 1964 Rivers and Harbors Omnibus Bill. The group's official motto was "Build Rampart Now," and its goal was to prove that the project would have overwhelming economic benefits not only for Alaska, but also for the nation at large.

Yukon Power for America published a pamphlet, "The Rampart Story," touting the dam's ability to provide Alaska with "a stable and growing economy" and to give the nation "a physical and scenic asset with untold commercial and recreational promise."[31] It was not long before Alaska's newspapers were headlined with these optimistic predictions, and children all over the state were writing school reports about the great Rampart Dam.[32] Yukon Power also raised sufficient funds to hire a hydroelectric consulting firm, Ivan Bloch and Associates, to conduct a private feasibility study for the project. The firm quickly concluded that "Rampart's output will be urgently required by the Nation to help meet electric power needs. . . . No other source of electric power will be as low cost."[33]

Senator Gruening, an ex-officio member of Yukon Power for America, was the spiritual leader of the pro-Rampart camp. He often gave keynote addresses at YPA meetings and rallied supporters to believe that "the project [looks] favorable from every standpoint." Gruening believed that the dam could produce the cheapest power available anywhere in the United States (three mills per kilowatt-hour), and there seemed to be no end to the list of additional benefits that Rampart would bring. As he later wrote in his autobiography:

> In addition to vastly improving living conditions, the project would assure the Natives a variety of new employment. There would be jobs during the construction of the dam and of the new community which the construction would bring into being; timber would have to be cleared in the area behind the dam; sawmills would be established and local residents trained in a variety of new skills. . . . Further, a freshwater fishery to be developed on the lake would also attract tourism. And the ever-present danger of floods after the spring break-up would be eliminated.[34]

Gruening even claimed that the existence of the dam would raise temperatures in the region, boosting the area's agricultural productivity.[35] As enthusiastic and committed as Gruening and his followers were, however, they would soon meet an opposition equally committed to defeating the extraordinary dam proposal. Rampart was about to become one of the bloodiest political battles in the history of Alaska.

In 1961, the Army Corps of Engineers had embarked upon a feasibility study for the Rampart project, but in 1962, after much bureaucratic wrangling, the primary responsibility for studying hydroelectric projects in Alaska was handed over to the Department of the Interior. The Corps would complete the study it had started, but after that, its role would be reduced to engineering and implementation matters. As part of the new Interior study, the Fish and Wildlife Service began an environmental assessment of the dam's potential impacts on the region's mammals, fish, and waterfowl. In 1963, the same year that Yukon Power for America was founded, the group released the preliminary results of its studies, predicting tremendous wildlife losses if the project were to proceed.

On March 4, Ira Gabrielson, a conservationist who had recently left his position as head of Fish and Wildlife to work for an environmental organization called the Wildlife Management Institute, delivered a speech at the North American Wildlife and Natural Resources Institute in Detroit during which he made the results of the environmental study of Rampart public. He warned the audience:

> There is a new proposal now for a project that dwarfs all previous [hydroelectric] projects in the unprecedented magnitude of fish and wildlife resources and habitat that would be destroyed. It is the proposed Rampart Dam on the Yukon River in Central Alaska. . . . The 500-foot dam would block sizable upstream migration of salmon in the Yukon. . . . Moose and furbearers would also suffer, and the dam would alter the annual water cycle that makes the Yukon delta an important waterfowl breeding and concentration ground. Rampart Dam is synonymous with resource destruction.[36]

In April 1964, the Fish and Wildlife Service officially released its report, and the statistics it cited were overwhelming. According to the service's environmental study, if the Rampart Dam were built, 2.4 million acres of premium waterfowl nesting area would be flooded. The wetlands that would be destroyed included 400 miles of river and more than 30,000 creeks and ponds. Because of this habitat destruction, 1.5 million ducks, 12,000 geese, 10,000 cranes, 20,000 loons, and substantial populations of ptarmigan and grouse would be lost. Populations of salmon would be reduced by up to 400,000, and mammals would also suffer: Black bears and grizzly bears, moose, lynx, wolverines, minks, beavers, foxes, otters, and muskrats would all lose important habitat and food sources. The report concluded that the dam should not be built and ended with what would soon become the rallying cry for Rampart's environmental opponents: "Nowhere in the history of water development in America have the fish and wildlife losses anticipated to result from a single project been so overwhelming."[37]

Environmental opposition to the Rampart Dam came from two camps. Conservation organizations—including Olaus Murie's Wilderness Society, the Sierra Club, and the Alaska Conservation Society—were major sources of protest. Sportsmen's groups, such as the Izaak Walton League and the Boone and Crocket Club, worried about the projected decreases in the populations of waterfowl available for hunting (many of the birds were migratory and spent much of their time in the Lower 48); consequently, sportsmen from all over the country also vocally condemned the dam. By the time the environmental opposition mobilized, however, Ernest Gruening and the members of Yukon Power for America had largely succeeded in convincing the media—even in the Lower 48—that Rampart would be a panacea for both Alaska and the nation.

After the Army Corps of Engineers released its own report in enthusiastic support of the dam, a member of the Wilderness Society explained, "Rampart [became] a 'motherhood' issue. To be opposed to it was tantamount to being for Communism or against Progress."[38] Arguments about loss of nesting habitat had a difficult time competing with the romantic frontier rhetoric of supporters. One of the proponents, Governor William Egan, said:

> All of us share a similar dream for Alaska. We see an Alaska of busy factories, modern cities, crowded ports. We see the vast potential wealth of Alaska being utilized to improve the material well-being of the people of our State and our Nation. This is the Alaska my parents hoped to see—it is a dream of long-standing, shared by all who know Alaska's enormous potential for economic and social growth.[39]

Rampart Dam advocates took control of the media debate by ridiculing the environmentalists at every opportunity. Ernest Gruening described any opposition to Rampart as "weeping and wailing by wholly uninformed people in our country who have seen the misleading publicity about Rampart which has come from the so-called conservation organizations."[40] He completely dismissed the concerns of hunters, arguing that there must "be a higher and nobler form of conservation to save [ducks] so they be slaughtered in the other 48 states." Gruening mocked the Fish and Wildlife study's contention that fur-bearing animals would suffer, snickering, "I can just picture the moose standing there for 18 years and not moving as these waters advance and the animals slowly drown. . . . It seems to me that the animals are more intelligent than some of our conservationists. They know enough to move out."

As for fish and waterfowl, it was common for Rampart proponents to argue that the reservoir would provide more water and consequently more habitat for these species. Ignoring the project's potential effect on the salmon population, Gruening repeatedly celebrated the flooded area's potential to support significant populations of lake trout and whitefish.[41] Completely ignoring conservationists' arguments about the importance of wetland areas, one booster famously dismissed any concern for waterfowl with the simple retort: "Who ever heard of a duck drowning?"[42]

As environmentalists worked to combat this "pop ecology," other groups were also organizing against the construction of the dam. In February 1964, the Bureau of Land Management (BLM) held hearings in Fairbanks and Fort Yukon to determine whether 8.9 million acres of land should officially be reserved for the dam site. The vast majority of Fairbanks residents—primarily businessmen—testified in favor of this measure. The hearings in Fort Yukon the following day, however, did not go so smoothly. Thirteen Native villages in the area would be significantly affected by the project, and seven—Beaver, Birch Creek, Chalkyitsik, Fort Yukon, Rampart, Stevens Village, and Venetie—would be completely submerged by the reservoir, and their residents would have to be relocated.

Though some Natives argued in favor of the project, citing the many local jobs that would be created, most were at least ambivalent about the proposal. The dam would bring the villagers further away from subsistence hunting and fishing and into a cash economy, which many Natives feared.[43] As elder Philip Peter put it, "this land is dear. There has been a day in the past that our grandfather has made a living in this land with a bow and arrow. . . . Millions and millions of dollars wouldn't mean a thing to us, wouldn't do us no good. If they take those millions and millions of dollars and distribute them among men, women, and children, they would only be shortening their lives."[44]

The approximately 2,000 Alaska Natives living along the central Yukon River—organizing themselves as "Gwitchya Gwichin Ginkhye" (Yukon Flats People Speak)—officially came out in opposition to the project. Gruening and other Rampart supporters made numerous trips to the villages, trying to convince the residents that the dam would bring untold benefits in terms of jobs, money, and modern amenities.[45] Behind the scenes, however, the boosters were no kinder to the Natives than they were to the environmentalists. Gruening called the area in which the villagers lived a "miserable swamp." He saw the Natives' subsistence lifestyle as proof of their need for government help, arguing that they "would be benefited

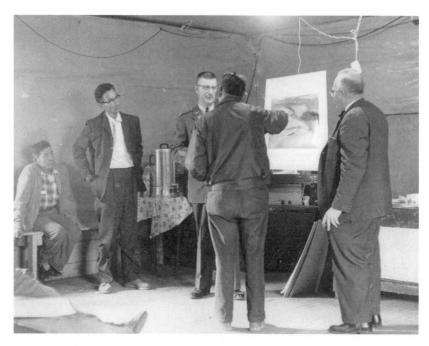

The Army Corps of Engineers explaining the Rampart Dam project to Native leaders, 1962. Bear Ketzler Photograph Collection, UAF-1992-202-15, Archives, University of Alaska–Fairbanks.

by being relocated, for they could scarcely be worse off than they are now."[46] George Sundborg, author of a book on the Grand Coulee dam and Gruening's chief aide on the Rampart project, dismissed the Yukon Flats as a pitiful area with "not more than ten flush toilets. . . . Search the whole world over and it would be difficult to find an equivalent area with so little to be lost through flooding."[47]

As comments such as these got out to the local and national media, the Yukon Natives did some flooding of their own, inundating Gruening's office with petitions and letters of protest. John Kameroff, the president of the Alakanuk Village Council, typified the resolve of most Natives when he wrote, "Please [do] not respond to this petition by sending us a large volume of official propaganda designed to convince us of the beneficial effects of the Rampart project. . . . Those in Alaska and elsewhere who support Rampart do so either through ignorance or selfishness. Rampart Dam will be the bane of the Yukon. *It must not be built.*"[48]

The Department of the Interior concluded its studies in 1965, and department secretary Stewart Udall took up a review of the findings.

Group of Natives from Fort Yukon, 1920s. Dr. Ernest A. Cook Photograph Collection, UAF-2003-109-62, Archives, University of Alaska–Fairbanks.

Although the report noted the many negative effects the project was likely to have on Natives and the environment, Gruening's aide dismissed the opposition as coming from "wholly uninformed persons living outside of our state."[49] In the wake of the report, Rampart boosters turned their attention to promoting what they believed were the ecological "benefits" of the dam, such as the creation of a large lake, which they repeatedly claimed would make both ducks and fish happy. In focusing exclusively on the environmental aspects of the project, however, Rampart Dam supporters were missing other, equally powerful objections to their project.

Economically, few experts believed that there would ever be a market for so much power in such a remote location. And with a $1.3 billion price tag, the dam just would not pay off financially—it would amount to a massive federal handout to boost Alaska's floundering economy in the short term. In March 1966, the Natural Resources Council of America, a coalition of national environmental groups, released a report it had commissioned from the University of Michigan. "The Spurr Report," as it became known (an economist named Stephen Spurr had led the investigation), concluded that Rampart would be "an all-or-nothing gamble. Only if all its power is used would the project prove economical. . . . Rampart should not be authorized at this time."[50] This economic assessment dealt a final blow to the project. One year later, Secretary Udall recommended against the construction of the Rampart Dam, and it died a slow political death thereafter.

The plan to construct the Rampart Dam collapsed for the same complex web of reasons that had ultimately doomed Project Chariot—environmental concerns, Native opposition, exorbitant cost, and lack of economic rationale. The legacy of the Rampart Dam, however, was to simplify debates over Alaska's future into the simple opposition of environment versus development. Gruening and his supporters effectively convinced the media that the issue was as simple as there being "two competing views of Alaska's destiny," as one reporter framed it. "The more common, perhaps, is a perspective of steady industrialization and urbanization on the model of the upper Midwest. The other, cherished by an articulate minority, perceives Alaska as the protector of the last great American wilderness, living from its fisheries and forests. The two destinies are not everywhere incompatible, but Rampart forces a hard choice between them."[51] By dismissing economic questions and refusing to engage meaningfully with Native objections, Rampart supporters simplified the dam into an issue of "ducks versus bucks" and simply mocked anyone who would seriously side with the former.[52]

This dynamic was typified in a pair of articles that appeared in *The Atlantic Monthly* in 1965. The first was by Paul Brooks, who summarized the case against the Rampart Dam in "The Plot to Drown Alaska." Brooks reiterated many of the findings from the environmental impact studies and explained the opposition of Native villagers. Interestingly, however, he spent the majority of the article arguing that the project made no sense economically. He quoted one independent study that found that Rampart would "produce a quantity of power many times the ability of present Alaskan industry, commerce, and population to absorb." Brooks explained that most economists believed that the idea that industries would flock to Alaska to utilize the excess power was "not a very realistic expectation."[53]

Ernest Gruening wrote a seething rebuttal to the article entitled, "The Plot to Strangle Alaska," in which he simply ignored all the economic arguments and focused on the question of potential wildlife losses. He reiterated his argument that more water would please the ducks, and he ridiculed the inclusion in Brooks's piece of "a photograph of a cow moose swimming." "The implication," he said, "is clearly that the moose is drowning."[54] Gruening briefly mentioned Brooks's argument that the majority of Natives did not support Rampart, but he implied that their opposition had been fabricated by the environmentalists: "Representatives of the opposition have prepared a letter for distribution to the Congress signed by the village residents protesting against Rampart which repeats all the Fish and Wildlife allegations in words not utterable by these natives."[55]

Gruening's single-minded quest to build the Rampart Dam caused him to overlook the fact that many "duck lovers" were sympathetic to his desire to strengthen Alaska's economy. In "The Plot to Drown Alaska," Brooks had concluded that thinking of development in Alaska "as a contest between cash and conservation is unreal. This is not an either-or choice, least of all in Alaska. . . . Orderly development of its waterpower will not necessarily destroy it. Spectacular but speculative ventures like Rampart Dam will surely do so."[56] In fact, many environmentalists supported another hydroelectric project, a smaller dam on the upper Susitna River near Devil's Canyon. The area was virtually uninhabited, the flooded area would be small, and the impact on the natural environment would be minimal. In addition, the area was located between the state's two major population centers—Fairbanks and Anchorage—so there was a guaranteed market for the power. Time and again, Rampart opponents suggested Devil's Canyon as a viable alternative to Rampart, but Gruening and members of Yukon Power for America were not interested—they were set on the "big one." As one environmentalist wittily remarked, "the trouble with Devil's Canyon dam, it doesn't cost enough."[57] Since Gruening and other Alaska leaders never got behind it, the smaller dam was never built. When the boosters lost Rampart, they lost their dam.

Although the Rampart Dam never happened, it had a lasting impact on the state of Alaska. Tourists who drive north on the Dalton Highway stop at the Yukon crossing and hear a grand tale of the great dam that might have been where now only mosquitoes bite and muddy waters flow. Environmentalists successfully introduced a new way of thinking about Alaska: It was the country's "last great wilderness." Natives along the Yukon organized themselves into a formidable political group (leading, in part, to Senator Gruening's political defeat in 1968). But perhaps most important, a new way of thinking about Alaskan development was introduced. Debates over how—and whether—to settle America's last frontier would now simplify themselves into "ducks versus bucks," a simple moral opposition that would ignore the complexity of life in a northern land. This new, simplified opposition would be put to the test when the biggest development scheme of all—something that really *did* happen—literally tore the Alaskan landscape apart.

A Crack in the Landscape:
The Trans-Alaska Pipeline

How to bring economic development to Alaska remained the big question for Alaska boosters for a few more years. Then, everything changed. There are a few moments in history—often wars, revolutions, or natural disasters—that have such a profound effect on people and places that they divide history into starkly different periods—"before anyone knew," and "after it happened." For Alaska, this monumental event was the discovery of oil at Prudhoe Bay, which led to the subsequent construction of the Trans-Alaska Pipeline.

Though the pipeline was far less bloody or tragic than most of these monumental historical events, it nevertheless forever divided the Alaskan narrative into "before oil" and "after oil," just as it symbolically cracked the Alaskan landscape into two portions. In February 1968, the Atlantic Richfield Company (Arco) dug an exploratory well in the northernmost part of Alaska. The amount of hot black gold that gushed onto the frozen landscape was astonishing.[1] Scientists estimated that the Prudhoe Bay oil field contained approximately 10 billion barrels of oil—making it the largest oil field in the United States and the fourth largest in the world. This discovery would prove to change Alaska in almost every conceivable way.[2] The controversy surrounding the construction of the pipeline would pit two distinctly different visions of Alaska against one another: Alaska as the nation's oil reserve versus Alaska as America's last great wilderness. The compromise decision that ensued implied that Alaska could be both of these things at once—but later events suggested that the balance between oil development and wilderness was precarious at best.

Oil exploration was nothing new in Alaska. Many nineteenth-century explorers reported seeing oil on the shores of the Arctic Ocean, and Eskimos had long used these oil seeps for fuel.[3] Consequently, both government and private interests had been exploring for major oil deposits in the western Arctic for decades, but to little avail. However, in the years immediately preceding statehood, significant amounts of oil had been discovered in the more southerly Kenai Peninsula, raising hopes that petroleum might indeed be an important resource for Alaska. During the 1960s, Cook Inlet became the focus of exploration, and by 1967 oil from the inlet region displaced fisheries as the leading source of Alaska's state income.[4] But all this was still a blip in terms of domestic or world production, and no oil discoveries thus far had even come close to the massive strike at Prudhoe Bay. The discovery unleashed oil fever in Alaska. In September 1968, the state opened up bidding for leases to drill on the North Slope. In a single day, Alaska grew $900 million richer, with the promise of an additional $200 million per year in royalties.[5]

The stage for this boom had been set years earlier. As part of the Alaska Statehood Act, the federal government had given Alaska the right to withdraw 104 of its 365 million acres for the purposes of economic development.[6] Hoping that the North Slope might contain significant oil deposits, the state asked the Bureau of Land Management for permission to withdraw the 2 million acres of land between the Colville and Canning rivers, an area that included Prudhoe Bay. The state argued that the land was uninhabited and unused by the Eskimos, and the BLM confirmed this "fact" by publishing a notice in an elite Anchorage newspaper (one that surely never made its way out to the Native villages) asking if any group claimed aboriginal title to the land. No one responded. Consequently, the state of Alaska was given control of the slope in 1964, and it put the land up for lease soon after. Before the Prudhoe Bay discovery, however, arctic oil exploration was still an unknown and expensive venture, so the state made less than $12 million on the initial sales.[7]

Another event that set the stage for the oil boom was the election of Republican governor Walter Hickel. Hickel—a self-made real-estate developer who famously claimed to have come to Alaska with only 37 cents in his pocket—narrowly defeated the Democratic incumbent, William Egan, in 1966, and his election marked a shift in Alaska's political allegiance away from Democratic candidates and toward Republicans and independents.[8] Hickel was an aggressive businessman, and one of his legislative priorities

Load of supplies heading north on the Hickel Ice Highway, 1970. Steve McCutcheon, McCutcheon Collection, Anchorage Museum, B81.36.15.

was to promote economic growth in the northern parts of Alaska. To his mind, "it was obvious . . . that finding our wealth and getting it to market would be the key to our freedom from Outside control."[9] In 1967, Hickel created the Northern Operations of Rail Transportation and Highways (NORTH) Commission to study opportunities for development in the Arctic. Little did he know that just one year later, those opportunities would make themselves abundantly clear at Prudhoe Bay.

With news of the strike, Hickel's development dreams came true, and he quickly sprang into action, authorizing the construction of a winter trail from Livengood, a small town north of Fairbanks and the end of the official road system, to the oil fields at Prudhoe Bay, a span of 300 miles. Construction took place in the winter of 1968, and the road was named the "Hickel Highway" in the governor's honor. With no time to investigate the proper engineering techniques for the trail, the construction crews plowed off the top layer of snow and removed ground cover to the permafrost, creating an "ice road" on which vehicles could travel in the winter, but which quickly became a river of mud come spring thaw.[10] When the surrounding snow melted, the Hickel Highway became the Hickel Canal, and the damage to the tundra was profound (attempts to reconstruct the road using a slightly different route in the winter of 1969 produced the same results). One critic at the University of Alaska bemoaned that "from an environmental point of view the [$766,000] Hickel Highway is the biggest screwup in the history of mankind in the Arctic."[11] The highly publicized disaster quickly demonstrated that there was going to be no clear way to get the valuable—but remote—Alaskan oil to market.

Meanwhile, Alaskans were struggling to comprehend the implications of the $900 million that had unexpectedly fallen into the state's hands. The state government, in conjunction with the Brookings Institution, scheduled a series of conferences in 1969 to discuss what should be done with the windfall. With a population of just under 300,000, the implications for Alaskan residents would be significant.[12] Over the course of several months, a cross section of Alaskans met to discuss the future of their state. Though many residents expressed a desire to preserve their lifestyle, "which affords the conveniences of technological innovation combined with the opportunity and values of living as close to nature as possible," they also believed that their way of life was compatible with the presence of the oil industry.[13] It was difficult to tame the euphoria felt by Alaskans, who now felt that they "had it all"—ducks *and* bucks—but the Brookings Institution warned the residents that their situation was not as simple as it seemed. The state had started with a severe financial deficit, and money from the oil leases simply brought Alaska's economy into line with those of many other states. Alaska's geographic remoteness and all the challenges that came with it would remain. In addition, members of the institution warned that there would be social and environmental costs to the presence of the oil industry; life in Alaska would indeed change, the only question was how. Money was only a small part of the equation.

While Alaskans were contemplating their new economic status, businessmen and engineers were thinking about how to move hot oil over a frozen landscape. So much petroleum in such a remote location—how would they ever get it to market? Humble Oil suggested that the fabled Northwest Passage could be the answer, and the company proposed that a fleet of ice-breaking tankers haul oil from the North Slope to New York by an all-marine route. In 1969, Humble chartered the S.S. *Manhattan*, the largest icebreaking tanker in the U.S. fleet, to complete an experimental run through the ice-ridden northern passage. After several improvements to the ship, it became the first commercial vessel to cross the Northwest Passage, although the expense and logistical difficulties involved made it apparent that this would not be a viable way to transport oil from the North Slope.[14]

Canadian engineers began studying the possibility of a pipeline west across the Arctic National Wildlife Range and through Canada's Mackenzie Valley, although most of the oil companies favored an all-Alaska pipe, one that would span the 800 miles from Prudhoe Bay to the ice-free port of Valdez, where oil would then be loaded onto tankers and shipped to California. Another group of developers argued for a shorter pipeline to Fairbanks, where oil could then be transported on trucks down the seldom-used Alaska Highway. Although the engineering challenges to the construction of any of these arctic pipelines would be monumental, there proved to be an even bigger political obstacle to getting Alaska's oil from the Arctic to the market.

The question regarding the legal relationship of Alaska Natives to their homeland had been slowly simmering since the United States purchased the territory from Russia in 1867. The treaty regarding the sale of Alaska only casually addressed the status of the Native inhabitants, stating that "the uncivilized tribes will be subject to such laws and regulations as the United States may, from time to time, adopt in regard to aboriginal tribes in that country."[15] This vagueness would remain the theme of federal Indian policy in Alaska for decades, and the white inhabitants never forced the issue. Alaska Natives never came into formal military conflict with white Americans, and although their homes were periodically trampled by gold miners or military personnel, the presence of these white invaders was usually temporary. Land conflicts tended to flare up periodically but deescalate with time. Technically, the territory to which Natives laid claim was not to be exploited; as the First Organic Act of 1884 stated, "the Indians or other persons in [Alaska] shall not be disturbed in the possession of any lands actually in their use or occupation or now claimed by them, but the terms under which such persons may acquire title to such lands is reserved for future legislation by Congress."[16] In reality, however, the lack of any formal title to the land meant that the Natives' rights were de facto nonexistent, and their interests were rarely—if ever—taken into consideration.

Even the Alaska statehood bill failed to address the issue. By the late 1950s and early 1960s, however, the controversies over Project Chariot and the Rampart Dam brought Native land claims to the forefront of Alaskan politics. With the state of Alaska now selecting lands to withdraw for economic development purposes, Natives and non-Natives alike began to realize that the issue must be addressed once and for all. In 1963, the Alaska Task Force on Native Affairs at the Department of the Interior made a formal statement that the settlement of Alaska Native land claims was long overdue. Natives started sending letters to the department protesting the withdrawal of certain areas by the state of Alaska, and in 1966, Secretary of State Stewart Udall imposed an informal land freeze in Alaska until the federal government settled Native land claims. From that point forward, no more land could be transferred into state or private hands until the Alaska Natives' rights to the land were legally defined. In 1969, following the discovery of oil at Prudhoe Bay, the land freeze was formalized by executive order.[17]

This federal intervention outraged the state of Alaska as well as the oil companies.[18] Stewart Udall was just the kind of national politician that Alaska boosters disliked. Appointed in 1960 by President John F. Kennedy, Udall sympathized with both conservationists and Native advocates, and he was willing to delay projects to make sure Alaskan development proceeded in a fair and thoughtful manner.[19] Although some Alaska leaders quietly agreed that Native land claims must be settled, Governor Hickel simply ignored Udall's injunction when he approved the sale of oil leases on Alaska's North Slope. Alaska Natives quickly realized that they were not going to get a fair settlement without a fight, and villages and local councils came together in Anchorage in 1966 to form the first statewide Native interest group, soon to be christened the Alaska Federation of Natives (AFN).

This important event can be traced largely to the existence of a Native newspaper, the *Tundra Times*, which had been created soon after the Inupiat Patiot meeting in Barrow to protest Project Chariot. In 1962, Henry Forbes, the new chairman of the Alaska Policy Committee of the Association on American Indian Affairs, visited Alaska and spoke with the Natives about the need for better inter-village communication. When no financial support for an all-Native newspaper could be found, Forbes offered to fund the paper himself, and he selected Howard Rock, an Eskimo artist from Fairbanks, to manage the project. Because of Rock's hard work, Natives in remote villages throughout the state began to realize that threats to their villages and hunting grounds were not isolated instances, but part of a larger phenomenon that would undoubtedly require the cooperation of all Alaska Natives to settle.[20]

Traditionally, Natives in Alaska had often been suspicious of one another, as their needs and wants varied from group to group and region to region. Even as the AFN came together, there were stark differences of opinion regarding the organization's proper mission. There was one thing that all the Natives agreed on, however: "It has now become necessary for the Native people of Alaska to make a determined stand to protect what is rightfully ours," as one Native told the *Tundra Times*.[21] The Natives' common goals included securing legal rights to their lands and to their subsistence lifestyles, stopping encroachment by white interests—and particularly the state of Alaska—onto traditional lands, and obtaining cash compensation for lands previously lost or about to be lost to oil development.[22]

Sensing the Natives' growing political determination, the Department of the Interior drafted a settlement bill in May 1967, proposing to award 50,000 acres of land to each Native village and to give a small cash award to each Native individual. The Department of the Interior, however, would manage the land and money in trust for the Natives, just as it did for Native Americans on reservations in the Lower 48. This offer did not even come close to compensating for the 380 million acres of land to which the Natives were claiming aboriginal title (this area was greater in size than the state of Alaska, as many groups held overlapping claims). The AFN quickly voted to reject the Department of the Interior's offer and decided to fight to the finish to get a settlement they believed was fair.[23]

Alaska Natives wanted something unique. They had long resisted the idea of Indian reservations held in trust by the federal government—they wanted actual control of their lands and their lifestyles, and they wanted to preserve their traditions while also participating fully in modern American life. A tall order, to be sure, but many legislators were sympathetic, as they did not want to repeat the many failures that had resulted from federal Indian policy in the continental United States. In addition, the national atmosphere for a generous settlement was right, as public opinion generally favored civil rights for minority groups at that time. In addition, the newly elected president, Richard Nixon, was known to be sympathetic to Native American causes.[24]

Wanting to settle the matter as quickly as possible, the state of Alaska set up a Land Claims Task Force under the leadership of State Representative Willie Hensley, an Inupiat Eskimo from Kotzebue. The task force held hearings and listened to the testimony of Native leaders from all over the state, trying to determine what kind of settlement would meet the needs of hundreds of communities with diverse lifestyles.[25] The specter of federal Indian policy in the continental West haunted each and every discussion

Alaska Native leaders meeting with Secretary of the Interior Walter Hickel to discuss the land claims dispute, Fall 1970. Alaska State Library, Alaska Native Organizations Photograph Collection, P33-05.

about what should be done for the Natives in Alaska, and this dark history motivated people to work together to overcome their differences.

After the strike at Prudhoe Bay, the oil companies joined the Alaska Natives in their fight. This sped up the legislative process considerably and facilitated a generous settlement. President Richard Nixon signed the Alaska Native Claims Settlement Act (ANCSA) on December 18, 1971. The bill was fully supported by the AFN, the oil industry, and the state of Alaska. The legislation extinguished all claims of aboriginal title by Indians, Eskimos, and Aleuts in Alaska, and in return the Natives were awarded more than $962 million and title to 40 million acres of land, which the Natives themselves would select from areas withdrawn from the public domain by the secretary of the interior.[26] Most innovatively—and most controversially—ANCSA created twelve state-chartered, profit-driven regional corporations to be run by the Natives for the benefit of their shareholders. In addition, the legislation mandated the creation of more than 200 village corporations to administer the land and cash awards of the settlement.[27] Although the full implications of this monumental legislation would not be felt for decades, in the short term, the Native question in Alaska was finally settled, and construction of the oil pipeline could proceed.

But then the environmental movement stepped in. There was no point at which the environmentalists believed that they could prevent the extraction of Prudhoe Bay oil, but they were horrified by how quickly and destructively things were moving forward in Alaska. In addition to the Hickel Highway disaster, reports of low-flying aircraft shooting wildlife near the oil fields, the discovery of unofficial "camps" being set up along the proposed pipeline corridor, and the lack of any formal discussions about the pipe's potential impact on the landscape enraged conservationists.[28] Environmentalists wanted the opportunity to slow the pace of activity to ensure that every possible ecological factor was taken into consideration. Fortunately for their cause, they had an important legal resource at their disposal.

In 1970, the same year the Trans-Alaska Pipeline System (TAPS, later called Alyeska, a consortium of several major oil companies) filed for the formal right-of-way to build a pipeline from Prudhoe Bay to Valdez, the National Environmental Policy Act (NEPA) had become law.[29] NEPA required that major development projects undergo environmental study, after which an Environmental Impact Statement (EIS) would be issued on which the public could comment. In 1970, the Environmental Defense Fund, the Wilderness Society, and Friends of the Earth sued the Department of the Interior on the grounds that the proposed pipeline violated the EIS provision of NEPA. The environmentalists also argued that the proposed pipeline corridor was too broad, violating the Mineral Leasing Act of 1920. The courts agreed on both counts and issued a preliminary injunction against construction.[30]

Alaskan officials were thoroughly annoyed. Republican governor Keith Miller (who had replaced Walter Hickel when he became secretary of the interior) called the injunction "an unwarranted interference in the sovereign state of Alaska."[31] While the environmental study went forward—supposedly examining all the various options for transporting Alaska's oil—Alyeska began a public relations campaign promoting the pipeline from Prudhoe Bay to Valdez, which it believed to be the most economically profitable option (the oil companies assumed this pipeline could be buried, as was the custom in other oil regions, such as Oklahoma and Texas). The other major possibility, a pipeline through Canada, would take longer to construct and would possibly subject the oil companies to additional taxes and regulations.

The environmentalists, however, worried about oil leaks along the marine portion of the all-Alaska route, and they believed that a pipeline through Canada would be preferable. In addition, they wanted to make sure that any line would be built with the prevention of oil spills as its top priority. The state just wanted to get the oil to market as quickly as possible. All sides soon had ammunition for their causes. The draft Environmental Impact Statement was completed in December 1970, and public hearings began the following February.[32]

The ensuing hearings generated 12,000 pages of public testimony and more than 8,000 letters to the Department of the Interior. The environmentalists were outraged with the initial EIS—although the Department of the Interior's study was supposed to consider all possible means of transporting the oil, it had only addressed Alyeska's preferred route from Prudhoe Bay to Valdez.[33] The report said nothing about the potential effects of oil spills along the pipeline corridor; it failed to address the pipeline's impact on the behavior of wildlife; and it completely ignored the marine portion of the route, stopping its study at the Valdez port.[34] While the environmentalists pointed to these and other gaps in the report, engineers and scientists argued about the implications of a hot pipeline buried in arctic permafrost. Traditional methods for burying oil pipes would never work in much of the Alaskan landscape, they argued; the oil would either have to be refrigerated, or much of the pipeline would have to be constructed above ground.[35]

Alaska Natives from the fishing village of Cordova worried about the presence of oil tankers in Prince William Sound. As an Alaska fisherman put it, "our way of life is threatened and nobody seems to give a damn."[36] Some Alaskans noted that the report failed to consider that the southern part of the pipe would cross one of the most earthquake-prone regions in North America. It would also traverse many rivers and streams that were vulnerable to major flooding. Finally, some economists suggested that a Canadian pipeline might be more profitable, since the oil could be brought directly to energy-hungry midwestern markets.[37] Critics accused President Nixon and the new secretary of the interior, Rogers Morton, of kowtowing to the oil industry by trying to slam the project through as quickly as possible. Proponents of the pipeline were suddenly on the defensive.

In the end, it was the Department of the Interior's failure to study the Canadian alternatives that forced the department to conduct a more complete environmental impact study. In January 1972, the appeals court of the District of Columbia ruled that the National Environmental Policy Act required "a broad consideration of alternatives to any proposed federal action."[38] When the Department of the Interior released its final EIS on

March 20, 1972, it considered all possible means of transporting the oil—consequently, the report was nine volumes and 3,550 pages long. Seeking to avoid another widespread attack on the project, the department argued that, despite the new information contained in the study, "another public hearing at this time is not necessary. . . . It is the Secretary's view that this complex report [on the Trans-Alaska Pipeline] needs to be read; needs to be understood; that a public hearing would be a *circus* in comparison to the kind of thoughtful, substantial comment that might come . . . [in government] offices."[39]

The environmentalists and other public interest groups were livid—there were only seven copies of the report available for public inspection in the Lower 48 states, and the window of time for public comment was less than two months. For those who did manage to get their hands on the report, its conclusions were confusing. As one historian put it, "it rated the Prudhoe-Mackenzie way (across the Arctic National Wildlife Range) as least damaging to the biotic environment, and Prudhoe-Fairbanks-Alaska Highway as least impactful on the marine environment. Prudhoe-Valdez would be superior only in doing the least damage to the abiotic (nonliving) environment."[40] As to the final option, the authors warned that the pipeline could have untold effects on large mammals, especially caribou; that even small oil spills from marine tankers could do irreparable damage to ocean life; and that seismic activity in southern portions of Alaska could ultimately destroy the pipe. The report pointed to the project's innumerable environmental risks but ultimately did not make a clear recommendation, instead raising as many questions as it answered.[41]

The second EIS had ostensibly fulfilled the requirements of NEPA, but another court ruling, in February 1973, found that the proposed pipeline remained in violation of the 1920 Mineral Leasing Act. When the U.S. Supreme Court refused to hear the appeal in this case, it ultimately left the fate of the pipeline project up to Congress, and once Congress got hold of the issue, talk turned from wildlife and engineering concerns to national security. In May 1973, Alaska Senator Ted Stevens introduced a bill authorizing the immediate construction of the Prudhoe Bay to Valdez pipeline, warning that "America's dependence on foreign oil to meet our increasing energy needs is threatening our economic health, placing our national security in jeopardy and questioning America's role in the international community."[42]

With the energy "crisis" moving to the forefront of national politics, statements like these resonated with the public.[43] Suddenly, the pipeline was a patriotic issue. While environmentalists and public-interest groups cried foul, senators from Alaska and other western states worked with the oil companies to assure passage of the bill, even including a controversial amendment that would prohibit any further challenges to the project under the National Environmental Policy Act. When the Middle East oil embargo began, the scales were firmly tipped in the direction of the swift construction of the pipeline. President Nixon signed the Trans-Alaska Pipeline Authorization Act in November 1973.

Equipment began moving north in January 1974, and construction was well under way by the end of the summer. Alaskans who had so optimistically believed that their way of life was compatible with the oil industry now began to understand why the Brookings Institution had questioned that assumption years earlier. Scores of men from the Lower 48 came looking for the highly paid jobs that the pipeline offered. And with these men came women—many of them prostitutes. Sleepy towns such as Fairbanks and Valdez saw a significant rise in crime, gambling, and alcohol abuse. While workers from the Lower 48 found this supposed replay of the "Wild West" exciting, local residents were distraught.[44] Traffic on Alaska's few roads skyrocketed, and stores could not keep enough food and supplies on the shelves. Prices at restaurants and hotels more than doubled. One popular bumper sticker read, "Happiness Is—10,000 Okies Going South with a Texan under Each Arm." This attitude contributed to the election of a conservation-minded Republican governor, Jay Hammond, in 1974.[45]

Construction involved not only building the pipeline, but also building an all-weather road to the oil fields (it was first simply called the "Haul Road" and later christened the "Dalton Highway"). Psychologically, the initial opening of the Haul Road was devastating to environmentalists— Alaska had been split in two, and from their point of view, it could never be made whole again.[46] If they had lost the war, however, they had still won some important battles. From an engineering standpoint, the Trans-Alaska Pipeline was much more environmentally friendly than it would have been if the environmentalists had not succeeded in delaying the project for almost five years.

Almost one-half of the pipeline's length (380 of about 800 miles) was elevated to avoid thawing the permafrost, and the terminal at Valdez was built to withstand even major earthquakes. The elevated pipeline was built in a zigzag pattern to absorb any shock from thermal expansion or seismic activity. The Haul Road was routed to avoid important spawning and nesting

Workers building the Tazlina River Pipeline Suspension Bridge, c. 1976. Steve McCutcheon, McCutcheon Collection, Anchorage Museum, B90.14.3.1253.

areas. Sections of the pipe were designated "wildlife crossings" and elevated to a minimum of 10 feet to allow for migrating animals to pass. From a design standpoint, these concessions were significant.[47]

The actual construction process was another matter. A swift completion of the project was Alyeska's top priority—the company promised the government "that Alaska oil [will] reach the U.S. West Coast Market during 1977."[48] Speedy construction meant that mistakes were often made—oil was spilled, fires were set, and wildlife and river crossings were not always built up to the promised standards. The Alyeska Company had hired Mechanics

Research, a contractor from Los Angeles, to survey pipeline activities, but since the company was on Alyeska's payroll, objective monitoring could not be guaranteed. Local environmental organizations—such as the Fairbanks Environmental Center, the Alaska Conservation Society, and the Alaska Center for the Environment—worked with the national conservation groups to create an independent surveillance team, but the enormity of the project and a scarcity of funds meant that their efforts were only marginally successful, at best. Alyeska was not terribly cooperative when conservation groups asked to see construction sites or to obtain engineering data, and it was not long before the environmentalists realized that they were fighting a losing battle.[49] As promised, the pipeline was completed quickly, and oil began flowing on June 20, 1977. The Trans-Alaska Pipeline was the largest privately funded construction project in history, with total costs reaching almost $9 billion.

Although, toward the end, the environmentalists may have given up on the pipeline, they had far from given up on Alaska. In fact, their greatest political fight was still to come. It began, in fact, the moment that the Alaska Native Claims Settlement Act was passed. The environmentalists largely supported a generous settlement for the Natives, but they also realized that "the great federal domain in Alaska—originally comprising all 375 million acres of the Alaskan land mass—is being disposed of rapidly":

> [ANCSA] will grant [the Natives] 40 million acres. Earlier, Congress granted rights to 103 million acres to the State of Alaska. Between them, under pressures from speculators and exploiters, they will compete in dividing up the best lands in Alaska—public lands. The results of this competition will be development of a chaotic land use pattern, in a "public-take-the-hindmost" land rush. [ANCSA] seemingly serves the interests of the Natives, of the State of Alaska, and of resource developers. But nowhere in this bill is the public interest accommodated—the interest of the 208 million people who own most of Alaska.[50]

Because of this reasoning, and the government's desire to do something to placate the environmentalists during this "scramble for Alaska," Congress included a provision in ANCSA—the 17(d)(2) section—that authorized the secretary of the interior to withdraw up to 80 million acres of unreserved and unappropriated lands for possible inclusion in the country's national parks, national forests, wild and scenic rivers, and wildlife refuges. After the Interior Department made its recommendations, the final decision about which lands to preserve would be left up to Congress. Secretary Rogers Morton formally withdrew 78 million acres of land for study in 1972. Alaska boosters were furious with this attempt to "lock up" lands by "outside interests." The ensuing battle between pro-development and pro-environment forces became known as the "d-2 controversy."

The d-2 conflict raged for almost a decade. National public hearings centered on the meaning of Alaska and whether it was a frontier to be exploited or a wilderness to be preserved.[51] Those who favored development wanted to see the national-interest lands subject to "multiple uses"—including foresting and mining—while those who wanted to leave Alaskan lands undisturbed favored the creation of national parks and wildlife refuges. Government agencies also scrambled to control the fate of d-2 lands, with the National Park Service, the National Forest Service, the Fish and Wildlife Service, and the Bureau of Land Management all vying for authority.[52] But nowhere was the debate more heated than in Alaska, where Governor Jay Hammond said that,

> without doubt, the most confused, divisive issue confronting Alaska . . . is that of d-2. Probably no issue has ever so torn the state apart. Alaskans disagree on both the nature of the problem and what to do about it. We have the Alaska Coalition and the Real Alaska Coalition, [Citizens for the Management of Alaskan Lands], and the Conservation Society, two Senators who strongly disagree, and editorial writers who demand conflicting courses of action.[53]

Amidst all this chaos, the Joint Federal-State Land Use Planning Commission (a joint venture between the federal government and the state of Alaska) made its first recommendation in August 1973. "Reflecting its largely Alaskan composition," wrote two historians, "[the commission] stressed the 'multiple use' concept for the 78 million acres the secretary had withdrawn in 1972."[54] The Department of the Interior, working closely with the environmental movement, made a more preservationist-minded recommendation in December 1973. Secretary Morton asked Congress to add approximately 64 million acres to the national park and wildlife refuge system. Congress had until December 1978 to decide how to act on these recommendations.

When President Jimmy Carter and a new Congress were elected in 1976, environmentalists rejoiced. Strongly preservationist Alaska lands bills, which would protect approximately 100 million acres as national parks or wildlife refuges, were introduced in both the House and the Senate.[55] Not everyone was so happy, though, and Alaskans began staging protests all over the state. The majority of the state's newspapers came out in strident opposition to the proposed federal "lock up." One Alaskan argued that if an Alaska lands bill passed, "Alaska must secede from the Union, become an independent country where men are free, not penned up behind yards of laws telling them they can't do here and they can't do there. . . . When I first came to this country I hunted when I damn well felt like it, where I damn well felt like it, and that's how it ought to be."[56] Alaska Natives were divided. Village corporation leaders saw a lands bill as a chance to protect their subsistence lifestyles, whereas regional corporation leaders felt that such a bill would interfere with their ability to make a profit for their shareholders. Opinions were strong on all sides.

Alaska Senator Mike Gravel lobbied hard to keep the Alaska Lands Bill in the Senate from passing. The December 1978 deadline was fast approaching, and if he could delay the vote, he could effectively kill the bill. Recognizing Gravel's intentions, the environmental movement convinced President Carter to designate 56 million acres of the proposed National Interest Lands as National Monuments, a right given to him as president under the 1906 Antiquities Act. Carter hesitantly agreed, and on December 1, 1978, the lands included in the Alaska Lands Bill were designated as national monuments by an executive order. Carter claimed that he was forced to act because of Congress's refusal to do so, but it was not long before Alaskans were burning Carter's image in effigy in towns throughout the state. Many Alaskans armed themselves against the National Park Service and prepared literally to fight it out on the ground.

Meanwhile, a more conservative Congress was elected in 1978, and proponents of National Interest Lands realized that they might have to compromise to get a legislative settlement, which would be preferable to Carter's executive order, as it would allow for better protection and management of the land. Both sides battled it out, but when President Ronald Reagan was elected in 1980, the conservationists realized that they would have to accept a weaker Alaska Lands Bill, if they were to get anything at all. The compromise bill protected 43 million rather than 100 million acres as national parks or wildlife refuges, and in total, it put 104 million acres under some kind of federal land management. Congress passed the Alaska National Interest Lands Conservation Act (ANILCA) in November 1980, and President Carter signed the bill into law the following month. Despite compromises made by the environmentalists, the legislation remained the largest conservation act in history, more than doubling the total acres in the U.S. Wilderness Preservation System.[57]

By 1980, Alaska was a completely different place than it had been in 1968. The state had been divided into federal, state, private, and Native lands. From the public's point of view, Alaska was a success—a place that had it all, that protected the interests of everyone. The "last frontier" was now an "enduring frontier," a place where economic development peacefully met a wilderness landscape, where Natives coexisted with non-Natives, and where national and state interests had been brought into balance. On the ground, however, Alaskans struggled with "having it all"—Natives wondered how to balance traditional lifestyles with corporate structures; the state struggled with the economic dominance of the oil industry; and Alaskans fought the many new regulations that came with federal land management. During the 1980s, these battles became local concerns, however, and Alaska once again faded into the background of national politics.

Alaska dramatically reentered the national consciousness on March 24, 1989, when the oil tanker *Exxon Valdez* hit Bligh Reef in Prince William Sound. Thirty million gallons of crude oil spilled into the ocean, washing up on 1,200 miles of Alaskan coastline.[58] As images of black water, drowning seabirds, and oil-covered sea mammals hit the national media, the country worked to comprehend the magnitude of the greatest environmental disaster in American history. While environmentalists could not help but say, "We told you so," most Americans wondered how this could have happened. Alaska was the nation's enduring frontier, and the disaster was made all the more dramatic by its location in this beautiful, remote region, teeming with wildlife. In reality, this had been just one of more than 400 spills in Prince William Sound since oil had been leaving Valdez on tankers, but it took a disaster of this magnitude to capture the attention of the national media.[59]

If the American public was shocked by the *Exxon Valdez* disaster, Alaskans were less so. They were aware of contradictions inherent in being, in the words of Jay Hammond, "at once . . . oil barrel for America and National Park for the World."[60] Local media focused on the impacts the spill would have on the commercial fishing communities of Cordova and Valdez and on the crisis faced by the Native residents of Tatitlek, who relied on the sound's resources for subsistence. For those Alaskans who had long resented the presence of the oil industry, the spill provided the ultimate

The U.S. Coast Guard cleaning up Cook Inlet after the *Exxon Valdez* spill, c. 1989. Alaska State Library, U.S. Coast Guard Activities, 17th Division, Photograph Collection, Ed Moreth, P313–08–01.

ammunition for their hatred. Other Alaskans, by contrast, took the news in stride, quietly celebrating the high-paying jobs that would come with the cleanup. Environment and development debates raged once again in Alaska. What did the oil spill really mean? Was the presence of the oil industry ruining Alaska? Or was the nation's desire to keep Alaska a pristine wilderness unrealistic and unfair?[61]

Exxon spent over $2 billion cleaning up the spill and over $1 billion to settle civil and criminal charges related to the case. Litigation is still ongoing, and oil from the spill can still be seen on the water and the shores of southern Alaska. From the national point of view, the "disaster" may have passed, but the questions raised by the *Exxon Valdez* spill linger everywhere in Alaska. What does it mean to be the nation's enduring frontier? Does Alaska truly have it all, or, as Alaska was divided into pieces, was the state left with an environment and development model that literally rips the land in two? While Alaskans debate these questions in a post-pipeline economy, the residents of the Lower 48 often see things quite differently. Once clearly thought of as "the last frontier," Alaska is now more likely to be described as

America's "last great wilderness," a place to be preserved rather than exploited. Ironically, it was the construction of the pipeline and the subsequent major oil spill that pushed the Alaska of America's cultural imagination away from the western-frontier image and toward the notion of a fixed and unchanging place of wilderness.

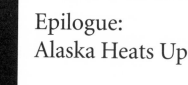

Epilogue:
Alaska Heats Up

In the summer of 2003, as I sat sipping coffee in that bookstore café in Fairbanks, I could scarcely have imagined how much media attention Alaska would receive between my project's inception and its conclusion. Over the past several years, Alaska has appeared time and again on the national radar screen in ways I could not have predicted. The nomination of Alaska Governor Sarah Palin as John McCain's vice presidential running mate in 2008 surprised the nation, and as she drew crowds and paparazzi, appeared in television interviews, and showed up on *Saturday Night Live*—after being impersonated on that show by comedienne Tina Fey in segments viewed by millions on the Internet—all sorts of issues in Alaska life and politics came under scrutiny. Attitudes about Alaska in the Lower 48 shifted yet again as a result (a topic to which I shall return later in this Epilogue). Alaska was also the subject of two major films, *Grizzly Man*, directed by Werner Herzog, in 2005, and *Into the Wild*, directed by Sean Penn, in 2007. Both films capitalized on the idea of Alaska as America's "Last Great Wilderness," drawing attention to the forty-ninth state even before Palin's rise on the national scene.

Although the films did not receive the same widespread attention that Palin's candidacy did, they are worth examining in some detail because of what they demonstrate about American attitudes toward the Alaska wilderness. Herzog's *Grizzly Man* documents the story of Timothy Treadwell, a young man who traveled to Alaska for thirteen consecutive summers to study grizzly bears in Katmai National Park and Preserve. Seen as an outlaw by the park officials, he nevertheless considered himself a protector of these creatures and claimed a spiritual bond with them, filming his interactions with the bears on a daily basis. Herzog fashions Treadwell's films into an interpretive narrative of his sojourns into the wilderness. In the summer of 2003, Treadwell and his girlfriend were both mauled and eaten by a bear.

Penn's *Into the Wild* recalls the environmental journey of Christopher McCandless, a story first made famous in a nonfiction book of the same name by Jon Krakauer. McCandless was an idealistic college student who traveled to Alaska in search of a nonmaterialistic life, living off the land. After a long cross-country trek, McCandless hiked into a remote area of Alaska, near Denali National Park and Preserve, and found an abandoned bus that was often used as a shelter for moose hunters. After several months of camping out, his food supply dwindled, and he found himself trapped, unable to leave. He eventually died of starvation during the summer of 1992.

Although both protagonists die, these films nonetheless celebrate the Alaskan landscape as a unique and majestic wilderness. Unlike most movies set in Alaska, Penn shot *Into the Wild* on location, believing that McCandless's story could only truthfully be told in the great wilderness in which it happened. And because of Alaska's natural splendor, the directors give the protagonists a fairly sympathetic portrayal. Although Treadwell and McCandless might have been careless, they were on environmental quests that could only happen in a place like Alaska. And audiences—in the Lower 48 at least—responded accordingly. In fact, the story of Christopher McCandless created a phenomenon of environmental pilgrimage, whereby his admirers routinely hike out to the bus in which he died.[1] Before his death, Timothy Treadwell founded an organization called Grizzly People, and its members continue to celebrate his memory and his pursuit of an intimate relationship with grizzly bears.[2]

Despite the fact that a significant percentage of the national audience quickly grew fond of these environmental seekers, Alaskans themselves were less impressed. They resented the celebration of two Outsiders who had come to their land, acted carelessly, and left yet another exaltation of Alaska's wilderness in their wakes. I watched the debut of *Grizzly Man* in Anchorage, privy to the audience's quiet heckling of the protagonist's foolishness and the verbal lamenting of the absence of any scenes of urban life in Alaska. One Alaskan who reviewed *Into the Wild* said, "Remember how at the start of *Rocky Horror Picture Show*, the audience would throw rice at the screen? I thought we [Alaskans] all should have done the same during the opening scene of *Into the Wild*."[3] Of course, not all Alaskans reacted this way, and Alaskans love their natural landscape, too. But Alaska's cultural designation as America's "Last Great Wilderness" often irritates them.

The designation bothers Alaskans because it directly affects the development options available to the state. Alaska's cultural designation as wilderness was solidified in the years following the construction of the pipeline, and at that time environmental debates about Alaska largely settled around one question: how much America could afford to lose "something that's as close to an intact wilderness as we're likely to get."[4] Although the wilderness idea has influenced a myriad of recent debates about environment and development in Alaska, there is one debate that distills that question down to its essence, while also driving Alaska boosters crazy: that of whether to open the Arctic National Wildlife Refuge (ANWR) to oil drilling. The political battle over drilling began with the passage of the Alaska National Interest Lands Conservation Act (ANILCA) in 1980 and continues to the present day.

ANILCA created ANWR, but it deferred the question of whether the coastal plain would be open to oil exploration. Countless studies later, no one can agree on how much recoverable oil is on the plain and what effects drilling would have on the area's wildlife, particularly the Porcupine Caribou Herd, which uses the coast as its calving grounds. In 1998, the U.S. Geological Survey (USGS) published a report estimating the amount of recoverable oil as somewhere between 4.3 billion barrels (95 percent certainty) and 11.8 billion barrels (5 percent certainty).[5] But without physical exploration, there is little way to know for sure. The USGS never revealed its methods for obtaining these estimates. Environmental proponents, on the other hand, claim that the area is too valuable as wilderness for it to be drilled. According to the Natural Resources Defense Council:

> The Arctic National Wildlife Refuge is called America's Serengeti, and for good reason. This South Carolina–sized chunk of pristine wilderness contains some of the finest examples of northern forests, glaciered peaks, and windswept tundra left in the United States. At 18 million acres, it is one of the largest sanctuaries for arctic wildlife in the world . . . [including] the 180,000-member Porcupine caribou herd. The sanctuary also provides habitat for polar bears, grizzlies, wolves, musk oxen, and millions of birds.[6]

Dozens of bills authorizing drilling in ANWR were introduced in the House and Senate between 1981 and 2008. Often they would pass one chamber of Congress but not the other; President Bill Clinton vetoed a bill authorizing drilling in 1996. Each and every time, the fight came down to a simple conflict of values—oil versus wilderness—and opponents fought extremely hard on both sides. Proponents of drilling included most Alaskans (including certain groups of Alaska Natives), oil industry workers, and others concerned with securing the domestic oil supply. Opponents of drilling mostly lived Outside and considered themselves environmentalists.[7] Ironically, most of them have never been to the refuge, and most will never go there. But they are convinced of its value as sublime wilderness, and they are determined to keep the oil industry out.[8]

The drilling issue has figured prominently in public debates over the nation's energy supply for years, but after the nomination of Sarah Palin as John McCain's running mate it was given new life. It was not the only issue involving Alaska that Sarah Palin's selection brought to the fore once again, however. While much of the media frenzy surrounding Palin concerned her personality and experience, her nomination also had an impact on the nation's image of Alaska and its inhabitants.

After Palin's nomination, late-night comedians (and comediennes) made jokes about hunting moose, snowmobiling to work, and building bridges to nowhere. Common misperceptions about Alaska—that it has six months of darkness in the winter, that it snows year-round, that Alaskans all "live off the land"—were reintroduced into cultural circulation. Jokes, spoofs, and skits about Governor Palin (who had been elected as governor in 2006) and the state of Alaska were intertwined with typical election-year quips. Alaska was portrayed as a backward place, and as the leader of this remote state, Palin was caricatured as a hillbilly. Prior to the 2008 election, the late-night comedian Conan O'Brien joked, "Alaska Governor Sarah Palin is out on the campaign trail. Today, she attended a rally in Wisconsin. The Alaska governor said she was thrilled to visit Wisconsin because she has never been to the Deep South." Talk-show host Bill Maher mused, "Are you kidding me, the mayor of Wasilla, Alaska? Yeah, that's who you want in the White House during a time of crisis. When she got a phone call at three in the morning, it was because a moose had gotten in the garbage can." Popular comedian Jimmy Kimmel added, "Three years ago, Sarah Palin was the mayor of a town with nine thousand people in it. Never mind national security, they barely have mall security in a town of that size."[9]

Many of the political quips attacking the vice presidential nominee had the same simple theme: Alaska is a land of moose and ice, and governing such a remote state does not give someone much insight into the larger

American experience. At the heart of this simplistic assumption, however, lies a more complicated question that went almost entirely unanswered: What *is* the relationship between the state of Alaska and the nation as a whole? Which is, ironically, a contemporary version of the historical questions that I have explored in this book: How have ideas of landscape and nature in the Lower 48 shaped development in Alaska? And, in turn, how have environmental changes in Alaska influenced larger American ideas about land use and preservation? The answers to these questions have changed over time and will continue to change into the future. Clearly, these topics need more in-depth exploration than they received on late-night television during the campaign of 2008.

While campaigning for the 2008 election, Palin repeatedly advocated for drilling in the Arctic National Wildlife Refuge (McCain opposed drilling in the refuge itself, but supported drilling offshore). A common (and often parodied) component of their political rallies was a group chant of "Drill, baby, drill!" And as part of her advocacy for drilling in ANWR, Palin argued that the place had little, if any, "wilderness" value. She also challenged her environmentalist critics by arguing that global climate change was not caused by fossil-fuel use or human activity of any kind (a claim that the nation's most respected scientists actively refuted), but, unlike some conservative politicians, Palin never once denied that climate change was happening. Being from Alaska, she knew all too well that the planet was warming. All Alaskans do. In fact, Alaska has been dubbed America's "Climate Change Frontier," which may soon replace its primary cultural designation as the "Last Great Wilderness."[10] After all, as I argued in the Introduction, the idea of wilderness is one of an *unchanging* nature, and no one can deny that the natural environment in Alaska is changing—and quickly.

Since polar regions warm the fastest, Alaska is well ahead of the rest of the nation on the climate-change curve. Polar regions have long been kept frigid because their heavy cover of snow and ice reflects about 70 percent of the sun's energy back into space. But higher temperatures have been shrinking this protective cover; arctic sea ice has shrunk 15–20 percent in the past thirty years alone. Overall, temperatures in Alaska have risen 3.6 degrees Fahrenheit since 1950. Winter temperatures have risen 6 degrees Fahrenheit.[11] Ponds and lakes are disappearing as less of Alaska's ground is covered by permafrost. The spruce budworm, spruce bark beetle, and aspen leaf miner—insects once kept in check by the winter cold—have killed

Signs show the rapid retreat of the Exit Glacier in Kenai Fjords National Park, 2003. Image provided courtesy of Craig Pynn, www.craigshots.com.

more than 4 million acres of forest in less than two decades. As summers get longer and hotter, forest fires burn longer and more rapidly—and the trees are having a hard time coming back. "Soon people will be coming to the great plains of Alaska," says forest ecologist Glenn Juday.[12] Perhaps the Matanuska Colony will actually be revived sometime in the near future.

While this idea might seem far-fetched, it is just this kind of rapid environmental change that global warming will bring to Alaska. The environment that Alaskans faced in the past will not be the one they face in the future. A warming planet will change where the caribou roam, whether waterfowl will continue to nest on the Yukon River, and the possibilities for a profitable agricultural enterprise in the state. As Eric Post, an associate professor of biology at Penn State, has argued, "the Arctic as we know it may soon be a thing of the past."[13] Boosters are already buying remote arctic lands, hoping that one day the climate might make them attractive to development. Some investors are hopeful that arctic shipping lands may soon become viable, speeding the global transport of goods between the East and the West.[14] The "frontier" part of America's "Climate Change Frontier" appeals to the development mind-set.

But while boosters wait and see if there might be money to be made from climate change, many Alaskans are already facing the devastating consequences of their warming state. Alaska Natives, in particular, have begun to suffer from living on America's frontier of climate change. Although Alaska Natives have historically been successful at adapting to Alaska's changing environment, since the 1970s they have witnessed an acceleration of natural changes that are becoming difficult to accommodate. According to their collective observations, many northern lakes and rivers have been running lower, decreasing fish populations. The tree line has been moving further north, affecting caribou migrations. The walrus and polar-bear hunts have become difficult; the ice moves too quickly, and the animals are soon out of reach. Hunters have been falling through the sea ice with increasing frequency, as what was formerly pack ice has now become unpredictably thin. Perhaps most devastatingly, whole villages are at risk. As the sea ice disappears, coastal communities are becoming the victims of erosion. Some Alaska Natives have had to relocate their homes, and likely many more will need to move in the near future. As Jerry Wongittilin, Sr., a Yup'ik Eskimo man from the village of Savoonga, explained, "our elders tell us that our earth is getting old and needs to be replaced by a new one."[15]

Of course, Alaska is not the only northern place that is experiencing the accelerated effects of climate change. If there was ever any question as to whether global northern communities had anything in common, there is no doubt now. While the fashioning of Alaska as "Seward's Folly," "The Last Frontier," or "The Last Great Wilderness" might be uniquely American, the designation of "Climate Change Frontier" is shared by northern communities across the globe.

More than a decade ago, a Canadian historian called for the formation of a more unified field of "Northern Studies." He argued that "the North, land of legend, mystery and misconception, remains as much a conceptual wasteland. After decades of scholarship, much of it excellent, insightful, and methodologically import, the vast circumpolar region is still typically explained within the conceptual frameworks and intellectual paradigms of the Southern, or 'outside' world."[16] And in the many years since his challenge, much work has been done to bring scholars of the north together. Still, northern scholars largely work on the margins of scholarship.

But now the call for a prominent and vocal "Northern Studies" field has become more urgent. Since all scholars of the north are working on the frontier of climate change, their research has become even more important.

The global environment of the future will happen first in the north—not just in the American north, but in the larger circumpolar north. But to understand what the environmental future might hold, we first must understand what happened in the past. And teaching Americans about both the environmental history and the environmental future of global climate change is yet another important role for Alaska, as our nation—and the world—heats up.

NOTES

INTRODUCTION: A PLACE FOR ALASKA

1. Susan Kollin, *Nature's State: Imagining Alaska as the Last Frontier* (Chapel Hill: University of North Carolina Press, 2001), 8.
2. I am committing my own sin of omission here by not acknowledging that many of these arguments might also be applied to Hawaii (and other American islands) in different forms. This would be a worthwhile subject for another scholar to investigate.
3. Stephen Haycox, *Alaska: An American Colony* (Seattle: University of Washington Press, 2002), xi–xii.
4. Preston Jones, *Empire's Edge: American Society in Nome, Alaska, 1898–1934* (Fairbanks: University of Alaska Press, 2007), 2.
5. I am borrowing this concept from William Cronon, "Kennecott Journey: The Paths out of Town," in *Under an Open Sky: Rethinking America's Western Past*, edited by William Cronon, George Miles, and Jay Gitlin (New York: W. W. Norton, 1992), 35.
6. Haycox, *Alaska*, 317.
7. Ibid.
8. Claus-M. Naske, "Some Attention, Little Action: Vacillating Federal Efforts to Provide Territorial Alaska with an Economic Base," *Western Historical Quarterly* 26, no. 1 (Spring 1995): 38.
9. Cronon, "Kennecott Journey," 32.
10. This is perhaps another way of formulating the "frontier history" versus "western history" question that has long plagued scholars of the American West. For a summary of this debate and a response to it, see David M. Wrobel, "Beyond the Frontier-Region Dichotomy," *Pacific Historical Review* 65, no. 3 (August 1996): 401–429. Although I do not position myself directly within this scholarly dialogue, I hope successfully to heed Wrobel's call to see how "place and process are inextricably linked" (426).
11. Richard White, "The Nationalization of Nature," *Journal of American History* 86, no. 3 (December 1999): 977.
12. Joel Wainwright, "The Geographies of Political Ecology: After Edward Said," *Environment and Planning* 37 (2005): 1037.
13. For more on the natural features of Alaska, see Joan M. Antonson and William S. Hanable, *Alaska's Heritage*, Alaska Historical Commission Studies in History, no. 133 (Anchorage: Alaska Historical Society, 1992), 1–35. For information on the causes and consequences of permafrost, see Neil Davis, *Permafrost: A Guide to Frozen Ground in Transition* (Fairbanks: University of Alaska Press, 2001).
14. In my writing, and in accordance with standard convention, the terms "Alaska Native" or "Native" (with the "N" capitalized) always refer to the Indian, Eskimo, and Aleut inhabitants of Alaska. "Alaska native" (without capitalization of the "n") refers to anyone born in Alaska, whether Native or white. In 1977, participants in the

Inuit Circumpolar Conference officially rejected the term "Eskimo" as having pejorative connotations and adopted the term "Inuit" as their preferred designation. Unlike their Canadian and Greenlandic brethren, however, most Alaska Natives continue to refer to themselves as Eskimo rather than Inuit in both speech and writing, which is why—along with the ease of historical consistency—I have chosen to use the term here. For a brief discussion of the term "Eskimo," see David Damas, ed., *Arctic*, vol. 5, *The Handbook of North American Indians*, edited by William C. Sturtevant (Washington, D.C.: Smithsonian Institution, 1984), 1–7.

15. The Aleuts once called themselves Ungangan, which means "the original people." The term "Aleut" was first introduced by the Russians, who borrowed it from a Native Siberian language, probably Chukchi or Koryak. The Aleuts quickly adopted the term for themselves, and the majority of them still use it today.

16. For more on the Native cultures of Alaska, see Steven J. Landon, *The Native People of Alaska* (Anchorage: Greatland Graphics, 1993). An older anthropological sketch is H. Dewey Anderson and Walter Crosby Eells's *Alaska Natives: A Survey of Their Sociological and Educational Status* (Stanford: Stanford University Press, 1935). For information on the contemporary lives of Alaska Natives, see Alexandra J. McClanahan, ed., *Growing Up Native in Alaska* (Anchorage: Ciri Foundation, 2000).

17. Wainwright, "Geographies of Political Ecology," 1039.

18. See, for example, C. C. Georgeson, *Fourth Report on the Agricultural Investigations in Alaska*, Bulletin no. 94, Office of Experiment Stations, U.S. Department of Agriculture (Washington, D.C.: Government Printing Office, 1901); and A. M. Goodman, "Report of Present, and Estimate of Future, Agriculture of the Matanuska Valley of Alaska," 1935, Ernest Gruening Papers, Alaska and Polar Regions Collection, Elmer E. Rasmuson Library, University of Alaska–Fairbanks.

19. Richard E. Welch, Jr., "American Public Opinion and the Purchase of Russian America," *American Slavic and Eastern European Review* 17 (1958), 481–494; Frank A. Golder, "The Purchase of Alaska," *American Historical Review* 25 (April 1920): 411–425; Ronald J. Jensen, *The Alaska Purchase and Russian-American Relations* (Seattle: University of Washington Press, 1975).

20. John Muir, *Travels in Alaska*, with a foreword by John Haines (San Francisco: Sierra Club Books, 1988), 11–12.

21. Charles Nordhoff, "What Shall We Do with Scroggs?" *Harper's New Monthly Magazine* 47 (June 1873): 41–44.

22. For a discussion of the various business schemes for Alaska during this period, see Ted C. Hinckley, *The Americanization of Alaska, 1867–1897* (Palo Alto, Calif.: Pacific Books, 1972). For more on the idea of Alaska as a "storehouse," see Peter Coates, *The Trans-Alaska Pipeline Controversy: Technology, Conservation, and the Frontier* (Fairbanks: University of Alaska Press, 1993), 27–62.

23. Frederick Jackson Turner, *Rereading Frederick Jackson Turner*, with commentary by John Mack Faragher (New York: Henry Holt, 1995), 31.

24. For more on frontier anxiety during the 1890s, see David M. Wrobel, *The End of American Exceptionalism: Frontier Anxiety from the Old West to the New Deal* (Lawrence: University Press of Kansas, 1993), 29–41.

25. *Philadelphia Inquirer*, April 17, 1867; quote from Dudley C. Wooten, Congressman from Texas, in *Facts on Alaska* (United States: n.p. [1902?]), Beinecke Rare Book and Manuscript Library, Yale University, New Haven, Connecticut.

26. James H. Ducker, "Gold Rushers North: A Census Study of the Yukon and Alaskan Gold Rushes, 1896–1900," in *An Alaska Anthology: Interpreting the Past*, edited by Stephen W. Haycox and Mary Childers Mangusso (Seattle: University of Washington Press, 1996), 206. When I call Alaska a "territory," I mean so only in the general sense. Alaska was officially a military "district" until 1912, when the federal government granted it territorial status.

27. As scholars frequently point out, the Klondike is actually part of Canada, although the region is often conflated with Alaska in literary works of the gold rush period, such as Jack London's *Call of the Wild*. For a discussion of this phenomenon, see Kollin, *Nature's State*, 65–71. Like London, most Americans of the time imagined the Klondike as part of Alaska, their unfamiliarity with northern landscapes transcending national boundaries.

28. For more on the construction of the railroad, see Edwin M. Fitch, *The Alaska Railroad*, with a foreword by E. L. Bartlett (New York: Frederick A. Praeger, 1967). Because of the difficulty of construction, The Alaska Railroad was not completed until 1923.

29. Special thanks to Kathryn Morse for her insight here.

30. William Cronon, "A Place for Stories: Nature, History, and Narrative," *Journal of American History* 78, no. 4 (March 1992), 1375.

31. Douglas Coe, *Road to Alaska: The Story of the Alaska Highway* (New York: Julian Messner, 1952), 16, 175.

32. White, "Nationalization of Nature," 980.

33. The reservoir would be approximately 2,800 miles long and up to 80 miles wide. Irene E. Ryan, "The Rampart Project," 1963, Box 531, Ernest Gruening Papers, Alaska and Polar Regions Collection, Elmer E. Rasmuson Library, University of Alaska–Fairbanks.

34. Ivan Bloch, "Summary Notes Regarding the Promotion of the Rampart Project," September 7, 1963, Box 531, Ernest Gruening Papers, Alaska and Polar Regions Collection, Elmer E. Rasmuson Library, University of Alaska–Fairbanks.

35. Yukon Power for America, "The Rampart Story" (Fairbanks: Yukon Power for America, 196?), Alaska and Polar Regions Collection, Elmer E. Rasmuson Library, University of Alaska–Fairbanks.

36. Claus-M. Naske and William R. Hunt, *The Politics of Hydroelectric Power in Alaska: Rampart and Devil Canyon—A Case Study* (Fairbanks: University of Alaska, Institute of Water Resources, 1978), 16.

37. U.S. Fish and Wildlife Service, *A Report to the Secretary of the Interior, Rampart Canyon Dam and Reservoir Project Committee* (Washington, D.C.: Government Printing Office, 1964), 13.

38. For more on mobile natural resources and their challenges for environmental history, see Mark Fiege, "The Weedy West: Mobile Nature, Boundaries, and Common Space in the Montana Landscape," *Western Historical Quarterly* (Spring 2005), 22–47, and Robert Wilson, "Directing the Flow: Migratory Waterfowl, Scale, and Mobility in Western North America," *Environmental History* 7 (2002): 247–266.

39. For more on the months preceding the pipeline construction, see Ken Ross, *Environmental Conflict in Alaska* (Boulder: University Press of Colorado, 2000), 145–162.

40. Robert Weeden, "Alaska's Oil Boom: From Swanson to Prudhoe Bay and Beyond," *Alaska Conservation Review* (December 1968): 3.

41. For a thorough discussion of the debate between boosters and environmentalists during this period, see Peter Coates, *The Trans-Alaska Pipeline Controversy: Technology, Conservation, and the Frontier* (Fairbanks: University of Alaska, 1993).

42. William Cronon, "The Trouble with Wilderness; or, Getting Back to the Wrong Nature," in *Uncommon Ground: Rethinking the Human Place in Nature*, edited by William Cronon (New York: W. W. Norton, 1996), 79.

43. This idea of an exceptional Alaska will continue in a slightly different form during the more contemporary debates over oil drilling in the Arctic National Wildlife Refuge (ANWR) and the effects of global climate change. I will discuss these more contemporary debates in my epilogue.

CHAPTER 1. A NEW GAME IN THE NORTH: ALASKA NATIVE REINDEER HERDING

1. James M. O'Toole, *Passing for White: Race, Religion, and the Healy Family, 1820–1920* (Boston: University of Massachusetts Press, 2002), 197–198.

2. The Organic Act of 1884 provided Alaska with a governor and a U.S. District Court, staffed by a judge appointed by the president, who was to enforce the laws of the state of Oregon in the district, "so far as the same may be applicable."

3. Elizabeth A. Tower, *Reading, Religion, and Reindeer: Sheldon Jackson's Legacy to Alaska* (Anchorage: Privately printed, 1988), 25–26.

4. U.S. Bureau of Education, *Report of the Commissioner of Education for the Year 1889–90* (Washington, D.C.: Government Printing Office, 1893), 1291.

5. Senate Committee on Appropriations, *Mr. Teller Presented the Following Newspaper Communication of Sheldon Jackson, Urging the Importation by the Government of the Siberian Reindeer into Alaskan Territory*, 51st Cong., 2d sess., Mis. Doc. No. 39 (Washington, D.C., 1891), 4.

6. Richard O. Stern et al., *Eskimos, Reindeer, and Land* (Fairbanks: Agricultural Experiment Station, School of Agriculture and Land Resources Management, University of Alaska–Fairbanks, Bulletin 59, 1980), 21–23.

7. Dean F. Olson, *Alaska Reindeer Herdsmen: A Study of Native Management in Transition*, SEG Report No. 18 (Fairbanks: Institute of Social, Economic, and Government Research, University of Alaska–Fairbanks, 1969), 20–21.

8. John R. Bockstoce, *Whales, Ice, and Men: The History of Whaling in the Western Arctic* (Seattle: University of Washington Press, 1986); J. R. Bockstoce, *Eskimos of Northwest Alaska in the Early Nineteenth Century* (Oxford: Pitt Rivers Museum, University of Oxford, 1977).

9. For examples of the type of media coverage the reindeer project received (both positive and negative), see Jackson's collection of scrapbooks, particularly volumes 2, 3, and 4, Sheldon Jackson Papers, Presbyterian Historical Society, Philadelphia; Sheldon Jackson (*Third Annual*) *Report on the Introduction of Reindeer into Alaska*, 52d Cong., 2d sess., Mis. Doc. No. 22 (Washington, D.C.: Government Printing Office, 1893).

10. Analyses of Sheldon Jackson's work in Alaska almost universally ignore any connection to Indian policy in the continental United States. One short exception is Stephen W. Haycox, "Sheldon Jackson in Historical Perspective: Alaska Native Schools and Mission Contracts, 1885–1894," *Pacific Historian* 26 (1984): 18–28.

11. Helen Hunt Jackson, *A Century of Dishonor: A Sketch of the United States Government's Dealings with Some of the Indian Tribes* (New York: Harper and Brothers, 1881).

12. Quoted in Robert Laird Stewart, *Sheldon Jackson: Pathfinder and Prospector of the Missionary Vanguard in the Rocky Mountains and Alaska* (New York: Fleming H. Revell, 1908), 391.

13. Jackson *(Third Annual) Report*, 10.

14. Sheldon Jackson *(Fifth Annual) Report on the Introduction of Reindeer into Alaska*, 54th Cong., 1st sess., Senate Executive Doc. No. 111 (Washington, D.C.: Government Printing Office, 1896), 11–13.

15. Stern et al., *Eskimos, Reindeer, and Land*, 25.

16. Sheldon Jackson *(Fourth Annual) Report on the Introduction of Reindeer into Alaska*, 53d Cong., 2d sess., Senate Executive Doc. No. 70 (Washington, D.C: Government Printing Office, 1894), 59–61.

17. Ibid., 42.

18. Ibid., 46–63.

19. Stern et al., *Eskimos, Reindeer, and Land*, 25.

20. Jackson *(Fifth Annual) Report*, 10.

21. Lapps, or Laplanders, are a group of people who inhabit the area of land that extends from the Kola Peninsula in northwestern Russia through the northern part of Finland to the Arctic coast of Norway, traditionally known as Lapland. The term "Lapp" is derived from the Finnish word *lappi* and has been used by Europeans to describe this group of people for more than 700 years. The people to whom this term refers, however, have never accepted this appellation, regarding it as pejorative. They call themselves "Saami," the name by which I will also refer to them, while retaining the terms "Lapps" and "Laplanders" in the historical quotations that I cite.

22. Jackson *(Fifth Annual) Report*, 45.

23. *Evening Star* (Washington, D.C.), September 4, 1894.

24. *The Record* (Chicago), September 11, 1894.

25. *Commercial Gazette* (Pittsburgh), September 7, 1894.

26. *San Francisco Chronicle*, June 10, 1894.

27. *Evening Bulletin* (San Francisco), June 9, 1894.

28. Jackson *(Fifth Annual) Report*, 65; "The Reindeer Project Families: Kjellmann Expedition 1894, Manitoba Expedition 1898," *Baiki: The North American Sami Journal* 19 (Spring 1999): 1–28.

29. Jackson *(Fifth Annual) Report*, 67–68.

30. Ibid., 17.

31. This trading relationship ceased in 1902 when the czar forbade all further reindeer exports from Russia.

32. For a portrait of Sinrock Mary's life, see *The Reindeer Queen: Once the Richest Woman in Alaska—The True Story of Sinrock Mary*, produced and directed by Maria Brooks, 28 minutes, Waterfront Soundings Production, 2000, videocassette. Some Inupiat Eskimos claim that Sinrock Mary's reindeer can still be heard running across the tundra.

33. Keith A. Murray, *Reindeer and Gold*, Occasional Paper 24 (Bellingham, Wash.: Center for Pacific Northwest Studies, 1988), 11. For an example of the media coverage of the "crisis," see the *New York Times*, October 18, 1897.

34. Sheldon Jackson to John G. Brady, September 1, 1897, John G. Brady Papers, Beinecke Rare Book and Manuscript Library, Yale University, New Haven, Connecticut, 3–4.

35. The majority of these herders were Saami, but a few were Finnish or Norwegian.

36. Sheldon Jackson *(Eighth Annual) Report on the Introduction of Reindeer into Alaska*, 55th Cong., 3d sess., Senate Executive Doc. No. 34 (Washington, D.C.: Government Printing Office, 1898), 145–146.

37. Ibid., 40–41.

38. Stern et al., *Eskimos, Reindeer, and Land*, 28.

39. Sheldon Jackson *(Fifteenth Annual) Report on the Introduction of Reindeer into Alaska*, 59th Cong., 1st sess., Doc. No. 499 (Washington, D.C.: Government Printing Office, 1905), 34.

40. Olson, *Alaska Reindeer Herdsmen*, 10.

41. Frank C. Churchill, *Reports on the Condition of Educational and School Service and the Management of Reindeer Service in the District of Alaska*, 59th Cong., 1st sess., Senate Executive Doc. No. 483 (Washington, D.C.: Government Printing Office, 1906), 26, 40.

42. Olson, *Alaska Reindeer Herdsmen*, 38.

43. Stern et al., *Eskimos, Reindeer, and Land*, 33–36.

44. "Reindeer Conference Journal: Mary's Igloo," 1915, Vertical File, Small Manuscript, Alaska and Polar Regions Collection, Elmer E. Rasmuson Library, University of Alaska–Fairbanks.

45. Cudluk Oquilluk, "Cudlook Oquillok Will Tell You about Reindeer," *The Eskimo: A Monthly Magazine Published by the Bureau of Education and Devoted to the Interest of Eskimos of Northern Alaska* 1, no. 3 (November 1916): 1.

46. G. J. Lomen, "Views on the Development of the Reindeer Industry," *The Eskimo (A Monthly Magazine concerning the Eskimo of Northwestern Alaska)* 2 (November 1917): 5–6.

47. "Notes—Reindeer Report 1916—Shields," Clarence Leroy Andrews Papers, Special Collections and University Archives, University of Oregon–Eugene, 4.

48. George Bird Grinnell to Carl S. Lomen, May 5, 1922, Lomen Family Papers, Alaska and Polar Regions Collection, Elmer E. Rasmuson Library, University of Alaska–Fairbanks.

49. "The Reindeer Industry," n.d., Anthony J. Dimond Papers, Alaska and Polar Regions Collection, Elmer E. Rasmuson Library, University of Alaska–Fairbanks, 7.

50. Stern et al., *Eskimos, Reindeer, and Land*, 45.

51. Olson, *Alaska Reindeer Herdsmen*, 47.

52. John G. Brady, "Reindeer in Alaska," n.d., John G. Brady Papers, Beinecke Rare Book and Manuscript Library, Yale University, New Haven, Connecticut, 2.

53. Untitled Document, October 11, 1929, Ben Mozee Papers, Alaska and Polar Regions Collection, Elmer E. Rasmuson Library, University of Alaska–Fairbanks.

54. "From Carl Lomen's Diary," 1935, Lomen Family Papers, Alaska and Polar Regions Collection, Elmer E. Rasmuson Library, University of Alaska–Fairbanks.

55. Olson, *Alaska Reindeer Herdsmen*, 14.

56. Ibid., 48.

57. This quote is attributed to Judge James Wickersham, then the Alaska delegate to Congress. "From Carl Lomen's Diary," 1926, Lomen Family Papers, Alaska and Polar Regions Collection, Elmer E. Rasmuson Library, University of Alaska–Fairbanks.

58. See Affadavits in Box 1, Alaska Reindeer Service Records, Record Group 75.21.1, National Archives and Records Administration, Pacific-Alaska Region, Anchorage. At this point, I am using the terms "Lomen Corporation" and "Lomen Company" as shorthand forms for all the Lomen-owned companies of the time, which included the Northwestern Livestock Corporation, the Alaska Livestock and Packing Company, the Lomen Commercial Company, the Nunivak Development Corporation, and the Arctic Transportation Company.

59. House Committee on Ways and Means, *Tariff Readjustment—1929: Statement of Carl J. Lomen, New York City, Representing the Lomen Reindeer Corporation*, 70th Cong., 2d sess., January 24, 1929.

60. "Minutes of the Cape Reindeer Company," n.d., Anthony J. Dimond Papers, Alaska and Polar Regions Collection, Elmer E. Rasmuson Library, University of Alaska–Fairbanks.

61. "The Reindeer Industry," Anthony J. Dimond Papers, 1–5.

62. Ibid., 4.

63. The results of this investigation are often referred to as the "Trowbridge-Gilman Report."

64. Stern et al., *Eskimos, Reindeer, and Land*, 63.

65. *Alaska Press* (Juneau), September 21, 1934.

66. For more on the Alaska Reorganization Act, see Kenneth R. Philp, "The New Deal and Alaskan Natives, 1936–1945," in *An Alaskan Anthology: Interpreting the Past*, edited by Stephen W. Haycox and Mary Childers Mangusso (Seattle: University of Washington Press, 1996), 267–286.

67. Stern et al., *Eskimos, Reindeer, and Land*, 69–70.

68. As quoted in ibid., 67–68.

69. The Alaskan Reindeer Act, 50 Stat. 900 (September 1, 1937).

70. Interview with Herman Toolie, "The Executive Council of the Reindeer Herders Association talks with Bill Schneider on September 26, 2002, in Nome, Alaska [sound recording]," Oral History Collection, University of Alaska–Fairbanks.

71. Olson, *Eskimo Reindeer Herdsmen*, 14–15.

72. "To The Eskimo People." *The Eskimo: A Quarterly Magazine Devoted to the Interest of Eskimos of Alaska* 5, no. 4 (October 1938): 1.

73. Interview with Ted Katcheak, "The Executive Council of the Reindeer Herders Association Talks with Bill Schneider on March 20, 2002, in Nome, Alaska [sound recording]," Oral History Collection, University of Alaska–Fairbanks.

74. Margaret Lantis, "The Reindeer Industry in Alaska," *Arctic* 3, no. 1 (April 1950): 27–44.

CHAPTER 2. ALASKAN PASTORAL: THE MATANUSKA COLONY

1. Although public opinion in the years immediately following the purchase of Alaska is most often remembered as being entirely negative, there were actually a significant number of early Alaska boosters who believed that Alaska would contribute to a growing American empire. See Richard Welch, "American Public Opinion and the Purchase of Russian America," *American Slavic and Eastern European Review* 17 (1958): 481–494.

2. James R. Shortridge, "The Alaskan Agricultural Empire: An American Agrarian Vision, 1898–1929," *Pacific Northwest Quarterly* 69 (1978): 145–158.

3. This perceived "lack of food" was not a problem for Alaska's approximately 30,000 Native residents, who survived on the land for thousands of years by hunting, fishing, gardening, trading, and gathering food.

4. For more on the international dimensions of the gold rush, see Adam Arenson, "Anglo-Saxonism in the Yukon: The Klondike Nugget and American-British Relations in the 'Two Wests,' 1898–1901," *Pacific Historical Review* 76 (August 2007): 373–404.

5. For a discussion of the demographic change that occurred during the gold-rush years, see Kirk H. Stone, "Populating Alaska: The United States Phase," *Geographical Review* 42, no. 3 (July 1952): 384–404.

6. For more on Alaskan food prices during this period, see Karl E. Francis, "Outpost Agriculture: The Case of Alaska," *Geographical Review* 57 (October 1967): 496–505. For a discussion of the politics of food during the gold rush, see Kathryn Morse, *The Nature of Gold: An Environmental History of the Klondike Gold Rush*, with a Foreword by William Cronon (Seattle: University of Washington Press, 1993), 138–165.

7. A. M. Goodman, "Report of Present, and Estimate of Future, Agriculture of the Matanuska Valley of Alaska," 1935, Ernest Gruening Papers, Alaska and Polar Regions Collection, Elmer E. Rasmuson Library, University of Alaska–Fairbanks, 3; C. C. Georgeson, *Fourth Report on the Agricultural Investigations in Alaska*, Bulletin no. 94, Office of Experiment Stations, U.S. Department of Agriculture (Washington, D.C.: Government Printing Office, 1901), 50–62.

8. James Wilson, Secretary of Agriculture, *A Report to Congress on Agriculture in Alaska, including Reports by Walter H. Evans, Benton Killin, and Sheldon Jackson*, Bulletin no. 48, Office of Experiment Stations, U.S. Department of Agriculture (Washington, D.C.: Government Printing Office, 1898), 35–36.

9. Wilson, *A Report to Congress on Agriculture in Alaska*, 3.

10. On this topic, see, for example, Jeannette Paddock Nichols, *Alaska* (Cleveland: Arthur H. Clark, 1924).

11. C. C. Georgeson, *Report on the Agricultural Investigations in Alaska for 1899*, Office of Experiment Stations, U.S. Department of Agriculture (Washington, D.C.: Government Printing Office, 1900), 9.

12. C. C. Georgeson, "Agriculture in Alaska," *Alaska-Yukon Magazine* 8 (1909): 300–302. Alaska boosters such as Sheldon Jackson, who were also attempting to establish reindeer herding in Alaska during this period, contributed to the body of literature espousing this philosophy.

13. C. C. Georgeson, "Agricultural Experiments in Alaska," *Yearbook of the United States Department of Agriculture 1898* (Washington, D.C.: Government Printing Office, 1899), 515.

14. James Wilson, Secretary of Agriculture, *A Second Report on the Investigations of the Agricultural Capabilities of Alaska for the Year 1898*, Office of Experiment Stations, U.S. Department of Agriculture (Washington, D.C.: Government Printing Office, 1899), 11.

15. Georgeson, *Report on the Agricultural Investigations*, 12.

16. Wilson, *A Second Report*, 11.

17. Ibid., 20.

18. Levi Chubbuck, "Alaska Agricultural Possibilities," *Bulletin of the American Geographical Society* 42, no. 12 (1910): 892–898.

19. Guy Mitchell, "Wonders of Alaskan Agriculture," *Illustrated World* 12 (1910): 526.

20. Alfred H. Brooks, "The Value of Alaska," *Geographical Review* 15 (January 1925): 25–50.

21. Middleton Smith, "Gardening in Northern Alaska," *National Geographic* 14 (September 1903): 355–357.

22. Gustav R. Stahl, "Farming in a Bowl of Ice," *Illustrated World* 20 (1913): 210–211.

23. William Wilson, *Railroad in the Clouds: The Alaska Railroad in the Age of Steam, 1914–1945* (Boulder, Colo.: Pruett, 1977), 18.

24. For details of the construction, see Edwin M. Fitch, *The Alaska Railroad* (New York: Frederick A. Praeger, 1967), 52–61.

25. "The Alaska Railroad" (with a capital "T") was the official name of the railroad.

26. In reality, the valley had been visited regularly by American whites since the 1890s, as prospectors would outfit themselves at the region's trading stores before setting off for the goldfields. Also, in the 1910s, the U.S. Geological Survey sent surveyors to map coalfields in the Matanuska region. See Don L. Irwin, *The Colorful Matanuska Valley* (published by the author, 1968), 14–32.

27. John Q. Adams, "This Is Matanuska!" *Alaska Sportsman* 4 (April 1938): 16–24.

28. Hugh A. Johnson and Keith L. Stanton, *Matanuska Valley Memoir: The Story of How One Alaskan Community Developed*, July 1955, Archives of the Palmer Public Library, Palmer, Alaska, 22.

29. Orlando Miller, *The Frontier in Alaska and the Matanuska Colony* (New Haven, Conn.: Yale University Press, 1975), 27.

30. The Alaska Railroad, U.S. Department of the Interior, *Alaska: The Newest Homeland* (Washington, D.C.: Government Printing Office, 1931), 1.

31. Scott C. Boone, *Annual Report of the Governor of Alaska* (Washington, D.C.: Government Printing Office, 1921), 41.

32. John F. Ballaine to Harold L. Ickes, January 25, 1935, Box 402, Office of the Territories, Classified Files, 1907–1951, Record Group 126, National Archives, College Park, Maryland.

33. U.S. Department of the Interior, *General Information regarding the Territory of Alaska* (Washington, D.C.: Government Printing Office, 1931), 36–37.

34. The few sectors of the Alaskan economy that were adversely affected by the depression included salmon fishing, copper mining, lumbering, and reindeer herding.

35. The most widely distributed of these was *Alaska: The Newest Homeland*, cited above.

36. For a discussion of the importance of Turner's frontier thesis, see John Mack Faragher, Introduction to *Rereading Frederick Jackson Turner* (New York: Henry Holt, 1994).

37. *Time*, May 6, 1935, 17. Admiration for Turner's ideas was not universal during this period, however, as there was also a class of academic historians who began to attack the frontier thesis during the 1920s and 1930s. See David M. Wrobel, *The End of American Exceptionalism: Frontier Anxiety from the Old West to the New Deal* (Lawrence: University Press of Kansas, 1993), 122–142.

38. Samuel I. Rosenman, ed., *The Public Papers and Addresses of Franklin D. Roosevelt*, vol. 1, *The Genesis of the New Deal, 1928–1932* (New York: Random House, 1938), 746–747, quoted in Orlando Miller, *The Frontier in Alaska and the Matanuska Colony* (New Haven, Conn.: Yale University Press, 1975), 2–3, n.5.

39. For more on the back-to-the-land movement during this period, see Paul K. Conkin, *Tomorrow a New World: The New Deal Community Program* (Ithaca, N.Y.: Cornell University Press, 1959); and David E. Shi, *The Simple Life: Plain Living and High Thinking in American Culture* (New York: Oxford University Press, 1985), 215–247.

40. Henry S. Anderson, "The Little Landers' Land Colonies: A Unique Agricultural Experiment in California," *Agricultural History* 5 (1931): 142.

41. Henry A. Wallace, *New Frontiers* (New York: Reynal and Hitchcock, 1934), 274.

42. "Matanuska Valley," October 24, 1935, Box 398, Office of the Territories, Classified Files, 1907–1951, Record Group 126, National Archives, College Park, Maryland.

43. Ernest Gruening, *Many Battles: The Autobiography of Ernest Gruening* (New York: Liveright, 1973), 181.

44. John W. Troy to Harry L. Hopkins, undated telegram, Box 8, Records of the Work Projects Administration, "State" Series, March 1933–1936, Record Group 69, National Archives, College Park, Maryland.

45. "Matanuska Project," Box 6, Uncataloged Matanuska Colony Papers, Record Group 69, National Archives and Records Administration, Pacific-Alaska Region, Anchorage, Alaska, 1.

46. Kirk H. Stone, *Alaskan Group Settlement: The Matanuska Valley Colony*, Bureau of Land Management, U.S. Department of the Interior, 1949, Alaska Resources Library and Information Services, Anchorage, Alaska, 8–11; Grant Heilman, "Matanuska: An Experiment in Rehabilitation," March 1941, Box 6, C. Earl Albrecht Papers, Archives and Manuscripts, Consortium Library, University of Alaska–Anchorage.

47. Reference to the quantity of letters is made in Gruening, *Many Battles*, 182. For examples of this correspondence, see letters in Boxes 61 and 62, Records of the Work Projects Administration, "Old General Subject" Series, March 1933–January 1935, Record Group 69, National Archives, College Park, Maryland; and letters in Box 415, Office of the Territories, Classified Files, 1907–1951, Record Group 126, National Archives, College Park, Maryland.

48. Annie Holdaway to Franklin D. Roosevelt, August 13, 1934, File No. 9 1 60 (Part 1), U.S. Department of the Interior, Office of the Secretary, February 13, 1933–November 5, 1934, Record Group 126, National Archives, College Park, Maryland.

49. David Westbrook, "Alaska: Matanuska Valley Project," January 1936, Box 396, Office of the Territories, Classified Files, 1907–1951, Record Group 126, National Archives, College Park, Maryland.

50. The final number of families chosen differs slightly from source to source. Sometimes the number is cited at 200, often at 202 or more. These discrepancies arise from last-minute cancellations and substitutions. The families totaled about 967 men, women, and children.

51. Miller, *The Frontier in Alaska*, 70–72.

52. Evangeline Atwood, *We Shall Be Remembered* (Anchorage: Alaska Methodist University Press, 1966), 33–34.

53. Alaska Rural Rehabilitation Corporation, "Letter to the Editor—Draft," December 28, 1939, Box 3, Uncataloged Matanuska Colony Papers, Record Group 69, National Archives and Records Administration, Pacific-Alaska Region, Anchorage, Alaska.

54. "Alaska Settlement," undated, Box 9, Technical and Personal File of David R. Williams, Records of the Deputy Executive Director and the Deputy Administrator, Records of the National Youth Administration, Record Group 119, National Archives, College Park, Maryland.

55. Melissa Susong to Franklin D. Roosevelt, May 25, 1935, File No. 9 1 60 (Part 1), U.S. Department of the Interior, Office of the Secretary, February 13, 1933–November 5, 1934, Record Group 126, National Archives, College Park, Maryland.

56. The Michigan and Wisconsin families traveled west about two weeks later. Their rail trip took them to Seattle, where they were treated with similar lavish hospitality. They then continued north by steamship.

57. Atwood, *We Shall Be Remembered*, 39–40.

58. Miller, *The Frontier in Alaska*, 76–77.

59. *20 Years of Progress in the Matanuska Valley, Alaska* (Palmer: Alaska Rural Rehabilitation Corporation, 1955), 2–5.

60. *Seward Gateway* (Seward, Alaska), May 7, 1935. In Alaska, the "Outside" is a common expression that refers to the continental United States—or anywhere else but Alaska.

61. *20 Years of Progress*, 6.

62. See the colonists' letters in Reel 6211, Works Progress Administration Microfilm, Federal Works Agency, Record Group 69, National Archives, College Park, Maryland.

63. Irwin, *The Colorful Matanuska Valley*, 17–18; Herbert C. Hanson, *Agriculture in the Matanuska Valley, Alaska*, U.S. Department of the Interior, Division of Territories and Island Possessions (Washington, D.C.: Government Printing Office, 1944), 2–8.

64. The Einer Huseby family to Mrs. Lundgren, May 27, 1935, Box 396, Office of the Territories, Classified Files, 1907–1951, Record Group 126, National Archives, College Park, Maryland.

65. Leo B. Jacobs to David R. Williams, June 4, 1935, Box 396, Office of the Territories, Classified Files, 1907–1951, Record Group 126, National Archives, College Park, Maryland.

66. Florance Barrett Willoughby, *Alaska Holiday* (Boston: Little, Brown, 1940), 242–250; *Saturday Evening Post* (Philadelphia), December 28, 1935.

67. Atwood, *We Shall Be Remembered*, 65–69; *Congressional Record*, 74th Cong., 2d sess., 1935, 74, Part 9, 9946–9947.

68. *Congressional Record*, 74th Cong., 1st sess., 1935, 74, Part 9, 10277–10286.

69. "The True Story of Matanuska," October 8, 1935, Box 398, Office of the Territories, Classified Files, 1907–1951, Record Group 126, National Archives, College Park, Maryland, 5–7.

70. *New York Times*, July 7, 1935.

71. "Matanuska Project," September 21, 1939, Box 6, Uncataloged Matanuska Colony Papers, Record Group 69, National Archives and Records Administration, Pacific-Alaska Region, Anchorage, Alaska, 3.

72. Miller, *The Frontier in Alaska*, 92–93, 130–131. After much debate, this promise to the colonists was finally kept in the summer of 1938.

73. See written correspondence in Box 399, Office of the Territories, Classified Files, 1907–1951, Record Group 126, National Archives, College Park, Maryland, 5–7.

74. Ross L. Sheely, July 14, 1936, quoted in Marvin Albert Halldorson, "The Matanuska Valley Colonization Project" (Master's thesis, University of Colorado, 1936), 113–114.

75. Ross L. Sheely, "News Article for the *Anchorage Times*," December 28, 1938, Box 5, Uncataloged Matanuska Colony Papers, Record Group 69, National Archives and Records Administration, Pacific-Alaska Region, Anchorage, Alaska; *Matanuska Valley Pioneer* (Palmer, Alaska), November 14, 1935.

76. Atwood, *We Shall Be Remembered*, 97–98. The bingle system was phased out after six months.

77. Herbert C. Hanson, *Agriculture in the Matanuska Valley, Alaska*, U.S. Department of the Interior, Division of Territories and Island Possessions (Washington, D.C.: Government Printing Office, 1944), 1.

78. *New York Times*, September 8, 1935.

79. Herbert C. Hanson to Anthony J. Dimond, October 22, 1940, Box 6, Uncataloged Matanuska Colony Papers, Record Group 69, National Archives and Records Administration, Pacific-Alaska Region, Anchorage, Alaska.

80. The exceptions to this were the years 1942–1946, when the fair was suspended because of World War II. Information about the fair was provided by the Alaska State Fair staff in Palmer, Alaska.

81. *Seward Gateway* (Seward, Alaska), May 7, 1935.

82. John Green Brady to Mary Brady, June 9, 1904, Box 5, John G. Brady Papers, Beinecke Rare Book and Manuscript Library, Yale University, New Haven, Conn.

83. Kirk H. Stone, *Alaskan Group Settlement: The Matanuska Valley Colony*, Bureau of Land Management, U.S. Department of the Interior, 1949, Alaska Resources Library and Information Services, Anchorage, Alaska, 38.

84. Stone, *Alaskan Group Settlement*, 44.

85. Ross L. Sheely to Sherwood Wirt, November 8, 1939, Box 5, Uncataloged Matanuska Colony Papers, Record Group 69, National Archives and Records Administration, Pacific-Alaska Region, Anchorage, Alaska.

86. U.S. Department of Agriculture, Alaska Statistics, 2008, http://www.ers.usda.gov/stateFacts/ak.htm.

87. Ibid.

88. U.S. Department of Agriculture, Alaska Statistics, 2007, http://www.ers.usda.gov/stateFacts/ak.htm.

CHAPTER 3. THE ROAD TO NOWHERE: THE ALASKA HIGHWAY AS A NORTHERN DEVELOPMENT PROJECT

1. This is the historical measurement of the road; however, the mileage has changed, as the road has been upgraded and rerouted multiple times. Also, many writers include the additional 100 miles from Delta Junction to Fairbanks in their calculations of the road's length.

2. Some Canadian scholars have done better than their U.S. counterparts on this issue. See, for example, K. S. Coates and W. R. Morrison, *The Alaska Highway in World War II: The U.S. Army of Occupation in Canada's Northwest* (Norman: University of Oklahoma Press, 1992).

3. William R. Morrison, review of *Building the Alaska Highway*, directed by Tracy Heather Strain, *Journal of American History* 92 (December 2005): 1100.

4. "Report of the Alaskan International Highway Commission to the President—Draft," April 1940, Box 28, Ernest Gruening Papers, Alaska and Polar Regions Collection, Elmer E. Rasmuson Library, University of Alaska–Fairbanks, Section 5.

5. U.S. Department of State, Committee on Foreign Affairs, *Report of the International Highway Commission to the President* (Washington, D.C.: Government Printing Office, 1940), 3. Cyrus Field had laid a cable in 1858, but the service soon failed. The old telegraph trail was revitalized when some gold rushers used the old markers to reach the Klondike in 1898.

6. J. M. Wardle, "The Alaska Highway," n.d., Series 1, Vol. 69, File 21, Alaska Highway Part 1, Government Documents 1679, Yukon Archives, Whitehorse, Yukon Territory, Canada, 2.

7. U.S. Department of State, *Report of the International Highway Commission to the President*, 4.

8. "The Alaska Highway ('Alcan')," 1972, Box 11, Office of the Chief of Engineers, Army Corps of Engineers, Alaska District, Anchorage Installation, Record Group 77, National Archives and Records Administration, Pacific-Alaska Region, Anchorage, Alaska, 79.

9. Documents in Vol. 2448, Record Group 24, National Archives of Canada, Ottawa, Ontario; B. J. Nopek to G. J. Lomen, June 15, 1927, reprinted in Dean F. Sherman, ed., *Alaska Cavalcade* (Seattle: Alaska Life, 1943), 274–276.

10. Alaska Road Commission, *The Proposed Pacific Yukon Highway* (Juneau: privately printed, 1931), 10–20.

11. "Radio Address of Anthony J. Dimond on the Pacific-Yukon Highway," August 14, 1934, Box 23, Anthony J. Dimond Papers, Alaska and Polar Regions Collection, Elmer E. Rasmuson Library, University of Alaska–Fairbanks, 6.

12. For a cogent analysis of the international politicking of the British Columbia premiers during this period, see David Remley, "The Latent Fear: Canadian-American Relations and Early Proposals for a Highway to Alaska," in *The Alaska Highway: Papers of the 40th Anniversary Symposium*, edited by Kenneth Coates (Vancouver: University of British Columbia Press, 1985), 1–8.

13. U.S. Department of State, *Report of the Commission to Study the Proposed Highway to Alaska*, Conference Series no. 14 (Washington, D.C.: Government Printing Office, 1933), 8.

14. The British Columbia–Yukon–Alaska Highway Commission, *Report of Proposed Highway through British Columbia and the Yukon Territory to Alaska* (Ottawa: Edmond Cloutier, 1941), 7–10; "Radio Address of Anthony J. Dimond on the Pacific-Yukon Highway," August 14, 1934, Box 23, Anthony J. Dimond Papers, Alaska and Polar Regions Collection, Elmer E. Rasmuson Library, University of Alaska–Fairbanks, 4.

15. Anthony Dimond to Peter Norbeck, October 10, 1934, Box 23, Anthony J. Dimond Papers, Alaska and Polar Regions Collection, Elmer E. Rasmuson Library, University of Alaska–Fairbanks.

16. Ernest Gruening, *The State of Alaska* (New York: Random House, 1968), 457.

17. Anthony Dimond to Ernest Gruening, January 5, 1935, Box 3, Anthony J. Dimond Papers, Alaska and Polar Regions Collection, Elmer E. Rasmuson Library, University of Alaska–Fairbanks. See also Dimond's letter to the editor in the *Washington Herald* (Washington, D.C.), March 12, 1935.

18. U.S. Department of State, *Report of the Alaskan International Highway Commission*, 6. The Canadian commission was called the "British Columbia–Yukon–Alaska Highway Commission."

19. Robert G. McCandless, "Yukon Wildlife: A Social History, 1900–1950," December 28, 1978, MSS 096, Accession Number 19/13, Yukon Archives, Whitehorse, Yukon Territory, Canada, 123.

20. U.S. Department of State, *Report of the Alaskan International Highway Commission*, 1.

21. "Alaska," n.d., File 631–52–1, Vol. 2448, Record Group 24, National Archives of Canada, Ottawa, Ontario, 1–2.

22. U.S. Department of State, *Report of the Alaskan International Highway Commission*, 9–10; Anthony Dimond, "Alaskan International Highway," 1941, Box 17, Anthony J. Dimond Papers, Alaska and Polar Regions Collection, Elmer E. Rasmuson Library, University of Alaska–Fairbanks, 1–11.

23. The British Columbia–Yukon–Alaska Highway Commission, *Report of Proposed Highway*, 13.

24. For a concise history of the Northwest Staging Route, see Daniel L. Haulman, "The Northwest Ferry Route," in *Alaska at War, 1941–45: The Forgotten War Remembered*, edited by Fern Chandonnet (Anchorage: University of Alaska Press, 2007), 319–326. For a slightly different version of this essay, see Daniel L. Haulman, "The Northwest Staging Route," in *Three Northern Wartime Projects*, edited by Bob Hesketh (Edmonton, Alberta: Canadian Circumpolar Institute and Edmonton and District Historical Society, 1996), 31–46.

25. "The Alaska Highway ('Alcan')," 1972, Box 11, Office of the Chief of Engineers, Army Corps of Engineers, Alaska District, Anchorage Installation, Record Group 77, National Archives and Records Administration, Pacific-Alaska Region, Anchorage, Alaska, 80.

26. "Confidential: The Defence Aspect of the Proposed Alaska Highway," July 8, 1938, File 631-52-1, Vol. 2448, Record Group 24, National Archives of Canada, Ottawa, Ontario.

27. "Report to Council on the Proposal to Construct a Highway through British Columbia and the Yukon Territory to Alaska," n.d., File 463-40, Vol. 2742, Record Group 25, National Archives of Canada, Ottawa, Ontario.

28. "Secret Minute Sheet Re: Alaska Highway," August 9, 1940, File 463-40, Vol. 2742, Record Group 25, National Archives of Canada, Ottawa, Ontario.

29. Henry Stimson, as quoted in David A. Remley, *Crooked Road: The Story of the Alaska Highway* (New York: McGraw-Hill, 1976), 120.

30. George Marshall, as quoted in Edward S. Miller, *War Plan Orange: The U.S. Strategy to Defeat Japan, 1897–1945* (Annapolis, Md.: Naval Institute Press, 1991), 42.

31. "Secret Minute Sheet Re: Alaska Highway," August 9, 1940, File 463-40, Vol. 2742, Record Group 25, National Archives of Canada, Ottawa, Ontario. These local groups eventually came together as the "United States–Canada–Alaska Prairie Highway Association."

32. *Dawson Daily News* (Dawson City, Yukon Territory), October 23, 1941.

33. Vilhjalmur Stefansson, "Routes to Alaska." July 1941, File 463-40, Vol. 2742, Record Group 25, National Archives of Canada, Ottawa, Ontario.

34. M. V. Bezeau, "The Realities of Strategic Planning: The Decision to Build the Alaska Highway," in *The Alaska Highway: Papers of the 40th Anniversary Symposium*, edited by Kenneth Coates (Vancouver: University of British Columbia Press, 1985), 26–27. I am indebted to Bezeau's essay for honing my own theory about how and why the Alaska Highway was constructed. Bezeau argues that, despite appearances to the contrary, military strategy was only a minor factor in the decision to build the Alaska Highway. Although some of his arguments are based on hindsight (the fact that the highway was never used for military purposes), I believe there is good evidence to support his main argument. For a more conventional assessment of the military value of the highway, see Greg Johnson, "Strategic Necessity or Military Blunder? Another Look at the Decision to Build the Alaska Highway," in *Three Northern Wartime Projects*, edited by Bob Hesketh (Edmonton, Alberta: Canadian Circumpolar Institute and Edmonton and District Historical Society, 1996), 5–30.

35. Robert Coakley and Richard Leighton, *Global Logistics and Strategy* (Washington, D.C.: Center of Military History, U.S. Army, 1955), 101–102.

36. George Marshall, as quoted in Bezeau, "The Realities of Strategic Planning," 27.

37. Anthony Dimond, "'Note to Self': Statement Made before House Military Affairs Committee," February 13, 1935, Box 17, Anthony J. Dimond Papers, Alaska and Polar Regions Collection, Elmer E. Rasmuson Library, University of Alaska, Fairbanks.

38. George Murry, as quoted in Daniel St. Jean, *And Where Will You Build This Alcan Highway?* (Whitehorse, Yukon Territory: Black Horse, 1992), 1.

39. Ernest Gruening, as quoted in David A. Remley, *Crooked Road: The Story of the Alaska Highway* (New York: McGraw-Hill, 1976), 13.

40. "The Alaska Highway ('Alcan')," 1972, Box 11, Office of the Chief of Engineers, Army Corps of Engineers, Alaska District, Anchorage Installation, Record Group 77, National Archives and Records Administration, Pacific-Alaska Region, Anchorage, Alaska, 80.

41. Ernest Gruening, *The State of Alaska* (New York: Random House, 1962), 622.

42. Anthony Dimond, "Notes for Hearings before the Subcommittee of the Committee on Appropriations," 1943, Box 23, Anthony J. Dimond Papers, Alaska and Polar Regions Collection, Elmer E. Rasmuson Library, University of Alaska–Fairbanks, 1.

43. U.S. War Plans Division, as quoted in Shelagh Grant, *Sovereignty or Security? Government Policy in the Canadian North, 1939–1950* (Vancouver: University of British Columbia Press, 1988), 75.

44. Hugh Keenleyside, as quoted in M. V. Bezeau, "The Realities of Strategic Planning," 32.

45. U.S. Department of State, *Military Highway to Alaska: Agreement between the United States of America and Canada: Effected by Exchange of Notes, Signed March 17 and 18, 1942*, Executive Agreement Series 246 (Washington, D.C.: Government Printing Office, 1942).

46. The Alaska Highway was known by many names during the war years, including the Alaskan International Highway, the Tote Road, and the Fairbanks Freight. Early documents most often refer to it as the Alaska-Canada Military Highway, which people usually shortened to "Alcan" in colloquial speech. In 1943, Congress passed a joint resolution to change the name to the "Alaska Highway," and Canada eventually agreed. For the sake of consistency, I will use the term "Alaska Highway," except when another term seems more appropriate.

47. Harold Richardson, *Alcan: American's Glory Road* (New York: Engineering News-Record Report, 1943), Alaska and Polar Regions Collection, Elmer E. Rasmuson Library, University of Alaska–Fairbanks, 134.

48. U.S. Department of the Interior, *Recreational Resources of the Alaska Highway and Other Roads in Alaska* (Washington, D.C.: Government Printing Office, 1944), 22.

49. "The Alaska Highway ('Alcan')," 1972, Box 11, Office of the Chief of Engineers, Army Corps of Engineers, Alaska District, Anchorage Installation, Record Group 77, National Archives and Records Administration, Pacific-Alaska Region, Anchorage, Alaska, 81.

50. U.S. Congress, *Hearings before a Special Committee Investigating the National Defense Program*, 78th Cong., 1st sess., Part 22, "The Canol Project" (Washington, D.C.: Government Printing Office, 1944), 9594.

51. Former governor Thomas Riggs, as quoted in Office of the Chief of Engineers, Northwest Service Command, *The Canol Project* (Washington, D.C.: War Department, 1945), 62.

52. For an account of the ordeal of these hostages, as well as the American evacuation of the Aleutian Islands, see Dean Kohlhoff, *When the Wind Was a River: Aleut Evacuation in World War II* (Seattle: University of Washington Press, 1995).

53. For a labor history of these "soldiers as workers," see William Morrison and Kenneth Coates, *Working the North: Labor and the Northwest Defense Projects, 1942–1946* (Fairbanks: University of Alaska Press, 1994).

54. For a social history of northern life during the construction of the Canadian segment of the highway, see Coates and Morrison, *The Alaska Highway in World War II.*

55. *Building Alaska with the U.S. Army, 1867–1965*, Army Pamphlet, Beinecke Rare Book and Manuscript Library, Yale University, New Haven, Conn.; "African Americans and World War II," 1993, Box 1, Alaska-Canada Highway Collection, Alaska and Polar Regions Collection, Elmer E. Rasmuson Library, University of Alaska–Fairbanks.

56. For a short consideration of racial relations during highway construction, see Lael Morgan, "Race Relations and the Contributions of Minority Troops to Alaska," in *Alaska at War, 1941–45: The Forgotten War Remembered*, edited by Fern Chandonnet (Anchorage: University of Alaska Press, 2007), 271–276.

57. Harold Richardson, *Alcan: American's Glory Road* (New York: Engineering News-Record Report, 1943), Alaska and Polar Regions Collection, Elmer E. Rasmuson Library, University of Alaska–Fairbanks, 134.

58. "Construction of the Gigantic Alaska Highway," n.d., J. Aubrey Simmons Collection, Pamphlets and Small Manuscripts, Yukon Archives, Whitehorse, Yukon Territory, Canada; V. A. Sprouse to Mrs. V. A. Sprouse, June 17, 1942, File 463-4-40, Vol. 2745, Record Group 25, National Archives of Canada, Ottawa, Ontario.

59. Lloyd Gustafson to Carroll Smith, July 5, 1942, File 463-4-40, Vol. 2745, Record Group 25, National Archives of Canada, Ottawa, Ontario, 1.

60. Ibid., 2.

61. George Humphreys to Edward Carmody, July 5, 1942, File 463-4-40, Vol. 2745, Record Group 25, National Archives of Canada, Ottawa, Ontario.

62. Lael Morgan, "Remember Black Troops Who Built the Alcan Highway," in *Three Northern Wartime Projects*, edited by Bob Hesketh (Edmonton, Alberta: Canadian Circumpolar Institute and Edmonton and District Historical Society, 1996), 151.

63. "Memo," n.d., Box 1, 341st Engineer Regiment Collection, 1943–1946, Alaska and Polar Regions Collection, Elmer E. Rasmuson Library, University of Alaska–Fairbanks.

64. Heath Twichell, *Northwest Epic: The Building of the Alaska Highway* (New York: St. Martin's Press, 1992), 173.

65. For more on the highway as a media spectacle, see File 463-4-40, Vol. 2747, Record Group 25, National Archives of Canada, Ottawa, Ontario.

66. Donald MacDonald to Furth, August 7, 1943, Box 3, Donald MacDonald Papers, Alaska and Polar Regions Collection, Elmer E. Rasmuson Library, University of Alaska–Fairbanks, 1. For more on MacDonald's criticisms, see Donald MacDonald, "The Unfinished Fight for the Highway We Must Yet Build," *Alaska Life* (October 1944): 36–43,

67. Anthony Dimond, "The Alaska Highway," November 1942, Box 23, Anthony J. Dimond Papers, Alaska and Polar Regions Collection, Elmer E. Rasmuson Library, University of Alaska–Fairbanks, 3.

68. See documents in Government Records YRG 1, Series I-A, no. 466i, Yukon Archives, Whitehorse, Yukon Territory, Canada.

69. Robert and Dell Black, as quoted in Ken Coates, *North to Alaska! Fifty Years on the World's Most Remarkable Highway* (Toronto: McClelland and Stewart, 1992), 183.

70. Paul T. Dupell, "ALCAN 24th Anniversary," 1996, Box 12, Office of the Chief of Engineers, Army Corps of Engineers, Alaska District, Anchorage Installation, Record Group 77, National Archives and Records Administration, Pacific-Alaska Region, Anchorage, Alaska.

71. General Simon Bolivar Buckner, as quoted in Charles Hendricks, "Race Relations and the Contributions of Minority Troops in Alaska: A Challenge to the Status Quo?" in *Alaska at War, 1941–45: The Forgotten War Remembered*, edited by Fern Chandonnet (Anchorage: University of Alaska Press, 2007), 277, n.2.

72. Twichell, *Northwest Epic*, 211–212.

73. Everett Louis Overstreet, *Black on a Background of White: A Chronicle of Afro-American Involvement in America's Last Frontier, Alaska* (Anchorage: Alaska Black Caucus, 1988), 42–43.

74. Robert Platt Boyd, *Me and Company C* (Auburn, Ala.: Published by the author, 1992), 6.

75. Resident of Teslin, as quoted in Julie Cruikshank, "The Gravel Magnet: Some Social Impacts of the Alaska Highway on Yukon Indians," in *The Alaska Highway: Papers of the 40th Anniversary Symposium*, edited by Kenneth Coates (Vancouver: University of British Columbia Press, 1985), 178.

76. "The Alaska Highway ('Alcan')," 1972, Box 11, Office of the Chief of Engineers, Army Corps of Engineers, Alaska District, Anchorage Installation, Record Group 77, National Archives and Records Administration, Pacific-Alaska Region, Anchorage, Alaska, 84.

77. Because the highway did, indeed, prove useless during wartime, a series of congressional and presidential investigations of the project were conducted. For details, see Twichell, *Northwest Epic*, 257–276.

78. Austin Lefurge Johnston, *The Alaska Highway Guide*, British Columbia, 1948, available at the Alaska and Polar Regions Collection, Elmer E. Rasmuson Library, University of Alaska–Fairbanks, 14–15.

79. George W. Payton to Mr. Cumming, January 11, 1947, Vol. 96, Record Group 99, National Archives of Canada, Ottawa, Ontario, 1.

80. Joan M. Antonson and William S. Hanable, *Alaska's Heritage* (Anchorage: Alaska Historical Society, 1985), 493.

81. For more on the effects of World War II on Alaskan development, see Stephen Haycox, *Alaska: An American Colony* (Seattle: University of Washington Press, 2002), 257–272.

82. Again, most of this criticism is directed at American historians. Canadian historians have done some research on the highway's impact on local communities, although much more work remains to be done. See note 1.

**CHAPTER 4. ALASKA SUBMERGED:
THE RAMPART DAM CONTROVERSY**

1. For more on the natural and cultural history of the Yukon Flats region, see *Alaska Native Problems from Rampart Dam Report* (Alaska: n.p., [1963?]), Alaska and Polar Regions Collection, Elmer E. Rasmuson Library, University of Alaska–Fairbanks. For a broader history of the Yukon Basin, see Melody Webb, *The Last Frontier: A*

History of the Yukon Basin of Canada and Alaska (Albuquerque: University of New Mexico Press, 1985).

2. Claus-M. Naske and William R. Hunt, *The Politics of Hydroelectric Power in Alaska: Rampart and Devil Canyon—A Case Study* (Fairbanks: Institute of Water Resources, University of Alaska, 1978), 3.

3. M. C. Mapes to Ernest Gruening, April 20, 1959, Ernest Gruening Papers, Alaska and Polar Regions Collection, Elmer E. Rasmuson Library, University of Alaska–Fairbanks, 4.

4. Ibid., 1.

5. "Brief of Matters Pertinent to Review of Draft of Department of Interior Rampart Project Report," September 28, 1964, Alaska Resources Information and Library Services, Anchorage.

6. For more on reclamation projects during the postwar years, see Donald J. Pisani, "The Bureau of Reclamation and the West, 1945–2000," in *The American West in 2000: Essays in Honor of Gerald D. Nash*, edited by Richard W. Etulain and Ferenec Morton Szasz (Albuquerque: University of New Mexico Press, 2003), 52–68.

7. In typical Cold War rhetoric, during his campaign for the presidency, John F. Kennedy told his supporters that the Rampart Dam would have been built long ago if the Russians still owned Alaska. *New York Times*, September 14, 1960.

8. George Sundborg, "Among the Ramparts We Watch . . . The 'Biggest Dam on the Mighty Yukin,'" n.d., Box 529, Ernest Gruening Papers, Alaska and Polar Regions Collection, Elmer E. Rasmuson Library, University of Alaska–Fairbanks, 2.

9. For more on the battle over Alaska statehood, see Claus-M. Naske, *A History of Alaska Statehood* (Lanham, Md.: University Press of America, 1985), and John S. Whitehead, *Completing the Union: Alaska, Hawai'i, and the Battle for Statehood* (Albuquerque: University of New Mexico Press, 2004).

10. Paul Brooks, "The Plot to Drown Alaska," *Atlantic Monthly* (May 1965): 53–59.

11. Carl R. Gerber et al., *Plowshare* (Oak Ridge, Tenn.: Atomic Energy Commission, Division of Technical Information, 1966); Edward Teller, as quoted in Dan O'Neill, *The Firecracker Boys* (New York: St. Martin's Press, 1994), 92. O'Neill's work is the best and most complete record of Project Chariot to date, although, as one reviewer noted, the narrative has "more than a touch of wild-western, white-hat-black-hat history." Morgan Sherwood, "Atomic Energy vs. Eskimos," *Science*, New Series 266 (October 28, 1994): 663.

12. Peter Coates, "Project Chariot: Alaskan Roots of Environmentalism," in *An Alaska Anthology: Interpreting the Past*, edited by Stephen W. Haycox and Mary Childers Mangusso (Seattle: University of Washington Press, 2002), 380.

13. *New York Times*, June 5, 1959. The blast would come from four bombs—two 1-megaton and two 200-kiloton hydrogen devices. Even the smaller bombs were more than ten times larger than the one dropped on Hiroshima.

14. As quoted in Ken Ross, *Environmental Conflicts in Alaska* (Boulder: University Press of Colorado, 2000), 102, n.23.

15. *Fairbanks Daily News-Miner*, July 24, 1958.

16. *Bulletin of the Atomic Scientists* 15 (January 1959): 47.

17. *New York Times*, December 4, 1960.

18. The Committee for the Study of Atomic Testing in Alaska was part of a larger public movement against Operation Plowshare. For details on the broader controversy, see Scott Kirsch and Don Mitchell, "Earth Moving as the 'Measure of Man': Edward

Teller, Geographical Engineering, and the Matter of Progress," *Social Text* 54 (Spring 1998): 100–134.

19. Coates, "Project Chariot," 385.

20. *New York Times*, August 17, 1960.

21. For more on Alaska's economy prior to statehood, see Claus-M. Naske, "Some Attention, Little Action: Vacillating Federal Efforts to Provide Territorial Alaska with an Economic Base," *Western Historical Quarterly* 26 (Spring 1995): 36–68.

22. For more on Gruening's attitudes and policies during his years as territorial governor, see Claus-M. Naske, *Ernest Gruening: Alaska's Greatest Governor* (Fairbanks: University of Alaska Press, 2004).

23. Ernest Gruening, "Statement of Ernest Gruening on Construction of the Rampart Canyon Dam," n.d., Box 528, Ernest Gruening Papers, Alaska and Polar Regions Collection, Elmer E. Rasmuson Library, University of Alaska–Fairbanks.

24. *Anchorage Daily News*, October 6, 1959.

25. Claus-M. Naske and William R. Hunt, *The Politics of Hydroelectric Power in Alaska: Rampart and Devil Canyon—A Case Study* (Fairbanks: Institute of Water Resources, University of Alaska, 1978), 4.

26. U.S. Department of the Interior, Subcommittee on Power, *Rampart Dam, Yukon River, Alaska: A Power Supply and Market Potential Review* ([Washington, D.C.?], 1966), Alaska and Polar Regions Collection, Elmer E. Rasmuson Library, University of Alaska–Fairbanks.

27. *Washington Post*, September 16, 1963.

28. U.S. Senate, Committee on Public Works, *The Market for Rampart Power, Yukon River, Alaska*, 57th Cong., 2d sess. (Washington, D.C.: Government Printing Office, 1962), 6.

29. Jay S. Hammond, as quoted in Peter A. Coates, *The Trans-Alaska Pipeline Controversy: Technology, Conservation, and the Frontier* (Bethlehem, Penn.: Lehigh University Press, 1991), 146, n.70.

30. *Anchorage Daily News*, October 23, 1963.

31. Yukon Power for America, "The Rampart Story" (Fairbanks: Yukon Power for America, [196?]), Alaska and Polar Regions Collection, Elmer E. Rasmuson Library, University of Alaska–Fairbanks.

32. For examples of these school reports, see Box 3, Ralph J. Rivers Papers, Alaska and Polar Regions Collection, Elmer E. Rasmuson Library, University of Alaska–Fairbanks.

33. Ivan Bloch, "Summary Notes regarding the Promotion of the Rampart Project," August 30, 1963, Box 531, Ernest Gruening Papers, Alaska and Polar Regions Collection, Elmer E. Rasmuson Library, University of Alaska–Fairbanks, 6.

34. Ernest Gruening, *Many Battles: The Autobiography of Ernest Gruening* (New York: Liveright, 1973), 497.

35. Coates, *Trans-Alaska Pipeline Controversy*, 136. Although the Rampart Dam can largely be marked as the time when boosters started imagining Alaska as what Carlos Schwantes has termed "a wageworker's" rather than an agrarian frontier, the transition would never be complete, and dreams of Alaskan agricultural prosperity would continue into the twenty-first century.

36. Ira Gabrielson, as quoted in "Remarks by Senator Ernest Gruening at National Electrical Week Dinner, Anchorage, Alaska," February 13, 1964, Box 532, Ernest Gruening Papers, Alaska and Polar Regions Collection, Elmer E. Rasmuson Library, University of Alaska–Fairbanks, 2.

37. U.S. Fish and Wildlife Service, *A Report on Fish and Wildlife Resources Affected by the Rampart Dam and Reservoir Project, Yukon River, Alaska* (Juneau: U.S. Fish and Wildlife Service, April 1964), 120.

38. U.S. Senate, Committee on Public Works, *The Market for Rampart Power, Yukon River, Alaska*, 57th Cong., 2d sess. (Washington, D.C.: Government Printing Office, 1962); Ginny Wood, "Rampart—Foolish Dam," Spring 1965, Box 1, Brock Evans Papers, Accession Number 1776–006, Special Collections, University Libraries, University of Washington, 2.

39. William A. Egan, "Address to Alaska Rural Electric Cooperative Association, Homer, Alaska," August 11, 1961, Box 528, Ernest Gruening Papers, Alaska and Polar Regions Collection, Elmer E. Rasmuson Library, University of Alaska–Fairbanks.

40. Ernest Gruening to John Johnson, December 15, 1965, Box 335, Ernest Gruening Papers, Alaska and Polar Regions Collection, Elmer E. Rasmuson Library, University of Alaska–Fairbanks.

41. "Remarks by Senator Ernest Gruening at National Electrical Week Dinner, Anchorage, Alaska," February 13, 1964, Box 532, Ernest Gruening Papers, Alaska and Polar Regions Collection, Elmer E. Rasmuson Library, University of Alaska–Fairbanks, 5.

42. *Fairbanks Daily News-Miner*, November 30, 1963.

43. For more on the situation in each of the individual villages, see Paul L. Winsor to Ernest Gruening, August 14, 1961, Box 528, Ernest Gruening Papers, Alaska and Polar Regions Collection, Elmer E. Rasmuson Library, University of Alaska–Fairbanks.

44. Philip Peter, as quoted in Ross, *Environmental Conflicts in Alaska*, 128, n.24. See also *Alaska Native Problems (from Rampart Dam Report)*, n.d., Alaska and Polar Regions Collection, Elmer E. Rasmuson Library, University of Alaska–Fairbanks.

45. "Remarks by Senator Ernest Gruening at National Electrical Week Dinner, Anchorage, Alaska," February 13, 1964, Box 532, Ernest Gruening Papers, Alaska and Polar Regions Collection, Elmer E. Rasmuson Library, University of Alaska–Fairbanks, 8.

46. Ernest Gruening to William R. Wood, June 12, 1961, Box 528, Ernest Gruening Papers, Alaska and Polar Regions Collection, Elmer E. Rasmuson Library, University of Alaska–Fairbanks, 2.

47. Yukon Power for America, "Addresses Presented at Rampart Dam Conference, Mt. McKinely [sic] Hotel, McKinley Park, Alaska," September 7, 1963, Alaska and Polar Regions Collection, Elmer E. Rasmuson Library, University of Alaska–Fairbanks, 39–41.

48. John Kameroff to Ernest Gruening, February 15, 1965, Box 534, Ernest Gruening Papers, Alaska and Polar Regions Collection, Elmer E. Rasmuson Library, University of Alaska–Fairbanks, 2. Emphasis in original.

49. George Sundborg, as quoted in Coates, *Trans-Alaska Pipeline Controversy*, 149, n.91.

50. Ernest F. Brater et al., *Rampart Dam and the Economic Development of Alaska*. Vol. 1, *Summary Report* (Ann Arbor: School of Natural Resources, University of Michigan, 1966), 3.

51. *Washington Post*, September 16, 1963.

52. The phrase and concept of "ducks versus bucks" comes from Ginny Hill Wood, "The Ramparts We Watch," n.d., Box 1, Brock Evans Papers, Accession Number 1776–006, Special Collections, University Libraries, University of Washington.

53. Paul Brooks, "The Plot to Drown Alaska," *Atlantic Monthly*, May 1965, 58.

54. Ernest Gruening, "The Plot to Strangle Alaska," Box 535, Ernest Gruening Papers, Alaska and Polar Regions Collection, Elmer E. Rasmuson Library, University of Alaska–Fairbanks, 5.

55. Ibid., 4.

56. Brooks, "The Plot to Drown Alaska," 59.

57. Wood, "The Ramparts We Watch," 6.

CHAPTER 5. A CRACK IN THE LANDSCAPE: THE TRANS-ALASKA PIPELINE

1. ARCO did not officially confirm the finding until July 1968. Two other oil companies, Humble Oil (later Exxon) and British Petroleum (BP), also had drilling rights in the immediate area, and these "big three" maintained control over most of the Prudhoe Bay oil fields when the drilling leases were sold.

2. For details regarding some of these changes, see the following reports: B. Stephen Strong, "Alaska Pipeline: Social and Economic Impact on Native People," 1977, Published under the Authority of the Hon. J. Hugh Faulkner, Minister of Indian and Northern Affairs, Ottawa, Ontario, Canada; Jeff Floch, "The Socio-Economic Impact of the Trans-Alaska Pipeline System on Fairbanks and Anchorage," 1979, Alaska Resources Library and Information Services, Anchorage; and Mathematical Sciences Northwest, "A Study of the Economic and Sociological Impact of the Construction and Initial Operation of the Trans-Alaska Pipeline," 1972, Alaska Resources Library and Information Services, Anchorage.

3. William R. Hunt, "Notes on the History of North Slope Oil," *Alaska Magazine*, February 1970, 8–10.

4. Institute of Business, Economic, and Government Research, "Alaska's Economy in 1967," *Monthly Review of Alaska Business and Economic Conditions* 5 (1967): 2.

5. "Alaska Strikes It Rich," *U.S. News & World Report*, December 9, 1968, 48–53.

6. This figure was approximately 28 percent of Alaska's total landmass, or an area about the size of the state of California.

7. Luther J. Carter, "North Slope: Oil Rush," *Science* 166 (October 3, 1969): 87–88.

8. This shift was never complete, however, and independent-minded Alaskan politicians often fail to fit their parties' molds.

9. Walter J. Hickel, *Crisis in the Commons: The Alaska Solution* (Oakland, Calif.: Institute for Contemporary Studies, 2002), 97.

10. More sophisticated—and effective—techniques for building winter roads in northern environments include packing down the snow and then covering trails with water, which freezes into ice. This insulates the permafrost and does not damage the tundra come spring.

11. Tom Brown, *Oil on Ice: Alaskan Wilderness at the Crossroads*, edited and with an introduction by Richard Pollock (San Francisco: Sierra Club, 1971), 43.

12. Approximately 50,000 of these residents were Alaska Natives.

13. Brookings Institution, "Conference on the Future of Alaska," 1969, as quoted in Claus-M. Naske and Herman E. Slotnick, *Alaska: A History of the 49th State* (Norman: University of Oklahoma Press, 1987), 180–181.

14. For details regarding this venture, see Ross Coen, "Sailing through a Granite Quarry: The Northwest Passage and the Voyage of the S.S. *Manhattan*" (Master's thesis, University of Alaska–Fairbanks, 2005).

15. Archie W. Shiels, *The Purchase of Alaska* (College: University of Alaska Press, 1967), 130.

16. U.S. Congress, House Committee on the Territories, *Civil Government for Alaska*, 48th Cong., 1st sess. (Washington, D.C.: Government Printing Office, 1884), 2.

17. Lennard Sillanpaa, *Alaska Native Claims Settlement Act: The First Twenty Years* (Ottawa: Indian and Northern Affairs Canada, 1992), 2–3.

18. The state of Alaska challenged this land freeze in the courts, but it ultimately lost.

19. Robert Manning, "Secretary of Things in General," *Saturday Evening Post*, May 20, 1961, 38–42. Udall resigned from office when President Richard Nixon was elected in 1969.

20. Mary Clay Berry, *The Alaska Pipeline: The Politics of Oil and Native Land Claims* (Bloomington: Indiana University Press, 1975), 35–39. Most issues of the *Tundra Times* are now available on the Internet. See Tuzzy Consortium Library, Ilisagvik College, http://ttip.tuzzy.org/.

21. "Statewide Native Unity Achieved at Conference," *Tundra Times*, October 28, 1966, 1.

22. Janie Leask, "The Alaska Claims Settlement," lecture, Vancouver, August 19, 1984. The text of this lecture can be found at http://www.alaskool.org/projects/ancsa/ JLeask/Alaska_Claims_Settlement_JLeask.htm.

23. Berry, *The Alaska Pipeline*, 50.

24. Ironically, Richard Nixon selected Alaska Governor Walter Hickel—a vocal opponent of the land freeze—to replace Stewart Udall as the secretary of the interior. By this time, however, it was clear that Hickel would never receive confirmation unless he won over the support of the AFN by extending the land freeze, which he ultimately agreed to do. However, Nixon fired Hickel in 1970, partly over their disagreement about the war in Vietnam.

25. Sillanpaa, *Alaska Native Claims Settlement Act*, 4.

26. This title included subsurface drilling rights. The area awarded to the Natives was about one-ninth of the total acreage in Alaska.

27. Sillanpaa, *Alaska Native Claims Settlement Act*, 4–5. For an exhaustive history of the passage of ANCSA, see Donald Craig Mitchell, *Take My Land, Take My Life: The Story of Congress's Historic Settlement of Alaska Native Land Claims, 1960–1971* (Fairbanks: University of Alaska Press, 2001). For more on the consequences of ANCSA, see Brian Hirsch, "Alaska's 'Peculiar Institution': Impacts on Land, Culture, and Community from Alaska Native Claims Settlement Act of 1971" (Ph.D. dissertation, University of Wisconsin–Madison, 1998).

28. Jay Hammond, "Pipeline: Panacea or Profanity?" n.d., Jay S. Hammond Papers, Archives and Manuscripts, Consortium Library, University of Alaska–Anchorage.

29. NEPA was passed in 1969 but did not take effect until 1970.

30. Environmental Action Bulletin, n.d., Box 5, Friends of the Earth Papers, Accession Number 2548, Special Collections, University Libraries, University of Washington.

31. As quoted in Ken Ross, *Environmental Conflicts in Alaska* (Boulder: University Press of Colorado, 2000), 151–152, n.15.

32. "Trans Alaska Pipeline Briefing Book," 1977, Box 1, Fairbanks Support Center, Bureau of Land Management Papers, Record Group 49, National Archives and Records Administration, Pacific-Alaska Region, Anchorage, Alaska.

33. "Trans-Alaska Pipeline Hearings," February 24–25, 1971, Anchorage, Box 4, Alaska Conservation Society Papers, Alaska and Polar Regions Collection, Elmer E. Rasmuson Library, University of Alaska–Fairbanks.

34. Environmental Action Bulletin, n.d., Box 5, Friends of the Earth Papers, Accession Number 2548, Special Collections, University Libraries, University of Washington.

35. Harold Peyton, "Pipeline Design in the Arctic Environment," n.d., Alaska Center for the Environment Papers, Archives and Manuscripts, Consortium Library, University of Alaska–Anchorage.

36. Cordova District Fisheries Union Press Release, n.d., Box 5, Friends of the Earth Papers, Accession Number 2548, Special Collections, University Libraries, University of Washington.

37. "Fact Sheet on the Alaska Pipeline," February 1972, Alaska Center for the Environment Papers, Archives and Manuscripts, Consortium Library, University of Alaska–Anchorage.

38. Naske and Slotnick, *Alaska*, 257.

39. Undersecretary of the Interior William T. Pecora, as quoted in the Wilderness Society, "The Alaska Pipeline Reading Lesson," n.d., Box 5, Friends of the Earth Papers, Accession Number 2548, Special Collections, University Libraries, University of Washington. Emphasis in original.

40. Ross, *Environmental Conflicts in Alaska*, 154.

41. The state of Alaska did its own study that more succinctly summarized these findings. See the Alaska Pipeline Coordinating Committee, *Moving Alaska Oil* (Juneau: State of Alaska, 1973), Alaska and Polar Regions Collection, Elmer E. Rasmuson Library, University of Alaska–Fairbanks.

42. As quoted in Ross, *Environmental Conflicts in Alaska*, 155, n.44. For more on this argument, see U.S. Department of the Interior, "An Analysis of the Economic and Security Aspects of the Trans-Alaska Pipeline," December 1971, Alyeska Pipeline Service Company Papers, Archives and Manuscripts, Consortium Library, University of Alaska–Anchorage.

43. Environmentalists argued that the energy "crisis" was invented to justify big business projects, such as the pipeline, when conservation would be the preferable solution to any such crisis, if it existed. However, they lost that rhetorical war during the pipeline debate—and it could be argued that they continue to lose it in contemporary debates. See Harvey Manning, *Cry Crisis! Rehearsal in Alaska* (San Francisco: Friends of the Earth, 1974).

44. For the point of view of pipeline workers, see Dermot Cole, *Amazing Pipeline Stories: How Building the Trans-Alaska Pipeline Transformed Life in America's Last Frontier* (Fairbanks: Epicenter Press, 1997).

45. Ross, *Environmental Conflicts in Alaska*, 159.

46. Harvey, *Cry Crisis!* x.

47. Alyeska Pipeline Service Company, "Pipeline Design," n.d., Alyeska Pipeline Service Company Papers, Archives and Manuscripts, Consortium Library, University of Alaska–Anchorage.

48. As quoted in Naske and Slotnick, *Alaska*, 259, n.74.

49. Brock Evans, "Pipeline Surveillance Memo," May 30, 1975, Box 6, Gil M. Zemansky Papers, Accession Number 3534, Special Collections, University Libraries, University of Washington.

50. Dale Jones, "Alaska Native Claims Legislation," October 14, 1971, Box 1, Friends of the Earth Papers, Accession Number 2548, Special Collections, University Libraries, University of Washington, 1.

51. This diametric opposition was important to the pipeline debate as well. Peter Coates, who has written the most complete history of the pipeline to date, argued that the "frontier versus wilderness" formulation defined the controversy. Although

there is much truth to his argument, I believe that this period in Alaskan history is far more complex, especially when the views of local Alaskans and Alaska Natives are taken into consideration. (Coates largely sidesteps any discussion of Alaska Natives.) At the bottom of the "petroleum with preservation" period, as I define it, was a desire to create an "enduring frontier"—a place where everyone could have it all—nature and development (for non-Native residents), tradition and modernity (for Alaska Natives). See Peter Coates, *The Trans-Alaska Pipeline Controversy: Technology, Conservation, and the Frontier* (Fairbanks: University of Alaska Press, 1993).

52. The National Park Service conducted historical as well as environmental studies in Alaska. An important book that came out of the historical studies is Melody Webb, *The Last Frontier: A History of the Yukon Basin of Canada and Alaska* (Albuquerque: University of New Mexico Press, 1985).

53. Jay S. Hammond, "Statewide D-2 Radio Address, Juneau," January 5, 1979, Jay S. Hammond Papers, Archives and Manuscripts, Consortium Library, University of Alaska–Anchorage, 1.

54. Naske and Slotnick, *Alaska*, 225–226.

55. These bills were sponsored by Morris Udall (Democrat from Arizona) and John Seiberling (Democrat from Ohio) in the House and by Lee Metcalf (Democrat from Montana) in the Senate.

56. As quoted in Ross, *Environmental Conflicts in Alaska*, 197, n.26.

57. "Great Stakes in the Great Land: Alaska Lands for the Public Good," n.d., Box 1, Friends of the Earth Papers, Accession Number 2548, Special Collections, University Libraries, University of Washington. See also Doug Scott, *The Enduring Wilderness: Protecting Our National Heritage through the Wilderness Act* (Golden, Colo.: Fulcrum Publishing, 2004), 90–94.

58. Initial estimates were 10.8 million gallons, but those figures were later increased to 30 million gallons.

59. For a more thorough analysis of the national reaction to the spill, see Susan Kollin, *Nature's State: Imaging Alaska as the Last Frontier* (Chapel Hill: University of North Carolina Press, 2001), 2–22.

60. Jay Hammond, "Testimony before U.S. House Interior Committee," April 22, 1977, Jay S. Hammond Papers, Archives and Manuscripts, Consortium Library, University of Alaska–Anchorage, 3.

61. For more on Alaskans' reactions to the spill, see Alaska Oil Spill Commission, *Spill: The Wreck of the Exxon Valdez* (Juneau: State of Alaska, 1990), Alaska Resources Library and Information Services, Anchorage.

EPILOGUE: ALASKA HEATS UP

1. Sherry Simpson, "I Want to Ride on the Bus Chris Died In," in *Travelers' Tales Alaska: True Stories*, edited by Bill Sherwonit, Andromeda Romano-Lax, and Ellen Bielawski (Palo Alto, Calif.: Travelers' Tales, 2003), 243–265.

2. See www.grizzlypeople.com.

3. "Hikers Rescued in Alaska after Journey into Wild," *Fairbanks Daily News-Miner*, August 25, 2009, http://www.newsminer.com/news/2009/aug/25/two-hikers-rescued-stampede-trail/.

4. Rebecca Boren, "Tundra War," n.d., Box 1, Friends of the Earth Papers, Accession Number 2548, Special Collections, University Libraries, University of Washington.

5. U.S. Geological Survey, *The Oil and Gas Resource Potential of the Arctic National Wildlife Refuge 1002 Area, Alaska* (Washington, D.C.: Government Printing Office, 1998), 4. These estimates include some offshore drilling sites.

6. Natural Resources Defense Council et al., "Tracking Arctic Oil: The Environmental Price of Drilling in the Arctic National Wildlife Refuge," 1991, Alaska and Polar Regions Collection, Elmer E. Rasmuson Library, University of Alaska–Fairbanks, 8.

7. One group of Alaska Natives, the Gwich'in, actively opposes drilling. The Gwich'in would not stand to profit from any oil development, and drilling would undoubtedly threaten their caribou-hunting subsistence lifestyle. See Scott Wallace, "ANWR: The Great Divide," *Smithsonian* 36, no. 7 (October 2005): 48–56.

8. By no means is this an exhaustive description of the ANWR debate. For a more detailed history, see Ken Ross, *Environmental Conflict in Alaska* (Boulder: University Press of Colorado, 2000), 269–290; for a more sociological analysis of ANWR activists, see Julie Raymond-Yakoubian, "Distance Activism and Arctic National Wildlife Refuge" (master's thesis, University of Alaska–Fairbanks, May 2002), Alaska and Polar Regions Collection, Elmer E. Rasmuson Library, University of Alaska–Fairbanks.

9. See www.sarahpalinjokes.com (accessed February 8, 2010). For an analysis of how these parodies of Sarah Palin, "the Alaskan," may have affected her candidacy, see Leslie Dow, "I Can See Russia from My House: Tina Fey & Political Parody," *Commentary: The University of New Hampshire Student Journal of Communication* (2008–2009): 95–108.

10. *Christian Science Monitor*, August 28, 2008.

11. *Arctic Climate Impact Assessment—Scientific Report* (Cambridge: Cambridge University Press, 2005), 34–45; see also Eric Post et al., "Global Population Dynamics and Hot Spots of Response to Climate Change." *BioScience* 59 (June 2009): 489–497.

12. *USA Today*, May 31, 2006.

13. *New York Times*, September 10, 2009.

14. *New York Times*, September 11, 2009.

15. Alaska Native Science Commission, "Impact of Climate Change on Alaska Native Communities," n.d., www.nativescience.org/issues/climatechange.htm, 1–17.

16. Ken Coates, "The Rediscovery of the North: Toward a Conceptual Framework for the Study of the North/Northern Regions," *The Northern Review* 12/13 (Summer/Winter 1994): 15.

SELECTED BIBLIOGRAPHY

This list contains only the major sources that I directly cited in this book; it is not meant to represent all the material that I consulted during my research. Minor sources (pamphlets, proceedings, draft reports, and so on) without complete citations are most often part of the Alaska and Polar Regions Collection at the University of Alaska–Fairbanks, or the Alaska Resources and Library Information Services (ARLIS) in Anchorage. Although some minor sources do not appear in this bibliography, their footnotes indicate their location in addition to all the information I could obtain about their proper citations.

ARCHIVAL COLLECTIONS

Beinecke Rare Book and Manuscript Library, Yale University, New Haven, Connecticut
    John G. Brady Papers
    Felix S. Cohen Papers
National Archives of Canada, Ottawa, Ontario
    Alaska Highway Collection (R.G. 24, R.G. 25, and R.G. 99)
National Archives and Records Administration, College Park, Maryland
    Records of the Department of the Interior, Office of the Secretary (R.G. 126)
    Records of the National Youth Administration (R.G. 119)
    Records of the Office of the Territories (R.G. 126)
    Records of the Work Projects Administration (R.G. 69)
National Archives and Records Administration, Pacific-Alaska Region, Anchorage
    Records of the Alaska Reindeer Service (R.G. 75)
    Records of the Army Corps of Engineers (R.G. 77)
    Records of the Bureau of Land Management (R.G. 49)
    Uncataloged Matanuska Colony Papers (R.G. 69)
Presbyterian Historical Society Archives, Philadelphia (viewed on microfilm at Yale University)
    Sheldon Jackson Papers
Public Library Archives, Palmer, Alaska
    Matanuska Colony Collection
University of Alaska Archives, Anchorage
    Alaska Center for the Environment Papers
    Alyeska Pipeline Service Company Papers
    C. Earl Albrecht Papers

University of Alaska Archives, Fairbanks
  Alaska-Canada Highway Collection
  Alaska Conservation Society Papers
  Anthony J. Dimond Papers
  Ernest Gruening Papers
  Lomen Family Papers
  Donald MacDonald Papers
  Ben Mozee Papers
  Oral History Collections
  Ralph J. Rivers Papers
  341st Engineer Regiment Collection, 1943–1946
  Vertical File, Small Manuscript Collections
University of Oregon Archives, Eugene
  Clarence Leroy Andrews Papers
University of Washington Archives, Seattle
  Brock Evans Papers
  Friends of the Earth Papers
  Gil M. Zemansky Papers
The Yukon Archives, Whitehorse
  Alaska Highway Collection

PUBLISHED SOURCES

Adams, John Q. "This Is Matanuska!" *Alaska Sportsman* 4 (April 1938): 16–24.

Alaska Agricultural Experiment Stations. Annual Reports of the Alaska Agricultural Experiment Stations (titles vary). Washington, D.C.: Government Printing Office, 1898–1919.

Alaska Oil Spill Commission. *Spill: The Wreck of the Exxon Valdez*. Juneau: State of Alaska, 1990.

Alaska Pipeline Coordinating Committee. *Moving Alaska Oil*. Juneau: State of Alaska, 1973.

Alaska Road Commission. *The Proposed Pacific Yukon Highway*. Juneau: Privately printed, 1931.

Anderson, H. Dewey, and Walter Crosby Eells. *Alaska Natives: A Survey of Their Sociological and Educational Status*. Stanford, Calif.: Stanford University Press, 1935.

Andrasko, Kenneth, and Marcus Halevi. *Alaska Crude: Visions of the Last Frontier*. Boston: Little, Brown, 1977.

Antonson, Joan M., and William S. Hanable. *Alaska's Heritage*. Alaska Historical Commission Studies in History No. 133. Anchorage: Alaska Historical Society, 1992.

Arctic Climate Impact Assessment—Scientific Report. Cambridge: Cambridge University Press, 2005.

Arenson, Adam. "Anglo-Saxonism in the Yukon: The Klondike Nugget and American-British Relations in the 'Two Wests,' 1898–1901." *Pacific Historical Review* 76 (August 2007): 373–404.

Army Corps of Engineers, Office of the Chief of Engineers, Northwest Service Command. *The Canol Project*. Washington, D.C.: War Department, 1945.

Arnold, Robert D. *Alaska Native Land Claims*. Anchorage: Alaska Native Foundation, 1976.

Athearn, Robert G. *The Mythic West in Twentieth-Century America*. With a foreword by Elliott West. Lawrence: University Press of Kansas, 1986.

Atwood, Evangeline. *We Shall Be Remembered*. Anchorage: Alaska Methodist University Press, 1966.

Bancroft, Hubert Howe. *History of Alaska, 1730–1885*, reprint. New York: Antiquarian Press, 1960 [1886].

Berry, Mary Clay. *The Alaska Pipeline: The Politics of Oil and Native Land Claims*. Bloomington: Indiana University Press, 1975.

Black, Lydia T. *Russians in Alaska, 1732–1867*. Fairbanks: University of Alaska Press, 2004.

Bockstoce, John R. *Eskimos of Northwest Alaska in the Early Nineteenth Century*. Oxford: Pitt Rivers Museum, University of Oxford, 1977.

———. *Whales, Ice, and Men: The History of Whaling in the Western Arctic*. Seattle: University of Washington Press, 1986.

Boone, Scott C. *Annual Report of the Governor of Alaska*. Washington, D.C.: Government Printing Office, 1921.

Boyd, Robert Platt. *Me and Company C*. Auburn, Ala.: Published by the author, 1992.

Brater, Ernest F., Michael F. Brewer, Justin W. Leonard, A. Starker Leopold, William A. Spurr, and Stephen H. Spurr. *Rampart Dam and the Economic Development of Alaska*. Vol. 1, *Summary Report*. Ann Arbor: School of Natural Resources, University of Michigan, 1966.

The British Columbia–Yukon–Alaska Highway Commission. *Report of the Proposed Highway through British Columbia and the Yukon Territory to Alaska*. Ottawa, Ontario: Edmond Cloutier, 1941.

Brooks, Alfred H. "The Value of Alaska." *Geographical Review* 15 (January 1925): 25–50.

Brooks, Maria. *The Reindeer Queen: Once the Richest Woman in Alaska—The True Story of Sinrock Mary*. VHS. Anchorage: Waterfront Soundings Production, 2000.

Brooks, Paul. "The Plot to Drown Alaska." *The Atlantic Monthly* 215 (May 1965): 53–59.

Brown, Tom. *Oil on Ice: Alaskan Wilderness at a Crossroads*. Edited and with an introduction by Richard Pollock. San Francisco: Sierra Club, 1971.

Campbell, Robert. *In Darkest Alaska: Travel and Empire along the Inside Passage*. Philadelphia: University of Pennsylvania Press, 2007.

Carter, Luther J. "North Slope: Oil Rush." *Science* 166 (October 3, 1969): 87–88.

Catton, Theodore. *Inhabited Wilderness: Indians, Eskimos, and National Parks in Alaska*. Albuquerque: University of New Mexico Press, 1997.

Chandonnet, Fern, ed. *Alaska at War, 1941–1945: The Forgotten War Remembered*. Anchorage: University of Alaska Press, 2007.

Chevigny, Hector. *Russian America: The Great Alaskan Venture, 1741–1867*. New York: Viking Press, 1965.

Chubbuck, Levi. "Alaska Agricultural Possibilities." *Bulletin of the American Geographical Society* 42 (1910): 892–898.

Churchill, Frank C. *Reports on the Condition of Educational and School Service and the Management of Reindeer Service in the District of Alaska*. 59th Cong., 1st sess. Washington, D.C.: Government Printing Office, 1905.

Coakley, Robert, and Richard Leighton. *Global Logistics and Strategy*. Washington, D.C.: Center of Military History, U.S. Army, 1955.

Coates, Ken. *North to Alaska! Fifty Years on the World's Most Remarkable Highway.* Toronto: McClelland and Stewart, 1992.

———. "The Rediscovery of the North: Toward a Conceptual Framework for the Study of the North/Northern Regions." *Northern Review* 12/13 (Summer/Winter 1994): 15–43.

———, ed. *The Alaska Highway: Papers of the 40th Anniversary Symposium.* Vancouver: University of British Columbia Press, 1985.

Coates, Kenneth, and William Morrison. *The Alaska Highway in World War II: The U.S. Army of Occupation in Canada's Northwest.* Norman: University of Oklahoma Press, 1992.

———. *Working the North: Labor and the Northwest Defense Projects, 1942–1946.* Fairbanks: University of Alaska Press, 1994.

Coates, Peter A. *The Trans-Alaska Pipeline Controversy: Technology, Conservation, and the Frontier.* Bethlehem, Penn.: Lehigh University Press, 1991.

Coe, Douglas. *Road to Alaska: The Story of the Alaska Highway.* New York: Julian Messner, 1952.

Coen, Ross. "Sailing through a Granite Quarry: The Northwest Passage and the Voyage of the S.S. *Manhattan*." Master's thesis, University of Alaska, Fairbanks, 2005.

Cole, Dermot. *Amazing Pipeline Stories: How Building the Trans-Alaska Pipeline Transformed Life in America's Last Frontier.* Fairbanks: Epicenter Press, 1997.

Conkin, Paul K. *Tomorrow a New World: The New Deal Community Program.* Ithaca, N.Y.: Cornell University Press, 1959.

Cronon, William. "A Place for Stories: Nature, History, and Narrative." *Journal of American History* 78 (March 1992): 1347–1376.

———, ed. *Uncommon Ground: Rethinking the Human Place in Nature.* New York: W. W. Norton, 1996.

Cronon, William, George Miles, and Jay Gitlin, eds. *Under an Open Sky: Rethinking America's Western Past.* New York: W. W. Norton, 1992.

Davis, Neil. *Permafrost: A Guide to Frozen Ground in Transition.* Fairbanks: University of Alaska Press, 2001.

Dow, Leslie. "I Can See Russia from My House: Tina Fey & Political Parody." *Commentary: The University of New Hampshire Student Journal of Communication* (2008–2009): 95–108.

Etulain, Richard W., and Ferenc Morton Szasz, eds. *The American West in 2000: Essays in Honor of Gerald D. Nash.* Albuquerque: University of New Mexico Press, 2003.

Fedorova, Svetlana G. *The Russian Population in Alaska and California.* Translated and edited by Richard A. Pierce and Alton S. Donnelly. Kingston, Ontario: Limestone Press, 1973.

Fiege, Mark. "The Weedy West: Mobile Nature, Boundaries, and Common Space in the Montana Landscape." *Western Historical Quarterly* 36 (Spring 2005): 22–47.

Fitch, Edwin M. *The Alaska Railroad.* With a foreword by E. L. Bartlett. New York: Frederick A. Praeger, 1967.

Francis, Karl E. "Outpost Agriculture: The Case of Alaska." *Geographical Review* 42 (July 1952): 384–404.

Georgeson, C. C. "Agricultural Experiments in Alaska." *Yearbook of the United States Department of Agriculture 1898.* Washington, D.C.: Government Printing Office, 1900.

———. "Agriculture in Alaska." *Alaska-Yukon Magazine* 8 (1909): 300–302.

Gerber, Carl R., Richard Hamburger, and E. W. Seabrook Hull. *Plowshare.* Oak Ridge, Tenn.: U.S. Atomic Energy Commission, Division of Technical Information, 1966.

Gibson, James R. *Imperial Russia in Frontier America: The Changing Geography of Supply of Russian America, 1784–1867*. New York: Oxford University Press, 1976.

Godsell, Philip H. *The Romance of the Alaska Highway*. Toronto: Ryerson Press, 1946.

Goetzmann, William H. *Looking Far North: The Harriman Expedition to Alaska, 1899*. New York: Viking Press, 1982.

Golder, Frank A. "The Purchase of Alaska." *The American Historical Review* 25 (April 1920): 411–425.

Grant, Shelagh. *Sovereignty or Security? Government Policy in the Canadian North, 1939–1950*. Vancouver: University of British Columbia Press, 1988.

Gruening, Ernest. *Many Battles: The Autobiography of Ernest Gruening*. New York: Liveright, 1973.

———. "The Plot to Strangle Alaska." *Atlantic Monthly* 216 (July 1965): 56–59.

———. *The State of Alaska*. New York: Random House, 1968.

———, ed. *An Alaskan Reader: 1867–1967*. New York: Meredith Press, 1966.

Gutfeld, Arnon. *American Exceptionalism: The Effects of Plenty on the American Experience*. Portland, Oreg.: Sussex Academic Press, 2002.

Halldorson, Marvin Albert. "The Matanuska Valley Colonization Project." Master's thesis, University of Colorado, 1936.

Hanrahan, John, and Peter Gruenstein. *Lost Frontier: The Marketing of Alaska*. With an introduction by Ralph Nader. New York: W. W. Norton, 1977.

Hanson, Herbert C. *Agriculture in the Matanuska Valley, Alaska*. U.S. Department of the Interior. Washington, D.C.: Government Printing Office, 1944.

Hawden, Seymour, and Lawrence L. Palmer. *Reindeer in Alaska*. U.S. Department of Agriculture Bulletin 1089. Washington, D.C.: Government Printing Office, 1927.

Haycox, Stephen. *Alaska: An American Colony*. Seattle: University of Washington Press, 2002.

———. *Frigid Embrace: Politics, Economics, and Environment in Alaska*. Corvallis: Oregon State University Press, 2002.

———. "Sheldon Jackson in Historical Perspective: Alaska Native Schools and Mission Contracts, 1885–1994." *Pacific Historian* 26 (1984): 18–28.

Hesketh, Bob, ed. *Three Northern Wartime Projects*. Edmonton, Alberta: Canadian Circumpolar Institute and Edmonton and District Historical Society, 1996.

Hickel, Walter J. *Crisis in the Commons: The Alaska Solution*. Oakland, Calif.: Institute for Contemporary Studies, 2002.

Hinckley, Ted C. *Alaskan John G. Brady: Missionary, Businessman, Judge, and Governor*. Columbus: Ohio State University Press, 1982.

———. *The Americanization of Alaska, 1867–1897*. Palo Alto, Calif.: Pacific Books, 1972.

———. *The Canoe Rocks: Alaska's Tlingit and the Euramerican Frontier, 1800–1912*. Lanham, Md.: University Press of America, 1996.

Hirsch, Brian. "Alaska's 'Peculiar Institution': Impacts on Land, Culture, and Community from Alaska Native Claims Settlement Act of 1971." Ph.D. dissertation, University of Wisconsin–Madison, 1998.

Holbo, Paul S. *Tarnished Expansion: The Alaska Scandal, the Press, and Congress, 1867–1871*. Knoxville: University of Tennessee Press, 1983.

Hunt, William R. "Notes on the History of North Slope Oil." *Alaska Magazine*, February 1970, 8–10.

Institute of Business, Economic, and Government Research. "Alaska's Economy in 1967." *Monthly Review of Alaska Business and Economic Conditions* 5 (1967): 2.

Irwin, Don L. *The Colorful Matanuska Valley*. Published by the author, 1968.

Jackson, Helen Hunt. *A Century of Dishonor: A Sketch of the United States Government's Dealings with Some of the Indian Tribes*. New York: Harper and Brothers, 1881.

Jackson, Sheldon. *(Third Annual) Report on the Introduction of Reindeer into Alaska*. 52d Cong., 2d sess. Washington, D.C.: Government Printing Office, 1893.

——. *(Fourth Annual) Report on the Introduction of Reindeer into Alaska*. 53d Cong., 2d sess. Washington, D.C.: Government Printing Office, 1894.

——. *(Fifth Annual) Report on the Introduction of Reindeer into Alaska*. 54th Cong., 1st sess. Washington, D.C.: Government Printing Office, 1896.

——. *(Eighth Annual) Report on the Introduction of Reindeer into Alaska*. 55th Cong., 3d sess. Washington, D.C.: Government Printing Office, 1898.

——. *(Fifteenth Annual) Report on the Introduction of Reindeer into Alaska*. 59th Cong., 1st sess. Washington, D.C.: Government Printing Office, 1905.

Jensen, Ronald J. *The Alaska Purchase and Russian-American Relations*. Seattle: University of Washington Press, 1975.

Jones, Preston. *Empire's Edge: American Society in Nome, Alaska, 1898–1934*. Fairbanks: University of Alaska Press, 2007.

Kirsch, Scott, and Don Mitchell. "Earth Moving as the 'Measure of Man': Edward Teller, Geographical Engineering, and the Matter of Progress." *Social Text* 54 (Spring 1998): 100–134.

Kohlhoff, Dean. *When the Wind Was a River: Aleut Evacuation in World War II*. Seattle: University of Washington Press, 1995.

Kollin, Susan. *Nature's State: Imagining Alaska as the Last Frontier*. Chapel Hill: University of North Carolina Press, 2001.

LaFerber, Walter. *The New Empire: An Interpretation of American Expansion, 1860–1898*. Ithaca, N.Y.: Cornell University Press, 1963.

Landon, Steven J. *The Native People of Alaska*. Anchorage: Greatland Graphics, 1993.

Lantis, Margaret. "The Reindeer Industry in Alaska." *Arctic* 3 (April 1950): 27–44.

Lazell, J. Arthur. *Alaskan Apostle: The Life Story of Sheldon Jackson*. New York: Harper, 1960.

Lomen, G. J. "Views on the Development of the Reindeer Industry." *The Eskimo: A Monthly Magazine Published by the Bureau of Education and Devoted to the Interest of Eskimos of Northern Alaska* 2 (November 1917): 5–6.

London, Jack. *Call of the Wild*. Illustrated by Philip R. Goodwin and Charles Livingston Bull. New York: Macmillan, 1903.

MacDonald, Donald. "The Unfinished Fight for the Highway We Must Yet Build." *Alaska Life*, October 1944, 36–43.

Mangusso, Mary Childers, and Stephen W. Haycox, eds. *An Alaska Anthology: Interpreting the Past*. Seattle: University of Washington Press, 1996.

——, eds. *Interpreting Alaska's History: An Anthology*. Anchorage: Alaska Pacific University Press, 1989.

Manning, Harvey. *Cry Crisis! Rehearsal in Alaska*. San Francisco: Friends of the Earth, 1974.

Manning, Robert. "Secretary of Things in General." *Saturday Evening Post*, May 20, 1961, 38–42.

McClanahan, Alexandra J., ed. *Growing Up Native in Alaska*. Anchorage: Ciri Foundation, 2000.

McPhee, John. *Coming into the Country*. New York: Noonday Press, 1977.

Miller, Edward S. *War Plan Orange: The U.S. Strategy to Defeat Japan, 1897–1945*. Annapolis, Md.: Naval Institute Press, 1991.

Miller, Orlando W. *The Frontier in Alaska and the Matanuska Colony*. New Haven, Conn.: Yale University Press, 1975.

Mitchell, Donald Craig. *Sold American: The Story of Alaska Natives and Their Land, 1867–1959*. Hanover, N.H.: University Press of New England, 1997.

———. *Take My Land, Take My Life: The Story of Congress's Historic Settlement of Alaska Native Land Claims, 1960–1971*. Fairbanks: University of Alaska Press, 2001.

Mitchell, Guy. "Wonders of Alaskan Agriculture." *Illustrated World* 12 (1910): 526.

Mitchell, William L. *The Opening of Alaska*. Edited by Lyman L. Woodman. Anchorage: Cook Inlet Historical Society, 1982.

Mood, Fulmer. "Notes on the History of the Word Frontier." *Agricultural History* 22 (1948): 78–83.

Morse, Kathryn. *The Nature of Gold: An Environmental History of the Klondike Gold Rush*. With a foreword by William Cronon. Seattle: University of Washington Press, 2003.

Muir, John. *Travels in Alaska*. With a foreword by John Haines. San Francisco: Sierra Club Books, 1988.

Murray, Keith A. *Reindeer and Gold*. Bellingham, Wash.: Center for Pacific Northwest Studies, 1988.

Naske, Claus-M. *Ernest Gruening: Alaska's Greatest Governor*. Fairbanks: University of Alaska Press, 2004.

———. *An Interpretive History of Alaskan Statehood*. Anchorage: Alaska Northwest Publishing Company, 1973.

———. "Some Attention, Little Action: Vacillating Federal Efforts to Provide Territorial Alaska with an Economic Base." *Western Historical Quarterly* 26 (Spring 1995): 36–68.

Naske, Claus M., and William R. Hunt. *The Politics of Hydroelectric Power in Alaska: Rampart and Devil Canyon—A Case Study*. Fairbanks: Institute of Water Studies, University of Alaska, 1978.

Naske, Claus-M., and Herman E. Slotnick. *Alaska: A History of the 49th State*, 2d ed. Norman: University of Oklahoma Press, 1987.

Nichols, Jeannette Paddock. *Alaska*. Cleveland: Arthur H. Clark Company, 1924.

Nordhoff, Charles. "What Shall We Do with Scroggs?" *Harper's New Monthly Magazine* 47 (June 1873): 41–44.

Olson, Dean F. *Alaska Reindeer Herdsmen: A Study of Native Management in Transition*. Fairbanks: Institute of Social, Economic, and Government Research, University of Alaska, 1969.

O'Neill, Dan. *The Firecracker Boys*. New York: St. Martin's Press, 1994.

Oquilluk, Cudluk. "Cudlook Oquillok Will Tell You about Reindeer." *The Eskimo: A Monthly Magazine Published by the Bureau of Education and Devoted to the Interest of Eskimos of Northern Alaska* 1 (November 1916): 1.

Overstreet, Everett Louis. *Black on a Background of White: A Chronicle of Afro-American Involvement in America's Last Frontier, Alaska*. Anchorage: Alaska Black Caucus, 1988.

Paine, Robert. *Herds of the Tundra: A Portrait of Saami Reindeer Pastoralism*. Washington, D.C.: Smithsonian Institution Press, 1994.

Post, Eric, Jedediah Brodie, Mark Hebblewhite, Angela D. Anders, Julie A.K. Maier, and Christopher C. Wilmers, "Global Population Dynamics and Hot Spots of Response to Climate Change." *BioScience* 59 (June 2009): 489–497.

Postell, Alice. *Where Did the Reindeer Come From? Alaska Experience, the First Fifty Years*. Portland, Oreg.: Amaknak Press, 1990.

Raymond-Yakoubian, Julie. "Distance Activism and Arctic National Wildlife Refuge." Master's thesis, University of Alaska–Fairbanks, 2002.

Reindeer Industry Act of 1937. Public Law 413. 75th Cong., 1st sess. September 1, 1937.

"The Reindeer Project Families: Kjellmann Expedition 1894, Manitoba Expedition 1898." *Baiki: The North American Sami Journal* 19 (Spring 1999): 1–28.

Remley, David A. *Crooked Road: The Story of the Alaska Highway*. New York: McGraw-Hill, 1976.

Roscow, James P. *800 Miles to Valdez: The Building of the Alaska Pipeline*. Englewood Cliffs, N.J.: Prentice-Hall, 1977.

Ross, Ken. *Environmental Conflict in Alaska*. Boulder: University Press of Colorado, 2000.

Saint John, Daniel. *And Where Will You Build This Alcan Highway?* Whitehorse, Yukon, Canada: Black Horse Publishing, 1992.

Scott, Doug. *The Enduring Wilderness: Protecting Our National Heritage through the Wilderness Act*. Golden, Colo.: Fulcrum, 2004.

Service, Robert. *The Complete Poems of Robert Service*. New York: Dodd, Mead, 1936.

Sherman, Dean F., ed. *Alaska Cavalcade*. Seattle: Alaska Life Publishing Company, 1943.

Sherwood, Morgan. "Atomic Energy vs. Eskimos." *Science* 266 (October 28, 1994): 663.

————. *Exploration of Alaska, 1865–1900*. New Haven, Conn.: Yale University Press, 1965.

————, ed. *Alaska and Its History*. Seattle: University of Washington Press, 1967.

————, ed. *Cook Inlet Collection: Two Hundred Years of Selected Alaskan History*. Anchorage: Alaska Northwest Publishing Company, 1974.

Shi, David E. *The Simple Life: Plain Living and High Thinking in American Culture*. New York: Oxford University Press, 1985.

Shiels, Archie W. *The Purchase of Alaska*. College: University of Alaska Press, 1967.

Shortridge, James R. "The Alaskan Agricultural Empire: An American Agrarian Vision, 1898–1929." *Pacific Northwest Quarterly* 69 (1978): 145–158.

————. "The Collapse of Frontier Farming in Alaska." *Annals of the Association of American Geographers* 66 (December 1976): 583–604.

Sillanpaa, Lennard. *Alaska Native Claims Settlement Act: The First Twenty Years*. Ottawa, Ontario: Indian and Northern Affairs Canada, 1992.

Simonson, Harold P. *The Closed Frontier: Studies in American Literary Tragedy*. New York: Holt, Rinehart and Winston, 1970.

Simpson, Sherry. "I Want to Ride on the Bus Chris Died In." In *Travelers' Tales Alaska: True Stories*, edited by Bill Sherwonit, Andromeda Romano-Lax, and Ellen Bielawski. Palo Alto, Calif.: Travelers' Tales, 2003, 243–265.

Smith, Henry Nash. *Virgin Land: The American West and Symbol and Myth*. Cambridge, Mass.: Harvard University Press, 1950.

Smith, Middleton. "Gardening in Northern Alaska." *National Geographic* 14 (September 1903): 355–357.

Stahl, Gustav R. "Farming in a Bowl of Ice." *Illustrated World* 20 (1913): 210–211.

Stephenson, William B., Jr. *The Land of Tomorrow*. New York: George H. Doran, 1919.

Stern, Richard O., Edward L. Arobio, Larry L. Naylor, and Wayne C. Thomas. *Eskimos, Reindeer, and Land*. Fairbanks: University of Alaska Agricultural Experiment Station, 1980.

Stewart, Robert Laird. *Sheldon Jackson: Pathfinder and Prospector of the Missionary Vanguard in the Rocky Mountains and Alaska*. New York: Fleming H. Revell, 1908.

Stone, Kirk H. *Alaskan Group Settlement: The Matanuska Valley Colony*. U.S. Department of the Interior. Washington, D.C.: Government Printing Office, 1949.

———. "Populating Alaska: The United States Phase." *Geographical Review* 42 (July 1952): 384–404.

Strong, B. Stephen. *Alaska Pipeline: Social and Economic Impact on Native People*. Ottawa, Ontario: Published under the Authority of the Hon. J. Hugh Faulkner, Minister of Indian and Northern Affairs, 1977.

"To the Eskimo People." *The Eskimo: A Quarterly Magazine Devoted to the Interest of Eskimos of Alaska* 5 (October 1938): 1.

Tower, Elizabeth A. *Reading, Religion, and Reindeer: Sheldon Jackson's Legacy to Alaska*. Anchorage: Privately printed, 1988.

Turner, Frederick Jackson. *Rereading Frederick Jackson Turner: "The Significance of the Frontier in American History" and Other Essays*. With commentary by John Mack Faragher. New York: H. Holt, 1994.

Twenty Years of Progress in the Matanuska Valley. Palmer: Alaska Rural Rehabilitation Corporation, 1955.

Twichell, Heath. *Northwest Epic: The Building of the Alaska Highway*. New York: St. Martin's Press, 1992.

U.S. Bureau of Education. *Report of the Commissioner of Education for the Year 1889–90*. Washington, D.C.: Government Printing Office, 1893.

U.S. Congress. *Hearings before a Special Committee Investigating the National Defense Program*. 70th Cong., 1st sess. Washington, D.C.: Government Printing Office, 1944.

U.S. Congress, House of Representatives, Committee on the Territories. *Civil Government for Alaska*. 48th Cong., 1st sess. Washington, D.C.: Government Printing Office, 1884.

U.S. Congress, House of Representatives, Committee on Ways and Means. *Tariff Readjustment—1929: Statement of Carl J. Lomen, New York City, Representing the Lomen Reindeer Corporation*. 70th Cong., 2d sess. Washington, D.C.: Government Printing Office, 1929.

U.S. Congress, Senate, Committee on Appropriations. *Mr. Teller Presented the Following Newspaper Communication of Sheldon Jackson, Urging the Importation by the Government of the Siberian Reindeer into Alaskan Territory*. 51st Cong., 2d sess. Washington, D.C.: Government Printing Office, 1891.

U.S. Congress, Senate, Committee on Public Works. *The Market for Rampart Power, Yukon River, Alaska*. 57th Cong., 2d sess. Washington, D.C.: Government Printing Office, 1962.

U.S. Department of the Interior. *General Information regarding the Territory of Alaska*. Washington, D.C.: Government Printing Office, 1921.

———. *Recreational Resources of the Alaska Highway and Other Roads in Alaska*. Washington, D.C.: Government Printing Office, 1944.

———. The Alaska Railroad. *Alaska: The Newest Homeland*. Washington, D.C.: Government Printing Office, 1931.

U.S. Department of the Interior, Bureau of Land Management. *Reindeer Grazing on the Seward Peninsula, Alaska*. Nome: Bureau of Land Management, Nome Field Station, n.d.

U.S. Department of State. *Military Highway to Alaska: Agreement between the United States of America and Canada: Effected by Exchange of Notes, Signed March 17 and 18, 1942*. Executive Agreement Series 246. Washington, D.C.: Government Printing Office, 1942.

U.S. Department of State, Committee on Foreign Affairs. *Report of the International Highway Commission to the President*. Washington, D.C.: Government Printing Office, 1940.

U.S. Fish and Wildlife Service. *A Report on Fish and Wildlife Resources Affected by the Rampart Dam and Reservoir Project, Yukon River, Alaska*. Juneau: U.S. Fish and Wildlife Service, 1964.

———. *A Report to the Secretary of the Interior, Rampart Canyon Dam and Reservoir Project Committee*. Washington, D.C.: Government Printing Office, 1964.

U.S. Geological Survey. *The Oil and Gas Resource Potential of the Arctic National Wildlife Refuge 1002 Area, Alaska*. Washington, D.C.: Government Printing Office, 1998.

U.S. National Resources Committee. *Alaska—Its Resources and Development*. 75th Cong., 1st sess. Washington, D.C.: Government Printing Office, 1938.

Vorren, Ornulv. *Saami, Reindeer, and Gold in Alaska: The Emigration of Saami from Norway to Alaska*. Prospect Heights, Ill.: Waveland Press, 1994.

Wainwright, Joel. "The Geographies of Political Ecology: After Edward Said." *Environment and Planning* 37 (2005): 1033–1043.

Wallace, Henry A. *New Frontiers*. New York: Reynal and Hitchcock, 1934.

Wallace, Scott. "ANWR: The Great Divide." *Smithsonian* 36 (October 2005): 48–56.

Webb, Melody. *The Last Frontier: A History of the Yukon Basin in Canada and Alaska*. Albuquerque: University of New Mexico Press, 1985.

Weeden, Robert. "Alaska's Oil Boom: From Swanson to Prudhoe Bay and Beyond." *Alaska Conservation Review*, December 1968, 3.

Welch, Richard. "American Opinion and the Purchase of Russian America." *American Slavic and Eastern European Review* 17 (1958): 481–494.

Wharton, David. *The Alaska Gold Rush*. Bloomington: Indiana University Press, 1972.

White, Richard. "The Nationalization of Nature." *Journal of American History* 86 (December 1999): 976–986.

Whitehead, John S. *Completing the Union: Alaska, Hawai'i, and the Battle for Statehood*. Albuquerque: University of New Mexico Press, 2004.

Whymper, Frederick. *Travel and Adventure in the Territory of Alaska, Formerly Russian America—Now Ceded to the United States—and in Various Other Parts of the North Pacific*. London: J. Murray, 1868.

Willoughby, Florance Barrett. *Alaska Holiday*. Boston: Little, Brown, 1940.

Wilson, Robert. "Directing the Flow: Migratory Waterfowl, Scale, and Mobility in Western North America." *Environmental History* 7 (2002): 247–266.

Wilson, William. *Railroad in the Clouds: The Alaska Railroad in the Age of Steam, 1914–1945*. Boulder, Colo.: Pruett, 1977.

Wrobel, David M. "Beyond the Frontier-Region Dichotomy." *Pacific Historical Review* 65 (August 1996): 401–429.

———. *The End of American Exceptionalism: Frontier Anxiety from the Old West to the New Deal*. Lawrence: University Press of Kansas, 1993.

Yukon Power for America. *The Rampart Story*. Fairbanks: Yukon Power for America, [196?].

INDEX